IN THE SERVICE OF THE TSAR AGAINST NAPOLEON

I take great pleasure in dedicating this book to my wife and best friend, Charlotte. She proof-read my manuscript, offered many valuable suggestions and ironed out my English prose.

IN THE SERVICE OF THE TSAR AGAINST NAPOLEON

The Memoirs of Denis Davidov, 1806–1814

Translated and Edited by Gregory Troubetzkoy

Greenhill Books, London

Stackpole Books, Pennsylvania

Greenhill Books

In the Service of the Tsar against Napoleon
First published 1999 by Greenhill Books, Lionel Leventhal Limited,
Park House, 1 Russell Gardens, London NW11 9NN
and
Stackpole Books, 5067 Ritter Road, Mechanicsburg, PA 17055, USA

British Library Cataloguing in Publication Data
In the service of the Tsar against Napoleon: the memoirs of Denis Davidov,
1806–1814
1. Davidov, Denis   2. Napoleonic Wars, 1800–1815 – Campaigns – Russia
3. Napoleonic Wars, 1800–1815 – Personal narratives, Russian
I. Title II. Troubetzkoy, Gregory
940.2′7′092

ISBN 1-85367-373-0

Library of Congress Cataloging-in-Publication Data available

Typeset by Wyvern 21, Bristol
Printed and bound in Great Britain by
Creative Print and Design (Wales), Ebbw Vale

Contents

List of Illustrations and Maps

Illustrations, pages 97–112

Maps

Introduction
Denis Davidov, 1784–1839

Denis Davidov, the famous partisan of the 1812 War, was a general of merit, a well-known poet, an authority on the theory of warfare and a chronicler of military history. He was, in addition, an astute landowner, a competent estate manager, a passionate hunter, a gifted conversationalist and a successful ladies' man. His literary activities earned him a deserved reputation and his personal attractiveness charmed many of his contemporaries, including the famous Russian poet Pushkin, despite a fifteen-year age difference. One of Davidov's witty remarks was used as an epigraph in *The Queen of Spades*. Pushkin, in the last year of his life, addressed Davidov in these terms:

To you, singer, to you, hero!
I could never gallop after you
On a mad steed into the fire
And roar of cannon . . .
I rode instead on steady Pegasus
Wearing the coat of ancient Parnassus.
But even here, in this heavy task
You, my marvellous rider,
Remain my father and commander.

Many Russian poets of the first third of the nineteenth century sang Davidov's praises; and a portrait of him even hung in the study of Sir Walter Scott. Finally he makes an appearance in Tolstoy's *War and Peace* in the person of Denisov, a devil-may-care character who is depicted cursing on a bridge in the course of a daring raid on a French convoy and dancing the mazurka with Natasha Rostov. The epigraph, 'My life is a struggle' – placed at the beginning of his memoirs on partisan warfare – symbolises not only his military activities but also his continual struggle against career officers, bureaucrats and adversaries.

Davidov organised his notes in 1814 when his recollections were still vivid. The astonishing feats, in 1809, of the Spanish guerrillas, which so confounded Napoleon and his marshals, inspired him to write:

Their achievements will always serve as an example for any guerrilla leader. He will learn from them how to use every advantage of the natural surroundings where fighting takes place and how to channel the anger of people who seek revenge.

A completely new method of warfare had suddenly emerged on the field of battle. Davidov was to become one of its brilliant and original pioneers in 1812, improvising its application in Russia to deadly effect.

Davidov's military career spans some 30 years (1801–31) with brief interruptions between various campaigns. He was only in his element while in uniform and on the move, sharing a pipe or a bottle around a campfire, riding his horse, charging sabre in hand – truly a colourful and romantic figure.

A collection of his poems and an autobiography were published twice in his lifetime, in 1828 and 1832; but this was done anonymously, and it was rumoured at first that they had been written by General Ermolov. Newspaper critics and readers, however, soon deciphered their true authorship, based mainly on the distinctive military idiom, which bore the familiar stamp of the 'bard of the bivouacs'.

The description of the battle of Eylau found its way separately into *The Library for Reading* in 1835. Davidov referred to it privately as the favourite of his children.

The chapter dealing with Tilsit was drastically altered and cut by the censors when first reproduced in 1839 in a collective publication that featured a hundred Russian writers. Excerpts from the 'Diary of Partisan Warfare', too, had suffered the same fate prior to their appearance in 1820 and 1822 in a journal called *Patriotic Notes*.

A growing sense of unease gripped Russia at the end of the Napoleonic wars. After the aborted coup against the monarchy in 1825, the climate was one of strict rule, repression, police intrusion and censorship, causing particular concern to former military heroes. Davidov and many others longed for the sense of freedom, adventure and independence that was now giving way to authoritarian attitudes. Forced into retirement and silence, the restless hussar reflects on his destiny:

> The sword has fallen from my hand
> And my fate has been trampled by the strong.
> Favoured by fortune, they now brush me aside
> And force me to bend behind the plough.

It is tempting to speculate on the circumstances or motives that prompted Davidov to embrace a military career. His father, a well-to-do landowner from a good family, had served under the famous Russian General Suvorov, and had attained the rank of brigadier before being suddenly cashiered from the army in 1798. This did not deter the young man; indeed, a chance meeting with the fabled Suvorov five years earlier, when only nine, had already helped to decide him on an army life. After greeting the famous field marshal and kissing his hand, Davidov was asked: 'Do you love soldiers, my boy?' The impulsive youngster boldly replied: 'I love Count Suvorov. In him there is everything – soldiers and victory and glory.' 'Good God,' exclaimed the field marshal, 'What a brave fellow! He will be an army man for sure. I shan't die before he wins three battles!' And Suvorov repeated his prediction before taking leave of the Davidov family. In the event, although Denis Davidov did not receive any army command that would enable him to win three battles, his mind was made up at that tender age to seek no other but the military profession.

As a writer, Davidov did not belong to any literary school. His poetry was never a mere exercise in rhyming and neat versification, but reflected a vital need to express deeply personal feelings. Poetry was another way to give free rein to the imagination and to pursue his story-telling on a loftier, more romantic level. It was a new pleasure, analogous perhaps to the effects, on heart and mind, of champagne.

His verses and his prose breathe fire and spontaneity – a veritable torrent of passion in which his rebellious nature finds comfort and true fulfilment.

As he reviews his military career, we are tempted to compare his adventures with those of other Napoleonic writers such as General Marbot and Sergeant Bourgogne. His accounts remain imbued with the smoke of campfire and battle, not sanitised or expurgated to placate nineteenth-century sensibilities. Like them, he was there – an eye-witness to history.

The translation which we now present to the reader is broken down into chapters dealing with a meeting with Suvorov; episodes centred on the 1807 campaign; recollections of the Russian campaign in Finland in 1808; Davidov's diary of partisan warfare during the French invasion of Russia in 1812; an analysis of Napoleon's comments on the 1812 campaign; and details of Davidov's role in the German campaign of 1813.

Apart from a few excerpts which appeared in the bulletins of the Napoleonic Society of America, the Napoleonic Alliance and the Journal of the International Napoleonic Society, this material has never been translated into English in its entirety until now.

Acknowledgements

I owe a debt of gratitude and special thanks to Ben Weider, CM, PhD, President of the International Napoleonic Society, and also to David Markham, editor-in-chief of the Society's journal. They both ceaselessly encouraged me and offered moral support as I worked on this project.

Gregory Troubetzkoy, 1999

Translator's Note

To get an idea of what the various cavalrymen were like, the reader should bear in mind that the Uhlans who fought in the French, Prussian, Russian and Austrian armies were basically lancers. This does not imply that they were restricted to carrying lances; usually the front rank bore lances and the second rank were armed with carbines. Some, too, were equipped with sabres and pistols, and even hatchets. The cossacks, on the other hand, favoured lances, muskets and swords, which usually lacked a hand-guard.

The heaviest cavalrymen were cuirassiers, with upper body armour, front and back. When completely armed and equipped, each man tipped the scales at over 300 pounds. Dragoons, with colourful horsetails streaming from their helmets, weighed about 270 pounds.

The hussars were the light cavalry *par excellence*, and when fully equipped and armed, weighed in at about 250 pounds.

As for the foot soldiers, it helps to remember that Jägers were light infantry. They did not operate independently, but were often incorporated into a grenadier company, so that the first platoon was made up of grenadiers proper and the second was composed of Jägers. This held true in the Russian army. However, in French battalions there were companies of grenadiers and *voltigeurs* (light infantry sharpshooters). The rule of thumb was that grenadiers were selected for their height and the smaller men were chosen as *voltigeurs*.

For further information concerning these terms, it is helpful to consult *Swords Around a Throne* by John R. Elting, which analyses the composition of Napoleon's Grande Armée in great detail.

CHAPTER 1

A Meeting with Suvorov, 1793

From the time I was seven years old, while my father was in command of the Poltava light-horse regiment, I lived in a soldier's tent. My boyhood pastimes were musket practice and marching, but the height of bliss was to go horseback riding on a cossack horse with the late Philip Mikhailovich Ezhov, a captain of the Don Cossack horse regiment.

How could a lively child fail to become excited by military matters when exposed daily to the sight of soldiers and encampments? And was not Suvorov himself the shining example of our own military way of life? He was the talk of the soldiers and of contemporary society, the universal object of admiration and praise. His secretive, unorthodox methods, counter to all accepted routine; his apparently quite reckless enterprises, his lightning marches, his resounding victories at places unforeseen either by us or the enemy – all these glorious, epic achievements, extending successively over decades, set a fresh and vigorous example for the youth of Russia.

Suvorov was the son of a commanding general, himself an intelligent, well-educated man. The father kept a close watch over the education of his son and daughter (Princess Gorchakov). The boy acquired a thorough knowledge of French, German, Turkish and also some acquaintance with Italian. He did not display any odd or peculiar traits before joining the service; but having accomplished great deeds during the Seven Years' War, and attaining high rank, despite the jealousy of powerful men, he began to attract notice for his strange quirks of behaviour. Those observers who envied his good fortune never suspected the true cause for his successes, which were fully appreciated by Catherine the Great, and attributed all his victories to blind luck.

Suvorov, in fact, embodied many traits of a hero of Shakespearean tragedy, who surprises people with alternate outbursts of comic wit and feats of bravery. Being a proud man, he was in constant conflict with influential court figures. He poked fun openly at the all-powerful Potemkin,[1] even though he wrote him polite letters, and he picked quarrels with the Austrian minister,

---

[1] Potemkin, the all-powerful minister of Catherine the Great, is now most often associated with the famous Potemkin Villages, which were sham 'stage-set' structures erected to impress the empress on her tour of southern Russia, but which were not real or permanent dwellings.

Baron Tugut. Yet he often referred to Potemkin and Count Razumovsky as his benefactors.

Before leaving for Italy, he prostrated himself at the feet of Emperor Paul. It is not clear whether this was deliberately calculated in order to mystify those who watched him closely, or simply another way to attract general attention by doing the unexpected.

If the entire life of this amazing man, with his generous heart, clever brain and lofty ideals was nothing more than play-acting and cold calculation, it would be interesting to know whether he ever acted naturally. For all his odd behaviour, he issued orders to his armies which were marvels of good sense. When conversing privately with Catherine about the most important military and political matters, he surprised this extraordinary woman with his original and remarkable mind and vast store of information on a multitude of subjects. He never ceased to amaze government officials with his actions and to startle them with his caustic humour.

Many have rushed to judgment and dismissed Suvorov as eccentric, ignorant, evil and as cruel as Attila and Tamerlane, even refusing to admit that he possessed any talent. Although I realise that I am ill-equipped and powerless to refute all the terrible slanders levelled at this great man, I feel I must attempt to set the record straight.

As head of the Russian armies for 55 successive years, Suvorov did not cause misery to any soldier or civil servant. Not once did he strike one of his men; and he punished the guilty only by poking fun at them and labelling them with nicknames which, like horse-brands, were attached to them permanently in the public memory. Sometimes he would resort to 'hauling over the coals' those who had incurred his displeasure. The bloodshed which occurred when Ismail and Praga had been taken by storm was simply the outcome of any prolonged siege and stubborn resistance.

During wars in Asia, where every individual is also a warrior, and in Europe, too, when garrisons are reinforced by the inhabitants of a town under siege, any assault is necessarily accompanied by bloodshed which does not spare the civilian population. We recall the siege and storm of Saragossa by the troops of Suchet, a general who was essentially a humane and noble man. The English like to dwell on the bloodshed which occurred during the assaults on Ismail and Praga by our troops, but whilst taking pride in their own civilised ways, they keep silent about the barbaric behaviour of their countrymen in India, which cannot be excused by any circumstance. There is no doubt that the more desperate the resistance of the defenders, the less inclined the besiegers will be to show any mercy once they force their way into the streets and houses; and their commanders are quite incapable of restraining them until the garrison is virtually wiped out.

That is what happened in the case of the attacks on Ismail and Praga. It is easy to sit in the comfort of a study, far from the scene of desperate fighting, and to criticise; but commanders, for all their Christian faith, conscience and humanity, are powerless to control the fierce determination of soldiers drunk with victory and success.

During the assault on Praga our troops were beside themselves with the burning desire to avenge the treacherous slaughter of their comrades at the hands of the Poles, and their fury knew no bounds. That is why Suvorov, when entering Warsaw, took with him only those troops who had not previously occupied the city with Ingelstrom (when our men were slaughtered without any warning). Those regiments which had been victimised were left in Praga so that they would not be tempted to seek vengeance. This decision, which is unknown to most people, says much for the humanitarian feelings of Suvorov.

Half a century ago, this great man took measure of the heart that beat in the breast of the Russian soldier. He became convinced that this soldier, no less than his foreign counterpart, was easily inspired and was well aware of his own dignity; and that was the basis of his relationship with the men. Whilst enforcing iron discipline, he instilled in his men the feeling of military pride and the conviction of their superiority to any opponent.

Some former commanders, on taking office, have chosen to address their troops with pompous and incomprehensible speeches. Suvorov preferred to live among his troops and get to know them well; his good nature, simplicity and popular mannerisms captivated many hearts. He talked with them continually during their campaigns and, while they were in camp, used unaffected language that they all could understand. Instead of numerous staff officers, he surrounded himself with a few ordinary individuals like Tishchenko and Stavrokov.

Suvorov was confronted by a military art built on very unsound foundations. Offensive tactics consisted of moving the troops in widely stretched and scattered lines in order to overrun both wings of the enemy and expose the centre to crossfire. The concept of defensive action was equally inept. Instead of taking advantage of the scattered forces facing them, striking in unison at the weakened line of the advancing enemy, ripping it into half and defeating the opponent piecemeal, the commander in charge of the defence would stretch his own forces to meet the enemy's advancing line and endeavour to defend each little gap or track that might be exploited. Even the most gifted military leaders would try to outdo the enemy by extending the defence lines and enveloping the attackers in an even broader pincer movement so as to catch them in a crossfire that would outgun theirs. All they accomplished was to thin out even further the numbers of the main body and reduce its fighting efficiency. This strategy also called for sham attacks that deceived no one. Such calculated manoeuvres only enabled the enemy to predict their exact arrival with great accuracy and to take necessary counter-measures.

Great care was devoted to the mechanical aspect of food supply trains and a strict timetable was observed before the battle. Subsequent military considerations were often subservient to the orderly flow of supplies that were in the hands of the quartermaster officials, and this did not help either.

The tactics that were in vogue made no better sense than the strategy. When the time came for battle, the most important consideration was deemed to be the choice of a more or less elevated location and the anchorage of both wings of the army to natural or artificial obstacles in order to repulse the enemy's efforts without moving or changing position. When taking the offensive, apart from the use of feigned attacks that deceived nobody, preference was invariably given to the use of firepower rather than a reliance on cold steel.[2] Decisiveness was always conspicuously absent, tentative probing the general rule. You can well imagine how an uncompromising, wilful and independently minded genius would deal with such problems.

While still a colonel in the Astrakhan Grenadier Regiment on manoeuvres near Krasnoe Selo, where one side was under the command of Count Panin and the other of Catherine herself, Suvorov (who had for some time expressed his disgust for the methodical troop movements that were then exalted throughout Europe as the perfection of the art of war, and for the practice of aimless firing during combat) resolved to impress the empress and the commanders with a daring action that better suited the spirit of the Russian soldier. He ruined the occasion with a surprising display of intransigence. In the midst of one of the most pedantic manoeuvres, accompanied by a show of artillery support, he suddenly ordered his regiment to stop firing, moved out of alignment and burst through into the ranks of his opponents, causing havoc to the dispositions of both sides that soon turned into chaos.

A few months later, when he received an assignment to march with his regiment from St Petersburg to Riga, he jumped at the chance to demonstrate the advantage of accelerated marches, despite the inflexible ways in which they were mapped out beforehand. Loading a platoon with the standard and treasury on horse-drawn carriages, he reached Riga in eight days and sent a staff officer to inform an astounded war college of his arrival. The rest of the regiment soon joined him, not in 30 days as planned, but in 14 days. Catherine alone understood the young colonel and how he had carried out his assignment, saying of him: 'He is my own future general!'

Given such encouragement, anyone, let alone Suvorov, would have set his eye firmly on his goal, undaunted by possible reverses. And this man of iron

---

[2] Suvorov's favourite dictum was: 'A bullet is a fool, but a bayonet, a fine fellow!'

will and bold enterprise was to take full advantage of the situation and go far indeed.

Suvorov, throughout the ensuing 40 years of his army life, voiced his utter disdain for negative, defensive methods, and concentrated exclusively on offensive action. He pooled together all his forces and always fought with a single body of troops, thus gaining decisive superiority in engagements with scattered detachments in the generally accepted European sense. His method would henceforth prove the order of the day as a guarantee of victory.

In the course of actual fighting, Suvorov would either remain quite immobile, trying to ascertain the enemy's plans of movement, or, once having perceived them, would resort to forced marches at full speed (to this day labelled 'Suvorovian') and fall on the enemy with the suddenness of snow out of the blue.

One consequence of these lightning strikes, which were designed to unsettle the enemy by achieving total surprise and catch him unprepared for battle, was Suvorov's predilection for cold steel over firepower. This was inevitable, because by not setting up firing lines and opening a cannonade, he retained that element of surprise, giving the enemy no opportunity to organise and come to order, which would put them on a par with the attackers. With a clear view of his line of operations, perfectly adapted to the terrain over which his men had to move, Suvorov kept his eye on the critical point of the battlefield on which his tactics were to hinge. He directed all his efforts towards that point, refusing to be distracted by anything else that was going on, just as nothing could distract him during his life from this sole passion for battles and military glory.

Suvorov's fondness for decisive action and speed was reflected in his favourite manner of speaking. He insisted on a straight 'yes' or 'no' and laconic sentences which expressed a thought in two or three words. He was the sworn enemy of those who claimed not to know and who tried to dodge the question: 'The cursed can't-sayers cause no end of trouble.' Once when he asked a grenadier how far it was to the nearest star, the man answered: 'Three Suvorov marches.' Disdaining any action that smacked of timidity, slackness, excessive calculation or circumspection, he strove to foster a spirit of resolution and audacity in keeping with his propensity for sweeping movements in the field.

Towards the end of his illustrious career he led the Russians and Austrians against the French and succeeded in conquering Italy, where many hotheads had refused to obey the legitimate authorities. Can his detractors say where and on what occasions did Suvorov display cruelty and inhumanity? Nearing the end of the campaign, half of the French army under Moreau, with Generals Grouchy, Perignon, Victor and others had been taken prisoner. Could his behaviour ever be compared with that of the Austrians and English who oppressed their captives in foul, humid dungeons and barges?

His determination and single-mindedness astonished many. Having chosen his profession, he strengthened his physical stamina by continually exercising and keeping fit. At the age of 70 he still walked about seven miles each day, ate simple food in moderate amounts, slept once a day on a bundle of fresh hay and every morning washed himself with buckets of icy water.

Suvorov dreamed only of glory, but in the purest and most elevated form. This passion engulfed everything else, so that when he was fully grown and reached the age when nature draws us more towards material than ideal considerations, he appeared as a sort of 'military monk'. He avoided the company of women and the characteristic distractions of youth, remaining insensible to matters of the heart.

Forseeing that the desire for worldly goods might increase with age, he renounced the cares of overseeing his estates in good time and studiously avoided contact with the precious metal which feeds this unworthy ambition. Although he owned 9,000 serfs, he never knew the amount of his income; at the age of 30 he entrusted the management of his estates to his family who conveyed to his adjutants that portion of the revenue necessary for his modest standard of living.

The main strands of his philosophy were the study of human weaknesses and constant observation of his own actions. When the concerns of old age covered his face with wrinkles and his head with grey hair, he developed an aversion to mirrors. He ordered them to be carried out of his rooms or covered with a sheet, and for the clocks to be removed from his quarters as well. Many were quick to ascribe these peculiarities to his whimsical character. The truth was that he still felt young and chose to avoid everything that reminded him of the passage of time, banishing the thought that his life was already nearing its end. His hatred of mirrors most likely stemmed from fear of seeing himself as an old man, the cooling of his youthful ardour, the extinction of the spark of enterprise which required all his moral strength, and the declining dedication to action so characteristic of earlier years. Frederick the Great of Prussia began to colour his face with cosmetics, probably for the same reasons.

Having hardened his body through physical exercise and having misled his detractors by his eccentric behaviour, he bore patiently every kind of insult, practising rigid self-control, committing himself fully to the passion for glory, supremely confident in the power of his own genius.

In his military career he only attained the rank of major general at the age of 41, when many others who had already acquired this title were preparing to leave the service. Which of us has not seen 33-year-old major generals busy complaining about the fate that has prevented them from reaching higher rank? At the time of his promotion, Suvorov was practically unknown, but how quickly he was to achieve undisputed renown! General Foix said of Napoleon: 'Like the gods of Homer he took three steps and stood already at the edge of the world.' The words of this famous general could apply equally to the great, unforgettable Suvorov.

This is the man whom I was destined to see and with whom I was privileged to exchange a few words on one of the happiest days of my life. This is how it happened.

A few months before the uprising in Poland, Suvorov commanded the army corps stationed in the Ekaterinoslav and Kherson provinces. The headquarters was located in Kherson itself. Four cavalry regiments, which formed part of this corps, were encamped near the River Dnieper at various points, but close to one another. The house in which my family lived was tall and spacious, but actually built in haste for Empress Catherine during her trip to the Crimea region. The Poltava light horse regiment was stationed near the village of Grushevka and its camp was within a hundred paces of our home.

One night I heard a great commotion in the camp. I ran out of my tent to see the whole regiment on horseback, our tent being the only one that had not been dismantled. Eventually I was told that Suvorov had just arrived in a simple 'courier' carriage and had stopped seven miles away at the camp of another regiment where we were ordered to appear for a review and manoeuvres. I was very young, but all my talk and dreams were of Suvorov. Imagine my joy!

I was not the only one to be caught up in the excitement. I remember that my late mother, all the relatives who lived with us, as well as the lackeys, drivers, cooks and servants, not to mention others in the village, gathered together and rushed over to the camp where Suvorov was staying in order to get a glimpse of our hero, our demigod of war. This, it should be noted, was at a time when neither his victories in Poland and Italy nor his triumph over nature herself in the Alps had yet taken place – deeds that were to crown the epic career of this marvellous man.

My mother and all of us soon joined the crowd following the regiment and found the camp empty because the troops were already on manoeuvres. Suvorov had detailed a small group of men from each regiment to set up the tents and was now participating in the manoeuvres which ended up some twelve miles from the encampment. Towards midday the troops finally returned. My father, covered with dust and quite weary, entered our tent with his fellow officers. The stories continued non-stop. Anecdotes about Suvorov, his 'bon-mots' and his peculiarities did the rounds. The only thing they complained about was the excessive speed that he demanded of them, and the hot pursuit of an imaginary enemy which exhausted both men and horses.

The officers expressed their special dislike of one particular manoeuvre. Suvorov treated the troops as a weapon and not a pretty toy; so he insisted that an army unit should subordinate anything not connected with the actual fighting – outward appearance, orderly formation and the like – to the sole purpose for which it was created. Because the primary obligation of the cavalry was to cut a path through enemy ranks, it should not be concerned with speed alone and maintaining line while on the gallop. It must surge into the midst of the enemy line or column and strike at anything close to hand, not turn about and break off the engagement alleging that the firing had frightened the horses, or retreat in good order without making actual physical contact with enemy fire. In order to stop this practice, Suvorov trained the horses of his cavalry to gallop at full speed and accustomed them to break through the central ranks of the opponent's firing line. To achieve this, he saved the manoeuvre for the end of the training period, relying on the memory of the animals, and reinforced with a verbal command that they knew would signal the conclusion of the exercise.

For this purpose he had half of his troops dismount and stand with carbines loaded with blanks. The soldiers were separated from one another by the distance necessary for one horse to gallop between them. The other half remained on horseback, aligned opposite the gaps of the facing infantry, and then were ordered to attack. The foot soldiers were told to discharge their weapons at the very moment when the horses galloped through their lines. The riders would then dismount and the training or manoeuvres were over. The theory was that instead of being frightened by the shots fired directly at them, the horses would look forward to the moment of facing the infantry fire, remembering that the sound of shots would be followed by their being reined in, haltered or returned to their stables. Indeed, they would neigh and be eager to charge!

Of course, these exercises were not without cost to the foot soldiers, because sometimes more than one horse or rider would burst through the narrow gap, causing injury, even death. That is why the soldiers so hated this exercise, especially if they were to play the role of infantry that day.

Such accidents, however, did not deter Suvorov from using this method which he found to be the best way to train cavalry to defeat infantry. When he received a report of casualties among the men trampled by the riders, his reaction would usually be something like: 'May the Lord have mercy on them! I may kill four, five, even ten men; but I'll train five or ten thousand!' So there was no way in which his officers could divert him from his chosen method of perfecting the cavalry and the purpose for which it was created.

The troops had marched out of the camp before sunrise and about an hour later we followed them in a carriage. But how could we hope to overtake cavalry led by Suvorov? Now and then we heard shouting at a distance or caught a glimpse of someone in a white shirt galloping in and out of the cavalry squadrons, at which a cry would go up from the scattered onlookers:

'There he is, there's our master, Aleksandr Vasilyevich!' That's all we managed to see and hear, and growing weary of this useless attempt to catch sight of the hero, we returned to the camp in the hope of seeing him upon his return from manoeuvres, which we were assured would end sooner today than on the previous day.

And indeed, around ten in the morning, the camp came alive as people started yelling: 'Here he comes galloping!' We ran outside the tent and saw Suvorov about 300 yards away, riding at full speed towards the camp in our direction. I remember my heart skipping a few beats as it later did when I actually caught sight of my hero. I felt intensely curious and filled with joy. I can still see that group – four colonels with several adjutants and orderlies and, ahead of them, Suvorov himself on a roan Kalmuck horse that belonged to my father, in a white shirt, linen trousers, Hessian boots and a small military helmet of the time, similar to those now worn by horse grenadiers of the guard. He wore no ribbons or crosses, and I remember very well his gaunt, wrinkled features, his high eyebrows and lowered lids. Although I was only a child, his image, as well as his dress, remains sharp in my memory. That is why I do not like his busts or any of his portraits, except one which was painted while he was in Italy and of which I have a good copy, and also the death mask that served as inspiration for the bust by Guichard.

As he galloped past us, his favourite adjutant Tishchenko, an uneducated man from whom Suvorov pretended to take advice, shouted to him: 'Count, why are you galloping away? Look, here are the children of Vasili Denisovich!' 'Where are they, where are they?' asked Suvorov. He turned towards us, reined in his horse and stopped. We approached him. He greeted us and asked my father our names. Calling us even closer, he blessed us gravely and extended his hand, which we kissed. Then he asked me: 'Do you love soldiers, my boy?' With the boldness of youth, I replied impulsively: 'I love Count Suvorov. In him there is everything – soldiers and victory and glory.'

'Good God,'Suvorov exclaimed. 'What a brave fellow! He will be an army man for sure. I shan't die before he wins three battles! And this one (pointing to my brother) will do well in the civil service.' Then he abruptly turned his horse around, whipped it and galloped off to his tent.

In this case Suvorov proved no prophet. My brother served in the army all his life, and quite honourably, as is demonstrated by the eight wounds he received, all but two from the bayonet in close encounters. As for me, I never got to command either an army or an individual corps, and therefore failed to win any victories. Even so, the words of the great man had something of a magical effect; when, seven years later, it was time for both of us to enter a profession, my father was invited to register us with the Foreign Service. But with my hero's words still ringing in my ears, I wanted no other career except the military. My brother, possibly perplexed by Suvorov's prediction, accepted his fate and served as a cadet in the Moscow archives of the Foreign Service before joining the army.

On that special day, all the colonels and several staff officers were dining at Suvorov's table. Upon his return, my father told us how they were discussing, before dinner, the day's manoeuvres and were exchanging comments. Because my father was in charge of the second line, Suvorov turned to him and demanded: 'Why did you lead the second line so slowly during the third attack of the first line? I sent you the order to pick up speed, but you continued your slow advance!'

Such a question from the lips of any commander is not amusing, but from Suvorov it could be quite unnerving. My father was famous for his sharp wit in society circles, and also for his composure under questioning. He answered Suvorov without faltering: 'Because I did not see any need for it, Your Excellency!' 'Why so?' 'Because the success of the first line did not call for it – it did not stop pursuing the enemy. The second line was only needed to relieve it if the pursuit slowed down. That's why I conserved the strength of the horses until they were called on to replace those which were worn out.' 'And what if the enemy had taken heart and repulsed the first line?' 'That could never happen. Your Excellency was leading it.' Suvorov smiled and kept quiet.

As a rule, he would simply turn his back in silent reply to elaborate praise and flattery, making an exception only for statements that might help to popularise his image and strengthen the idea of his invincibility in the public's mind. He appreciated and dearly loved that form of adulation, probably not out of vanity but as a moral support and incentive.

That evening we hurried back to Grushevka with mother and all the servants. As a special favour to my father, Suvorov had personally requested a dinner invitation. It was either during Lent or on a day of fasting. I can only remember the fuss and bustle in our home while they sought out the best fish and prepared his favourite dishes.

There was great excitement, too, over the reception and entertainment of our famous guest, in a manner calculated not to disturb in the least his ordinary way of life, his habits and his fancies.

Towards eight in the morning all was in readiness. A large round table in the salon was set up with all sorts of Lenten appetisers, including generous-sized vodka glasses and a decanter. In the dining room there was a table with 22 settings, but with no centrepiece, no bowls of fruit, titbits and hors d'oeuvres, and no china figurines. Suvorov did not care for these things. No soup plates were laid, because the food was supposed to be served, one dish after another, straight from the cooking pot on to the guest's plate. That is how it was done in his quarters. In one of the rooms beyond the dining area the servants set up ready for him a bathing tub with several buckets of cold water, several clean sheets, a change of underwear and clothing brought from the camp.

Manoeuvres ended that day at seven in the morning. My father left the regiment on the return march to camp and galloped back at full speed on the Circassian horse that he had ridden in the field to switch mounts and get home quickly to supervise arrangements before Suvorov's arrival. He was already half-way from the camp to Grushevka when, from the top of a hill, he suddenly spotted, some two miles ahead of him but to the side, two horsemen, one slightly behind the other. Both were galloping at full speed towards Grushevka. It was Suvorov with one of his orderlies heading there directly from manoeuvres. My father spurred on his horse but still did not manage to get back to our house before this 63-year-young/old man. He found him covered with dust, standing at the entrance, stroking his horse and praising its qualities to the curious crowd around. 'God forgive me, what a glorious horse! I never rode one like it. It hasn't got two lives, it has three!' At that point my father invited him in, led him to the room that had been prepared for him, and tried to clean up as well, because he, too, was covered with so much dust that he seemed to be disguised.

The other invited dinner guests began to arrive. I remember the duty general, Levashov, Major Tchorba and the afore-mentioned Tishchenko. There were also the colonels of the various regiments that had been gathered together for the manoeuvres, all Suvorov's staff officers and some from the Poltava regiment. All these guests were in full parade uniform with sashes and had joined my father (likewise fully uniformed) in the living room, together with my mother, us two youngsters and one elderly lady, an acquaintance of my mother who had arrived from Moscow. Suvorov, from the very beginning, took a dislike to her, and she became the butt of his mocking glances and jokes all the time he was there.

Everyone awaited Suvorov's entrance. This took about an hour. Suddenly the doors flew open and Suvorov appeared clean and neatly dressed like a baby after christening. His hair was arranged as it appears in all his portraits. He wore the uniform of general-in-chief, light cavalry dark blue with red collar and sleeves, richly embroidered in silver, opened in front and with three stars. On his white summer waistcoat was the ribbon of St George First Class, but he wore no other decorations. For the rest, light white summer trousers and light Hessian boots, with a dress-sword at his side: and he carried neither hat nor helmet. That is how I remember him on this second occasion.

My father came to meet him, led him to the salon and introduced my mother and ourselves. He approached her, kissed her on both cheeks, and murmured a few words about her late father, General Scherbinin who, a few years previously, had been governor of the Kharkov, Kursk and Voronezh provinces. He blessed each one of us, let us kiss his hand and exclaimed: 'They are my friends!' Then turning to me, he repeated: 'Oh, this will be a military man. He will win three battles before I die!'

Then my father presented to him my three-year-old sister, and he asked: 'What is wrong, my little dove? Why are you so thin and pale?' They told him she had been running a fever. 'God forgive me, that's terrible! We must take this fever and give it a good whipping so that it doesn't come back.' My sister thought that the whipping was intended for her and almost burst into tears. Then, turning to our elderly lady visitor, Suvorov remarked: 'And we don't have to ask anything about her; she must be a madam of some sort!' These words were uttered without the slightest smile and with complete composure, which almost caused us to burst out laughing. But he, without changing expression, and as coolly as ever, went over to the table laden with hors d'oeuvres, poured himself a glass of vodka, drank it in one gulp and proceeded to eat heartily.

After a while my father invited him to the dining table. Everyone sat down. They served boiling fish soup just the way he liked (he would often have it straight out of the pot cooking on the stove). I remember that he spent half the time at the table concentrating, with the utmost attention and application, and in complete silence, on his food and drink. Finally the time came for conversation. But what sticks most in my memory are the jokes he made at the expense of the elderly lady from Moscow, which amused us children no end and made it difficult for the grown-ups to restrain their laughter. During the most interesting discussions he would stare at her and the moment her head was turned away, he would tease her. When she heard his voice and turned in his direction he would lower his eyes towards his plate, the bottle or the glass, indicating that his attention was elsewhere. At other times he would come out with: 'Look how she keeps on staring', 'They go on talking, but she sits and stares!', or 'What a clumsy woman!'

His aide Tishchenko later admitted that it was only out of respect for my mother that Suvorov limited himself to these remarks about the lady to whom he took such a dislike. Ordinarily, to get rid of anyone he detested, he would shout: 'Smells bad, smells bad! Fumigate, fumigate!' His aides would quietly come over and invite the person in question to leave the room. Only then would his exclamations cease.

After dinner he started speaking again about the horse on which he rode during the manoeuvres and brought to our house. He praised her agility and strength and assured us he had never ridden on such an animal except one time during the battle near Koslugy. 'In this fight,' he said, 'I was cut off and pursued by Turks for quite some distance. I understand Turkish and heard them agree not to shoot or slash at me, but to try to capture me alive. They found out who I was. With this intention, they came so close that they kept trying to grab my coat, but each time they closed in, my horse would leap forward like an arrow and they would fall back a few yards. That's how I escaped!'

During the hour or so he spent with us after dinner, he was quite talkative and merry, showing no sign of any strange behaviour. He took his leave and got into his carriage, which took him back to camp. There he issued the following order of the day:

> The First Regiment is excellent; the Second is quite good; about the Third I won't say anything; the Fourth is totally useless.

Although I indicate them by number, he referred to each regiment by name. I cannot help mentioning that the First was the Poltava Light Horse Regiment led by my father. Afterwards Suvorov got back into his carriage and galloped back to Kherson.

A few months after the peaceful manoeuvres of the cavalry regiments (and the jokes about the old lady) on the banks of the Dnieper, the Polish kingdom was in turmoil and Praga, overflowing with blood, was wreathed in smoke.

CHAPTER 2

Lesson for a Madcap, 1807

Our army was retreating from Iankovo to Eylau. At that time the rearguard was divided in two parts. One was under the command of General Barclay de Tolly, the other was under General Prince Bagration.

On 23 January the former was fighting near Deppen, covering the retreat of the army towards Wolfsdorf. On the 24th it was Bagration's turn to cover the retreat from Wolfsdorf to Landsberg.

The individual commanders of the rearguard were major generals who later became quite famous: Count Pahlen, Marcoff, Baggovut, Count Lambert, and others already with a reputation, such as Ermolov, who commanded the entire rearguard artillery, Prince Dolgoruky, Gogel and Yurkovsky, who was in charge of the forward line.

The affair at Wolfsdorf was the first engagement of my long military career. I shall never forget the impatience with which I awaited the first shots of the actual fighting. As if unsure of my own courage, I tried to emulate the high spirits of the officers who surrounded Bagration, basking in their attention and fascinated by their conversation, which dealt so lightly with danger and which radiated a mood of carefree abandon. But it was Prince Bagration who had the most influence on me. I had not yet witnessed his lofty spirit at its finest, but I already sensed his moral strength and flashes of genius concealed under an outward calm: they would truly catch fire and erupt on the battlefield as hopes of success grew dimmer and the prospects of disaster became more certain.

At dawn, the enemy began to maul our forward line near Varlak, about four miles from Wolfsdorf. The rearguard took up arms at a spot parallel to the highway leading from Gutstadt to Liebstadt. This position protected a secondary road which led via Petersdorf to Dietrichsdorf and on to Arensdorf, Open and Kashauen, along which the rearguard was to follow the rest of the army. The edge of the woods between Wolfsdorf and Elditen swarmed with Jägers of the Fifth Regiment. A small cavalry unit moved swiftly to keep the enemy under observation on our left flank.

The French vanguard, with a screen of skirmishers before it and the whole army behind, opened fire from one or two cannon on our forward line; masses of troops were moving among the snow-covered hills and were streaming downhill towards Wolfsdorf.

Yurkovsky, under cover of the cossacks closest to the enemy, alternately halted and advanced at an angle to the battle line of the rearguard towards the right flank of the Fifth Jäger Regiment beyond the edge of the woods.

As adjutant to Prince Bagration and, therefore, without a command of my own, I begged to be sent to the front line, ostensibly to keep track of enemy movements, but really to prance about on my horse, fire my pistols, flourish my sword, and (if the chance arose) hack away at the enemy.

I galloped over to the cossacks who were busy exchanging fire with the enemy skirmishers. The man closest to me in a blue cape and bearskin cap appeared to be an officer. I had the notion of cutting him off from the line and taking him prisoner. But when I tried to persuade the cossacks to lend me a hand, they simply laughed at this cavalier who had appeared out of the blue with such a ridiculous proposition. No one was prepared to support me and, thank God, I thought, I still had enough sense not to take on single-handed a soldier who at that very moment was joined by other fellow riders. Unfortunately, in my youthful eagerness, common sense all too soon deserted me.

With growing defiance, like a man possessed, I spurred my horse forward and, once within range, let off a pistol shot at the officer. Without altering pace, he answered me with a shot of his own and other shots followed from the carbines of his colleagues. These were the first bullets ever to whistle past my ears.

I felt immensely proud of myself and excited at everything going on around me. Only the army mattered; civilian life suddenly seemed worthless. No longer expecting any help from the cossacks, I was supremely confident in the prowess of my horse. Anger suddenly welled up in me against a total stranger who, God knows, was simply carrying out his duty and obligations just like myself. I drew closer to him, flourishing my sword and swearing at him in French as loudly and expressively as possible. I invited him to engage with me unassisted in single combat. He swore back at me and offered the same conditions; but neither of us took up the challenge and we both stayed rooted to the spot. I had strayed quite a distance from the cossacks and was within only three or four steps of the French officer and his men. To be honest, I probably deserved to be yanked by the ears from my horse and smacked across the head.

At that moment a cossack sergeant galloped over and exlaimed: 'Why all the swearing, Your Excellency? That's a sin! Fighting is a sacred business. Swearing in battle is like swearing in church. God will punish you; you'll get killed and so will we. Please, better go back to where you came from!' Only then did I come to my senses. My parody of a Trojan hero seemed absurd, so back I rode to Prince Bagration.

It is quite a challenge to command the rearguard of an army while it is being hotly pursued. The basic duty of such a commander is twofold: while maintaining the safety and discipline of the army as it retreats under enemy attack, he must at the same time keep the rearguard orderly and in close contact with the main body of troops. But, in the course of every battle, enforced halts may cause an increasing distance to open up between the rearguard and the army proper. If the rearguard concentrates on keeping in close touch with the other troops, therefore avoiding clashes with the enemy, it invites attack. Bagration resolved this dilemma, mastering the rules for rearguard tactics which, fourteen years later were exemplified on the island of St Helena by the greatest exponent of the art of war, when he said: 'The vanguard must keep pushing relentlessly, while the rearguard must manoeuvre.' Bagration used this axiom as his guide for rearguard action in all his various later operations.

Under Bagration's command the rearguard never remained long in the same place, and never trailed along in the wake of the army. In essence, it would keep retreating from one defensive position to another without offering total battle, but maintained a threatening appearance by repeatedly repelling enemy thrusts, provoking a response with fierce and indiscriminate artillery fire. This is an operation that calls for a shrewd grasp of the situation, coolness, a sharp eye and quick reactions – qualities with which Bagration was so well endowed.

All this was quite beyond my comprehension. As a hussar company commander I hungered for a hot engagement. According to my strategy it was absolutely necessary, and its likelihood was guaranteed by the fearless nature of the prince, who, in my opinion, was obliged to defend the Wolfsdorf position by all possible means, even at the cost of sacrificing the entire rearguard.

I was so convinced that my reasoning was sound, so certain that everything would turn out differently if they only would listen to me, that neither Suvorov nor Napoleon would have been able to persuade me otherwise! This explains the stupid self-confidence which placed me in such a dangerous position and from which I was only saved by Providence.

Upon my return from the front line to the prince, I was immediately dispatched by him to the 5th Jäger Regiment with orders to abandon the woods they had occupied and fall back on Dietrichsdorf, where a second position had been chosen for the rearguard. 'How can it be,' I pondered, 'when so few troops have been committed to action, when no one in the regiment has even fired a shot, that we are to retreat? Is this the resolute, intrepid prince who has earned universal praise?' Nevertheless I galloped off to the Jägers and carried out my order.

In the meantime our forward line continued to exchange fire with the enemy skirmishers and fell back towards the woods which the Jägers were supposed to vacate. It happened that on my way back to my post, and reflecting on how I might correct Prince Bagration's erroneous decision to give up the

Wolfsdorf position without responding vigorously to the enemy attacks, I rode past the very front line where an hour earlier I had been exchanging swear-words with my French officer. As luck would have it, I spotted the same cossack sergeant who had interrupted my Homeric challenge with his prosaic good sense. As I trotted over to him, an even crazier idea suddenly struck me. I had read once, God knows where, that in some battles completely unknown soldiers had appeared and, by sheer willpower, had snatched victory from the foe despite strict orders to the contrary. My imagination ran rife. Perhaps I, too, was such a person, chosen by Providence to accomplish just such a feat.

What I planned to do was to launch a frontal attack on the enemy, send it reeling and break through with the 5th Jäger Regiment, which was prepar-ing to leave the woods. The prince, as witness to my success, would then reinforce me with the entire rearguard and inform Bennigsen, who would promptly come up with the whole army. In short, I aimed for nothing less than to defeat the entire enemy vanguard with a handful of horsemen and Jägers and take the credit for vanquishing Napoleon himself.

Passion spoke louder than reason, as was to happen, too, in other cir-cumstances. I could see the whole scene in my mind, the entire area from Wolfsdorf to Varlach covered with dense columns of infantry, cavalry and countless artillery pieces. I should have realised the foolishness of my under-taking, but obsessed with my audacious plan, I addressed the cossack sergeant: 'What do you say, brother, shall we have a go at them?' 'Why not, Your Excellency?' he replied, pointing at the skirmishers who were dashing about right under our nose, and added: 'There are not many of them here; we could deal with them easily. Yesterday we were on our own, but today our infantry are close by and could give us a hand.'

'Right! You sell the idea to the cossacks and I'll have a word with the hussars and Uhlans' (who made up two platoons of the cossack line).

We got our way. The troops all rose up, gave a shout and hurled them-selves at the enemy skirmishers. Swords clashed, bullets flew by and the fun began. I remember my sabre biting into live flesh and warm blood steam-ing from the blade.

The fight did not last very long. The French skirmishers who had been mauled by our men beat a hasty retreat, but in our eagerness to chase them we came up against their reserves who galloped to their aid. These were dragoons with horsetails streaming from their helmets. They swooped on us hungrily, fresh blows were exchanged and we in turn were beaten back towards the woods where the Jägers were no longer stationed and in a posi-tion to help us. The whole gigantic plan of my folly fell apart and I, like Napoleon after Waterloo, gloomy and despondent, made my way back to the prince, skirting Wolfsdorf towards Dietriechsdorf, where the whole rear-guard was headed.

I rode alone through a valley, quite safe from the enemy because the dragoons who had thrashed us were content with their success and did not pursue us. But as I climbed a hillock I came suddenly face-to-face with six French *chasseurs à cheval*, bound for Wolfsdorf to keep an eye on the movements of our rearguard. Startled, I galloped away. They fired their carbines after me and seriously wounded my horse, which, for the moment at any rate, did not slacken pace. I thought I had shaken them off, but they were gaining on me from either side. I looked around to see if there was any help nearby, but only caught a distant glimpse of our rearguard columns advancing on Dietrichsdorf, about three miles away. Otherwise, to the point where the woods began, there was not a soul in sight.

Disaster seemed imminent. I was wearing a pelisse, buttoned with one clasp at the throat, my sword was drawn and I had no time to reload the pistols at my saddle. One of my pursuers, probably riding a better horse than his friends, caught up with me, though not quite close enough to touch me with his sword. But he made a grab for the edge of my billowing cloak and almost managed to drag me off my horse. Luckily the pelisse came undone and he was left with it in his hand. I kept galloping at full speed towards the woods, but gradually the distance between me and my pursuers shortened as my wounded horse, fast wearying, slowed down.

The winter had been of short duration and as a result the swamps were treacherous and invisible under the snow. I could not keep to a path, but twisted and turned at random. To my misfortune, I entered the woods at a point where, unseen by me, they bordered a swamp. My horse crashed into the water up to its belly and gave up the ghost. Moments later a sharp blade was raised above my head. Death or capture stared me in the face!

At that very moment, brought here by Providence, a patrol of about twenty cossacks dispatched by Yourkovsky to observe the enemy, burst out of the nearby woods with a mighty yell and proceeded to chase the French back to Wolfsdorf. One of them, my true saviour, mounted me behind him and conducted me to Yourkovsky, who promptly gave me the horse of a dead hussar. And that's how I rejoined our rearguard, now in position near Dietrichsdorf.

Meanwhile, the prince, as considerate as he was heroic, had become worried about my safety and was asking for news from each man returning from the front line. No one could tell him what had happened to me.

Finally I appeared before him on a strange horse, without a coat, covered with mud, snow and blood, but with something like a triumphant expression that stemmed from recollection of my bold exploit and my unexpected rescue. Needless to say, I did not divulge to the prince and my friends the details of my grandiose plans which by now I had come to realise were thoroughly quixotic. I only told them about the enemy pursuit and my salvation thanks to the cossacks who had arrived in the nick of time. The prince, with an approving smile, chided me a little for my rash behaviour and arranged for me to have his own warm coat as replacement for my cape. Soon afterwards he recommended me for an award.

CHAPTER 3

The Battle of Eylau, 7–8 February 1807

Napoleon's successful campaign against Prussia in 1806 amazed everyone. There appeared to be no stopping his plans to hammer out new foundations for Europe and bend the continent to his will. Yet although he succeeded in destroying the Prussian military machine in the battles of Jena and Auerstädt, his diplomatic efforts met with little success.

Russia continued to refuse to join his crusade against England or to accept the new status quo imposed in central Europe.

The economic blockade proclaimed from Berlin in November 1806 did not have the hoped-for result and force England to her knees. Instead, it would gradually bring economic ruin to Napoleon's empire. His efforts to pin the Russians down and to destroy them were also proving elusive. A long winter war loomed ahead as the Russian and French armies prepared for the encounter.

The original Russian plan was to surprise and overwhelm the French troops under Bernadotte and Ney before Napoleon and his other army corps, about 80,000 strong, could come to their rescue and defeat the Russians separately. In his winter quarters, Bernadotte had 17,000 troops, almost out of touch with the military operations, in Elbingen. Ney had 22,000 infantry soldiers and the cavalry of Bessières in his corps, equally dispersed. Ney, however, was not at his winter quarters, but was actually pursuing L'Estocq's corps in the direction of Friedland. This placed him virtually along the route that was being followed by the Russian army! The plan was to cut off and destroy Ney's corps while on the march, but due to the Russians' slow progress and incorrect bearings, Ney was able to march through Eylau, follow the River Passarge, and join the main body of the French army.

Bernadotte, learning of the Russian movement to intercept Ney and Bessières, recognised the danger of remaining by the seashore near the fortified towns of Danzig and Graudenz, which were still occupied by the Prussians. So he left Elbing and marched to Mohrungen, where he could make a stand and avoid encirclement in the north.

After a skirmish of almost eight hours with Soult and Murat around the cemetery of Eylau on 7 February, Bennigsen, with about 50,000 men under his command, should have attacked the French at the crack of dawn on the 8th, before the arrival of Davout and Ney. The latter were respectively still 20 and 25 miles away when they were summoned urgently by Napoleon to join his forces. Davout hurried from Bartenstein with about 15,000 men.

Instead, the Russians opened a cannonade early in the morning with 500 artillery pieces of which one-third was of heavy calibre. At about 1.00 p.m., having arrived with fresh troops, Davout attacked the Russian left and threatened their rear. Bennigsen directed most of his troops against him. To prevent this, Napoleon ordered Augereau to attack, but both his divisions were mown down up by Russian artillery and he lost 12,000 of his 15,000 men. To stabilise the situation, Murat's cavalry (10,700 men) charged the Russian centre and forced them to withdraw, albeit in good order.

Ney failed to intercept the 15,000-strong Prussian army, which checked Davout's advance.

Although Bennigsen lost a large portion of his army, Eylau was no better than a draw.

The French lost between 20,000 and 25,000 killed and wounded and 1,200 men were taken prisoner. The Russians left 11,000 dead on the battlefield and about 2,500 were taken prisoner, mainly wounded. All told, there were almost 40,000 casualties at Eylau where some 70,000 troops confronted one another on each side.

Bennigsen had a chance to destroy Bernadotte and Ney while they were so far removed from Napoleon's main army. Ney in particular was in a precarious position, as he was strung out in pursuit of L'Estocq and the Prussians. Bennigsen's failure to grasp the moment thus proved a major missed opportunity that could have had a dramatic effect on the outcome of the overall action.

Davidov's memoirs, incidentally, contain ten pages of text describing the marches and counter-marches prior to the battle of Eylau, which are not included in this translation of his account of the battle itself.

The battle of Eylau has almost receded from contemporary memory after the storm of the battle of Borodino, and because many now feel that it was not an equally significant event. For a Russian, the issue that was debated by force of arms at Borodino was nobler, more involving and more passionate than the contest at Eylau because what was at stake was Russia's very survival. The object of dispute at Eylau was on quite a different level. True, it proved a bloody prelude to Napoleon's invasion of Russia, but no one could have foreseen this. It appeared rather as a contest of military prestige by both armies, in the spirit, say, of card players fighting it out with their wallets still crammed, not obliged to wager their last morsel of bread or contemplate shooting themselves through the head in the event they lost.

It is not really fair to compare the two battles on the basis of the number of contestants or casualties. This is because at Eylau different weapons and fighting methods prevailed. At the battle of Borodino the main weapon was firepower. At Eylau it was hand-to-hand fighting that took front stage. Bayonet and sword held sway, drinking their fill of blood. No other battle had witnessed clashes of infantry and cavalry and exchanges of musket fire on such a scale, and cannon bombardment merely played a supporting role here. As in other battles, too, the guns produced more noise than destruction and made a greater impression on the minds and morale of the troops, speeding up the destruction of the enemy by other means.

I was only about 20 years old, full of verve, looking forward to any kind of adventure and eager to confront every sort of danger. I must have been immune to the rain of cannonballs that hummed overhead, crashed around me and ploughed through the ranks by my side, or the hail of grenades that exploded above my head and under my feet!

It was a vast hurricane of death that seemed to smash and erase from the face of the earth everything in its path; and it continued from midday on 26 January until 1 o'clock in the early morning of 27 January 1807. Certainly, firepower is ineffectual in comparison with hand-to-hand fighting, where blows are not wasted, always find their mark, and do not require careful aim, whereas gunfire involves uncertainty and guesswork.

The disposition of our army, comprising 70,000–80,000 men, was as follows. The right flank was anchored to the main Königsberg highway near the village of Schloditen, extending towards the town of Eylau; half a mile or so short of its walls, it made an angle, so that the left flank lay adjacent to Klein-Sausgarten. The village of Serpalten, just before Sausgarten, was occupied by a weak detachment under Major General Baggovut. Five infantry divisions – the 2nd, 3rd, 5th, 7th and 8th – were arranged in two lines; two battalions of each regiment were deployed frontally and the 3rd behind them in a column; with them were arrayed over 200 cannon.

The reserve, consisting of the 4th and 15th divisions, was drawn up in two dense columns and had 50 pieces of horse-drawn artillery. At sunrise it was moved closer towards the centre of the army. The cavalry was divided into three sections and placed on the flanks and in the centre, where there were no more than 28 squadrons. The cossack regiments were positioned on the approaches to both flanks.

Independently of the artillery, which was deployed along the line and kept with the reserve, the 1st battery of 40 heavy pieces and 20 light pieces was at first stationed on the right flank of the army, next to the Königsberg highway; but when the town was occupied by the enemy it was moved 700 paces further away from it; the 2nd battery of 70 heavy pieces was positioned almost in the centre of the army, about a mile from the city, and the 3rd battery of 40 heavy pieces stood between the centre and Sausgarten. All three batteries were bolstered by troops of our first line, like bastions protruding from fortifications.

The Prussian corps under L'Estocq, strengthened by the Viborg Infantry Regiment and numbering 8,000 men, was still quite far off, but moving towards Altdorf, i.e. our right flank. One of its brigades under General Plotz was to entice Ney towards Kreitzburg and away from the area of decisive events, to prevent him taking part in the coming battle.

Our right flank was commanded by Lieutenant General Tuchkov (I), the centre by Lieutenant General Sacken, the left flank by Lieutenant General Osterman-Tolstoy, the reserve by Lieutenant General Dokhturov, the cavalry by Lieutenant General Golitzyn and the artillery by Lieutenant General Rezvoy.

Bagration, who was the youngest of the generals, had no independent command and was assigned to Dokhturov's reserve.

The French army on the eve of the battle was disposed as follows. At the approaches to Eylau and inside the town, the infantry division of General Legrand was on the right side, and the infantry brigades under Vivienne and Fère (both part of the infantry division under Leval) on the left. Adjoining the right flank of Vivienne's brigade was the infantry division of St Hilaire. All these three divisions were part of the corps commanded by Marshal Soult.

To the right of St Hilaire's division was the dragoon division under Milhaud. Behind the town, on either side of the Landsberg road, were the dragoon divisions of Klein and Grouchy; to the left, behind Fère's infantry brigade, was the cavalry division of the guard. Further to the left were the light cavalry brigades of Colbert, Guyot and Bruyère, and the cuirassier division under Haupoult.

The light cavalry brigade of Durosnel was at the very end of the left flank of the entire army, adjacent to the village of Altdorf.

Behind Haupoult's cuirassiers, on the road leading from Eylau to the village of Stroben, was the infantry corps of Augereau. Napoleon's Imperial Guard and its own bivouac were situated on the hill between Eylau and Gringhofshen.

Davout's infantry corps was located about 20 miles from the main body of the army on the road to Bartenstein, and Ney's infantry corps some 25 miles away on the road to Tzinten.

The infantry corps under the command of Bernadotte was several days' march behind the French army. The surrounding area, which was occupied by our positions, was a slightly undulating plain. On the left side several hills that overlooked the location of our left flank were very dangerous from the strategic point of view. Snow covered the ground, making it difficult to move the artillery, and the various small lakes, frozen and also snow-covered, which were scattered around the field of battle were very treacherous as they offered flat surfaces which appeared ideal but in fact were quite hazardous when moving artillery pieces. Swamps made the terrain impossible even for infantry. A forest of brambles stretched between the villages of Sausgarten, Kutschitten and Anklappen. The weather was clear on the whole, although marred by passing snow flurries, with light frost, no more than three or four degrees.

In the half-light of early morning, the army rose and prepared their muskets. The campfires were still smouldering where the men had slept, their formations crisscrossing the pristine snow-covered fields of the coming battle. None of them had yet fired a shot; all that was evident was a ripple of commotion among the lines and columns being summoned to final battle order. The 4th Infantry Division and the Archangel Town Regiment returned to their places as part of the general army reserve.

Suddenly it was daylight, and with it the 60-piece battery of our right flank opened up with a roar. Part of the enemy artillery which was sheltering behind the first buildings of the town emerged from cover and answered the challenge. Napoleon saw with his own eyes that it was no longer a matter of a fight with the rearguard alone, as he had first thought, but with our whole army. Surely at that moment the great commander must have reproached himself for allowing the corps of Ney and Davout to be removed to such a distance from the main army, and cursed the fact that fate had left him without Bernadotte's corps on such a decisive day. Staff officers were immediately rushed to Davout and Ney with orders to hurry to Eylau. In the meantime a heavy cannonade roared around the town, and the main French forces began to redeploy. The light cavalry brigades of Durosnel, Bruyère, Guyot and Colbert remained to the left of Eylau. The left flank of Leval's infantry division, pooling together all three brigades, was drawn up alongside these light cavalry brigades and its right flank abutted the town. The Legrand infantry division moved forward from there and connected with Leval's right flank. Augereau's corps formed two lines: Desjardin's division was in front and Heudelet's division behind. Their left flanks protected the church at the end of town where Napoleon remained for the duration of the battle.

Behind Augereau was deployed Haupoult's cuirassier division, alongside the guard infantry stationed on a rise to the rear of the church. Behind Haupoult was the mounted guard and to the right, lined up with them, was Grouchy's division of dragoons. St Hilaire, from Soult's corps, adjoined the right flank of Augereau's first line, screening Klein's dragoon division.

The cannonade from both sides increased as the French army deployed parallel to ourselves. It became general but seemed more concentrated near the town than elsewhere. This was because at that point we were trying to prevent Legrand attacking our right flank and the French were attempting to draw our attention away from our left to open up the way for Davout, whose arrival was intended to decide the outcome of the battle.

The first bombardment from several hundred guns had already lasted about three successive hours, but nothing remarkable had happened, either on the enemy's or on ours.

Having received the news of the impending arrival of Davout's corps, which was under orders to move from the Heilsberg road to the Bartenstein road,

Napoleon instructed the centre of his army to move to the right and combine operations with those of Davout. As the armies moved forward, a heavy snowstorm struck, making it impossible to see anything more than a few steps away.

Augereau's corps lost its bearings, thus losing contact with St Hilaire's division and all the cavalry, and suddenly appeared, much to their and our surprise, in front of our central battery just as the weather cleared. Seventy cannons belched hellfire and a hail of grapeshot rang against their musket barrels and bit into the live mass of flesh and bone.

In an instant the Moscow Grenadiers and the Schlusselburg Infantry Regiment, together with General Somov's Infantry Regiment, charged hungrily at them with lowered bayonets. The French wavered, but recovering, met bayonet with bayonet and stood their ground.

There then ensued an engagement the likes of which had never been seen before. Over 20,000 men from both armies were plunging their three-faceted blades into one another. They fell in masses. I was personal witness to this Homeric slaughter. It came to be described, justly, as the legend of our century, and I have to say in truth that over the course of the sixteen campaigns in my service record and throughout the period of all the Napoleonic campaigns, I have never seen anything to compare with it! For about half an hour you could not hear a cannon or a musket shot, only the indescribable roar of thousands of brave soldiers as they cut one another to pieces in hand-to-hand combat. Mounds of dead bodies were covered by new mounds; soldiers were tumbling in their hundreds on top of each other, so that this corner of the battlefield resembled a high parapet of some hastily erected barricade.

Then, finally, our side got the upper hand! Augereau's corps was crushed and hotly pursued by our infantry and the central cavalry of Prince Golitsyn who had galloped up to support the foot soldiers. Their fervour reached an incredible pitch: one of our battalions, in the heat of the pursuit, outflanked the enemy position and appeared at the church only a hundred paces away from Napoleon himself, as is mentioned in all the French war diaries of that time. It was a critical moment. Napoleon, whose resolve increased in proportion to present dangers, ordered Murat and Bessières, together with the three Haupoult divisions, Klein, Grouchy and the horse-guard, to strike at our troops as they charged forward with shouts of 'Hurrah!' This action was essential in order to save even a part of Augereau's corps and to head off our attack. More than 60 squadrons galloped around to the right of the fleeing corps and swept towards us, brandishing their swords. The field resounded to their cries, and the snow, ploughed up by the concerted force of 12,000 riders, swirled up in a tempest. The brilliant Murat, sporting his carnival-style uniform and followed by a large entourage, led the attack with bare sabre and plunged directly into the thick of the battle. Neither musket and cannon fire, nor levelled bayonets could stem the deadly tide. The French cavalry smashed its way through the front line of our army and its impetuous charge reached our second line and the reserve. Here, however, it shattered against the cliff of a stronger will. Our men stood their ground, did not waver and turned back the awesome tidal wave with concentrated battery and musket fire.

The French cavalry, pursued in turn by our horsemen right through our front ranks (which had taken an initial battering but which had now recovered and had resumed firing), was soon flowing back even beyond the line that it had occupied at the start of the day. Our cavalry charge was breathtakingly successful and followed through to the hilt.

The enemy batteries left on that line were seized by our several squadrons, and the gun crews, together with the carriage wheels, were hacked to pieces after the draught horses and their drivers had galloped away in panic.

In this hand-to-hand engagement and the flowing back and forth of the cavalry, Dalman of the guard, Desjardins of the infantry and Corbineau all fell on the field of battle. Marshal Augereau himself, along with Division General Heudelet and Brigade General Lochet, were wounded; several other brigade generals and staff officers such as Lacuyet, Marois, Bouvier and others shared the same fate. Two squadrons of horse-guard grenadiers which composed the tail of the retreating enemy cavalry were intercepted by ours and laid down their lives between the church and the second line. The 14th Regiment of the line lost all its officers and the 24th of the line had only five left alive. Augereau's entire corps, three cavalry divisions and the mounted guard represented mere fragments of their former selves. Six eagles were captured by us.

What a moment of opportunity was now offered for a determined, combined thrust by all our forces against St Hilaire's division, left without support and any hope of assistance! All units surrounding this division had either been destroyed or broken, and more importantly, were too demoralised to come to its aid or possessed of the will to fight back. Moreover, it was not quite 11 o'clock in the morning, and therefore it would be two hours before Davout arrived on the battlefield.

In order to take advantage of such opportunities, however, it is not enough to have a thorough knowledge of one's craft, to show a determined spirit or possess a sharp mind. None of this is of any avail without inspiration – that inexplicable impulse which is as instantaneous as an electric spark, and which is as essential to the poet as it is to the military commander. To Napoleon and Suvorov, inspiration was innate, just as it was to poets such as Pindar and Mirabeau, with their command over words.

The propitious moment, which held out so much hope of military advantage, soon vanished. Our troops, in pursuit of the enemy, were forced to return to the main body of the army from which not a single battalion had been sent forward in support; and the enemy, who had been in disarray, recovered, took advantage of this lull to re-form, and found new heart. The opposing armies resumed the very positions they had occupied prior to the bloody onslaught which had so uselessly wasted so many lives; and all the amazing feats of bravery, all the selfless examples of heroism displayed by those soldiers whose bodies lay scattered over the disputed battleground were turned to naught as if it had never happened!

The action was now confined to a severe cannonade which again engulfed the troops on either side and resulted in the slaughter of thousands more, whiling away the time until the French were reinforced by the arrival of the Davout corps and we ourselves by that of l'Estocq's Prussian corps.

Now came the second phase of the battle. Around 1 o'clock in the afternoon, on the crest of the hills that rose to the left of us and where our left flank was posted, there appeared a few isolated men on horseback. Behind them emerged ranks of cavalry, followed by masses of infantry and artillery. The horizon grew dark and rippled with motion. The hills of Sausgarten, hitherto silent, flashed, belched smoke and thundered.

Davout brought up 40 field-pieces and his troops poured over the battlefield to coincide with the arrival of St Hilaire's division. Reinforced by the cavalry division, Milhaud moved to meet him. To the left of St Hilaire came the cavalry divisions of Klein, Grouchy and Haupoult, which had already been mauled in battle and were now arrayed in three lines. Further to the left of this cavalry came the remnants of Augereau's corps in formation composed of two lines. Behind them marched the guard infantry, bringing up the rear of Haupoult's division. It was followed by the battered guard cavalry. However, the divisions of Legrand and Leval, as well as four light cavalry brigades, remained where they were.

Attention on both sides was now focused on Davout and our left wing. Adjutants galloped along the Altdorf road with orders for L'Estocq to hasten his arrival, no longer to reinforce our right flank, but to divert through Schmoditten to support our threatened left wing. A section of our cavalry and artillery also moved leftward from the right and the centre, as the enemy forced back our left wing, under heavy fire from the batteries deployed behind the stone walls of the city. The guns were by now firing along the length of our army from Eylau to Anklappen and from the woods between Sausgarten, Anklappen and Kutschitten.

The situation did not appear too hopeful. Davout, having pushed back our left flank behind the woods, now occupied the area between Kutschitten and Sausgarten, had deployed an enormous gun battery on the heights of Sausgarten and was shelling the entire army with the same sweeping enfilade fire that we were experiencing from Eylau. Davout's infantry poured into the village of Kutschitten, as did the troops of St Hilaire, who had captured Anklappen (where Bennigsen had set up headquarters the previous night). And although Count Osterman-Tolstoy and Count Pahlen heroically attempted to fend off the ever intensifying assault, it was to no avail.

Disorder was beginning to grip our troops. The whole field of battle from Kutschitten to Schmoditten was covered with scattered ranks of soldiers that stretched out towards the Königsberg highway, still protected by those of their comrades in arms who had not lost their spirit or discipline and were shedding their blood over every inch of contested ground. The intensified crossfire of the enemy guns ploughed through and blew up everything on the battlefield. Pieces of muskets, shreds of gun carriages, helmets and other headgear were flying all over the place; everything was cracking and falling apart.

Out of the storm of screaming shells and exploding grenades, the heaped corpses and the collapsing men and horses, surrounded by tumult and confusion, and enveloping clouds of smoke, emerged the dominating figure of Bennigsen. To him and from him streamed adjutants, messages and orders, followed by news and further orders. The activity was incessant and unflagging. Yet for all that, the situation of the army did not improve. Calculation and prudence were the hallmarks of our general's thinking and planning, the logical outcome of a sound, precise mind. But although equal to the task of grappling with minds of a similar type, he was not up to dealing with flashes of genius, sudden events which defy foresight, and touches of inspiration founded upon classic rules. Bennigsen's orders and consequent tactics were all concentrated on systematically resisting the attacks of Davout and St Hilaire: opposing bayonet to bayonet and firearm to firearm, but failing to address any unexpected, unconventional move or to forestall a strike out of the blue against some position deemed in no danger from the enemy.

What, in fact, was actually happening? Davout continued to press forward, overrunning more and more of our left flank, while the centre and right, absolutely immobile, were sacrificing small sections of infantry, cavalry and artillery to help out the retreating left wing, not venturing anything calculated to surprise the enemy. Yet while the fighting continued, our right flank was playing a positive role and delaying a decisive defeat by affording time for L'Estocq's corps to arrive on the battlefield. But to take full advantage of this, we should have been propping up this flank with large numbers of men, not just small units.

Bagration, who in moments of danger asserted himself through sheer willpower and innate talent, moved the reserve towards Anklappen so that it faced Davout and St Hilaire. Ermolov galloped to the same spot with 36 horse-drawn guns taken from the reserve, peppered Anklappen with incendiary shells, set it immediately on fire and forced out the enemy infantry.

Major General Count Kutaisov also arrived there with twelve guns, but some-what later: then, not losing a moment, he made for the stream that crossed the woods and attacked the batteries which had been stationed there, thus preventing the infantry columns from moving into the woods of Anklappen or Kutschitten, and reinforcing the troops pouring into the latter village. But these successes, or rather the postponement of the threatened disaster, could not last. To snatch decisive victory from the enemy it was vital not only to halt Davout but to defeat him by bearing down on his right flank, and simul-taneously threatening his rear by a general offensive against Augereau's corps and the cavalry backing up his forces.

Eventually the adjutants galloped over with news of the approach of L'Estocq, whom we had awaited so long and so patiently. Having kept the greater part of Ney's corps occupied by battling the brigade of General Plotz and pursuing him to Kreizburg, L'Estocq turned towards Leisen, Graventen and Altdorf with his main forces, consisting of nine battalions and 29 squadrons. It was already around 4.00 p.m. The road to Altdorf was dark with troops and Bennigsen galloped to meet them – to speed them up and to issue them with his own orders. It was noticeable that with the arrival of the commander-in-chief the entire corps began to move faster. L'Estocq was directed towards Schmoditten; he passed this village and just short of Kutschitten drew up his troops in battle order. The right column was com-posed of the Viborg Infantry Regiment, the left was Ruchel's regiment and behind came the reserve. The Fobetsky Grenadier Battalion deployed in a single line. The Shoning Infantry Regiment, marching in column, bypassed the village on the left, smashed the enemy infantry positioned there and chased them into the woods. General Kal, with cavalry and one cossack reg-iment which joined him from the main body of the army, attacked the enemy cavalry posted near Kutschitten, creating havoc in the village. He then turned on the infantry fleeing for the village in disarray, destroyed the greater part of it and prevented the survivors escaping into the woods where their com-panions had found refuge.

In this engagement, the Viborg Regiment won back three cannon that the French had captured on our left flank during its retreat. Having taken pos-session of Kutschitten, L'Estocq turned his troops to the right and drew them up to face the woods. The Shoning Infantry Regiment composed his right flank, the Fobetsky Grenadier Battalion and the Viborg Regiment the centre, and the Ruchel Regiment the left. A second line of defence was made up of the Wagenfeld Cuirassier Regiment and the dragoon regiments of Auer and Batchko. A light cavalry regiment composed of various elements was arranged to the left of the infantry.

Our left flank, which had been retreating, halted and came to order; its reserve under the command of Major General Count Kamenskoy and the reserve cavalry under Major General Chaplitz arrived to reinforce the Prussian corps.

The attack on the woods was carried out with great courage and in impeccable order. The woods were cleared partly by firearms, partly by cold steel. The moment was ripe for a combined effort by our centre and the reserve against the weakened remnants of Augereau's corps (battered that morning), the horse-guard and the three cavalry divisions of Klein, Grouchy and Haupoult, which had brought together the left and right flanks of the French army. Such a combination had given victory to Napoleon at Austerlitz. But our army remained on the spot, limiting its action to a cannonade. The pressure exerted by L'Estocq was strengthened by the addition of his own artillery, which hammered the troops of Davout and St Hilaire. Ermolov's artillery also concentrated fire along the whole enemy line from left to right.

Despite this general inactivity on our side, which relied solely on the artillery barrages of L'Estocq and Ermolov, the enemy was unable to withstand the pressure. Their retreat, which at first began with some semblance of order, turned into inexcusable confusion, so much so, in fact, that 28 cannon, some damaged and some not, were abandoned by them on the battlefield. The coming darkness and poor intelligence did not allow the Prussian general to crown this day with these important trophies. Having left the field of battle, Davout and St Hilaire drew up their troops on either side of Sausgarten: the front line and sentries were placed a few yards ahead. The whole enemy line segmented the battlefield from Sausgarten to Eylau. At Eylau the divisions of Leval and Legrand remained at their previous stations; but four light cavalry brigades moved forward to the Altdorf stream to keep open the line of communication with Ney, who was then approaching Altdorf.

On our side, the troops were disposed as follows. The front line, with its left wing flanking the road from Kutschitten to Domnau, followed the stream which flowed from Anklappen and cut the woods in two. From there, the line extended from in front of Anklappen to a point alongside our central battery, which had played such an important role in the first phase of the battle. The troops of our right flank likewise adjoined this battery, as they did in their original formation prior to the battle. This defensive battle order of the opposing forces at the end of the conflict proves that neither was able to impose decisive superiority of arms over the other. Both the French and ourselves remained essentially in the positions they originally occupied, with minor changes on our left flank, which gave a little ground to Davout's corps and St Hilaire's division because the coming darkness made fighting more difficult. If we had had one more hour of daylight, L'Estocq would inevitably have taken possession of the artillery abandoned by the French and would have compelled Davout and St Hilaire to retreat beyond Sausgarten. Late night deepened the darkness over the blood-saturated field of Eylau. All the surrounding villages were now in flames and the reflection of the fires illuminated the exhausted troops, still standing under arms and awaiting further orders. Here and there you could see campfires being lit, rallying points for thousands of crawling, wounded soldiers. The torn bodies of men and horses, broken wagons, powder cases and gun carriages, equipment and weapons – scattered here and heaped up there – gave the plain an aspect of terror and destruction worthy of the brush of the inspired creator of *The Last Day of Pompeii*, the painter Bryullov.

The engagement had ended but the minds of the leaders of both armies were gripped by uncertainty: renew the battle or retreat to Königsberg? The more obstinate of the two finally triumphed, not because he resumed the offensive but because he remained on the battlefield until dawn.

Bennigsen departed the field around midnight, posting several squadrons to keep surveillance on the enemy and to provide a screen for the army heading for Königsberg. L'Estocq retired through Allenburg to Byelo. There was no pursuit. The French, like a disabled man-of-war with torn sails and broken masts, bobbed about menacingly, but were unable to make any headway to fight or to give chase.

Suddenly, we heard musket-fire in Schmoditten. We were astonished. Our first thought was that it was Ney, whom we had forgotten about. Sure enough, Ney had arrived with part of his corps at Altdorf around 9 o'clock in the evening and had come across the Prussian battalion of Captain Kurowsky who, realising the disproportion of opposing forces, had abandoned the village and joined the rest of the army. The French general Liger-Belair, with the 6th and 39th Regiments, followed him and entered Schmoditten village, which was filled with our wounded and covering escorts who were there to protect them. They opened fire on the French and a fusillade ensued. To assist them we sent the Voronezh Infantry Regiment and a few cannon; but the enemy did not choose to await their arrival and retreated into Altdorf, and thus the alarm was over.

On the 9th, our army, having rested in Muhlhausen, continued its march to Königsberg, stopping outside the city, having left Prince Bagration as rearguard in Ludwigswald. The French army, fearing a new battle up ahead, chose to stay put near Eylau. Only 24 squadrons moved forward to keep under observation the shores of Frieshing, towards Mansfeld and Ludwigswald; and that happened only two days later when Napoleon was assured that our army had arrived at Pregel. On 17 February, Napoleon decided to retreat behind the River Passarge to take up his winter quarters. He left Eylau, pursued by our vanguard and all the cossack regiments under the command of their leader, Hetman Platov, who from that day forward won his European reputation.

The French withdrawal was no less costly in many respects than the enforced retreat five years later from Moscow to the Niemen River, even though the weather was only moderately cold; so although the French later ascribed their losses after Eylau to the cold, few people nowadays believe that to be true. Being in the vanguard myself, I was witness to the bloody trail from Eylau to Gutstadt. The whole road was littered continuously with débris. Hundreds of dying horses obstructed our path, as well as ambulances filled with dying or dead soldiers and officers, mutilated in the battle of Eylau.

The rush to get away had become so urgent that besides the victims left in the carriages we found many who had been simply dumped in the snow without covering or clothes, bleeding to death. For mile after mile they lay not in pairs but in tens and hundreds. Moreover, all the villages along the way were filled with sick and wounded, without doctors or food or the least care. In this pursuit, the cossacks captured many exhausted men and scavengers, as well as eight artillery pieces, stuck in the snow without harnesses.

Our losses in this battle amounted to almost half of the number of the fighting men, that is to say, 37,000 men killed or wounded. According to the military registers, our army was apparently composed of 46,800 men (regular army) and 2,500 cossacks. Such losses have never been equalled in military annals since the invention of gunpowder. The reader can imagine the extent of the casualties in the French army, since they possessed a smaller force of artillery than ours, and were beaten back in two fierce assaults by our centre and the left flank. Our trophies consisted of nine eagles seized from the enemy ranks and 2,000 prisoners. The Prussian king was presented with two eagles.

I was involved in a touching episode after the battle. Fourteen months previously, our army had been defeated at Austerlitz. The Horse Guard Regiment shared the defeat along with the others. My own brother, then a 20-year-old youth who served with this regiment, was grievously wounded: he received five sabre cuts, one bullet wound and a bayonet thrust, and had been left for dead in a mound of corpses on the battlefield. There he lay until late at night. He regained consciousness in the dark, got up and somehow hobbled towards a fire in a nearby village which he found overflowing with Russian wounded, among whom he found shelter.

After three days, two men from his regiment who had sustained much lighter wounds – Arapov and Barkovsky – persuaded him to set off with them to find our retreating army; not really knowing which direction it had taken, they wandered about in the typical manner of men exhausted by suffering and hunger. Their journey did not last very long. A squadron of mounted grenadiers of the guard, detached from the French army to collect the wounded from both sides, overtook them and informed them of their fate. There was nothing to be done; they had to obey. The squadron continued on, but its commanding officer arranged for my brother and his two comrades to be conveyed to Brünn, where Napoleon's headquarters were located.

As our proverb says, however, poor folk get lost but God looks after them. This particular officer was Second-Lieutenant Serugues, a nephew of Minister Maret (Duke of Bassano). The life or death of my brother depended on his mercy. I say life or death because the reciprocal hatred of the French and the Russians dated from about that time. The soldiers of both armies had adopted the habit of stripping prisoners of their last clothes and their boots and leaving them to die, overcome by hunger and exhaustion, cold or wounds.

Although this was not part of a system ordered from above, such acts were never questioned by superiors. A humane and compassionate man, Serugues had not yet been infected by this loathsome practice. Taking a heartfelt interest in the misfortune of his prisoner, he showed compassion; he even forbade him to walk on foot, mounted him on a horse and, seeing how weak he was from hunger, shared with him his last morsel of bread. Thus he brought him to the pastor of the nearest village, saw to it that he was properly fed, got a cart ready for him and sent him on to Brünn, encouraging him with a friendly, almost fraternal concern. Moreover, he gave his word to my brother that he would look for him and find him again in Brünn, where he hoped to return shortly; but failing that, he made him promise to apply to his uncle, Minister Maret, for all necessary assistance.

All this I learned from my brother upon his return from captivity and a few weeks before I myself left to join the army. Having arrived with the rearguard at Ludwigswald on 29 January, I begged permission from Bagration to visit Königsberg on personal business, and duly quartered myself with General Chaplitz, who had been appointed commander of the city. Chaplitz told me that there was a French officer, wounded in the last engagement, who was making enquiries about me, asking whether anyone knew Davidov, a lieutenant of the guard. I was the only guard officer by that name in the whole army and, curious to discover the identity of this French officer, I asked to see the list of prisoners of rank. You can imagine my surprise when the name of Second Lieutenant of the Horse Guard Regiment, Serugues, leapt out at me the instant I opened the enormous folio!

In a flash I was off to find this man whose face I had never seen, but whom I already considered a devoted brother and lifelong friend.

The inhabitants of Königsberg, incidentally, had learned of the arrival of our army under their walls, and feared that if we retreated further, their city would eventually be occupied by the French. Therefore, to earn the favour of Napoleon beforehand, they begged Bennigsen for permission to divide themselves up to provide quarters for the wounded French officers and keep them in their homes at their expense.

Needless to say, the nephew of the minister was treated with special favour. Serugues enjoyed the hospitality of one of the wealthiest citizens of Königsberg. I found him in a tall, luxuriously appointed house, the first floor of which had been put at his disposal. A bed with a large canopy, choice linen, screens, small tables and sofas, comfortable armchairs, semi-darkness and fragrant incense, a doctor and medicines – nothing was lacking. But he lay there pale, worn out and in great pain. Several sword slashes on his head and arms did not trouble him as much as a deep and, as it proved, mortal wound to the groin.

I approached the bed of the unfortunate patient quietly and told him my name. We embraced as true blood brothers. He asked about mine with genuine concern: I thanked him for having saved him and offered my services with deep emotion. He answered me: 'You see I am in the care of a good person and don't lack for anything. However, you can do me a great service. Undoubtedly, among the prisoners there are some wounded from my outfit. Could you possibly appeal to the authorities and arrange for two, or even one, of my horse grenadiers to remain by my side? Let me die, still resting my eyes to the end on the uniform of my regiment and the guard of a great man.' It goes without saying that I rushed to see Bennigsen and Chaplitz, and obtained their permission to choose from the crowd of prisoners two horse grenadiers from Serugues's own squad. Within two hours I returned to him, accompanied by two mustachioed fellows, crowned with bearskin hats and in full uniform. It is impossible to describe the joy of my ill-fated friend at the sight of his comrades-in-arms. I had to cut short his expressions of gratitude, too exhausting in his condition. For two days, I did not leave his side, day or night. On the third, everything came to an end: he died in my arms and was buried in the Königsberg cemetery. Behind the casket walked the two afore-mentioned French horse-grenadiers and myself, a second lieutenant of the Russian guard. A strange juxtaposition of uniforms! Deep sorrow clearly etched the faces of the old veterans, my companions in the procession. I, who was young, wept.

CHAPTER 4

Tilsit, 1807

The day of 2 June 1807 was noteworthy for the incredible courage and frantic efforts of our armies, yet it proved a calamity for our cause.[3] Arrayed in battle order that countered the basic rules of military science, overwhelmed by superior enemy forces in a restricted area strewn with the débris of battle, some of us hemmed in by gunfire into the narrow streets of Friedland, others swept from the confined banks of the River Alle, our army fell back towards Pregel to avoid further enemy action.

I shall never forget the hardships that we experienced during the night that followed this bloody day.[4] Our rearguard, worn out by fighting that had lasted for ten days, and reeling from the latest blow which fell harder on them than on other troops, had the assignment of covering the disorderly retreat of an army that only a few hours before had been so imposing. Our physical strength buckled under the strain of duties entailed in front-line guard service. Ever cheerful, vigilant and heedless of danger and disaster, Bagration was in command of this portion of the army; but like his subordinates, he was worn out from lack of sleep and food. His close associates, who were just setting out on the road to fame – Count Pahlen, Rayevsky, Ermolov and Kulnev – were carrying out their duties by sheer willpower; the infantry barely dragged their feet; the horsemen were dozing off and swaying in their saddles.

At sunrise the army arrived at Velau and during the day crossed the Pregel; the rearguard, joining up with the rest of the men, destroyed the bridge. The whole body of troops, as far as time would allow, regrouped and carried on towards Taplaken, Klein-Shirau and Popelken, heading for Tilsit. Our marching order was as follows: ahead were the guard and the whole battery of artillery; they were followed by two regiments of light cavalry belonging to our right flank (the remaining cavalry was used by Bennigsen to reinforce the rearguard). Then came the heavy cavalry gathered from both flanks and finally the whole of our infantry and light artillery, together with the main headquarters. The rearguard formed the tail end of the troops.

---

[3] Because Davidov follows the Julian calendar, 2 June corresponds to 14 June, according to the Gregorian calendar that was adopted in the West. At that time, the difference between the two was twelve days; today it has stretched to thirteen.

[4] At the cost of only 8,000 casualties, the French destroyed 30 per cent of Bennigsen's army at Friedland; he lost 80 guns and almost 20,000 men!

Before continuing this sketch of our retreat, however, we need to take a look at the strategic dispositions previously adopted by both commanders.

Napoleon was established on the River Passarge and the advance corps of his army under Marshal Ney was located at Guttstadt and its immediate surroundings.

Bennigsen, alarmed at the activity near Frisches Haff (Gulf of Danzig), where his army virtually had been bottled-up during the winter campaign, had chosen a new line of operations. He distributed his troops along the River Alle from the area around Guttstadt to Heilsberg and Bartenstein, designating Heilsberg as the rallying point for all his forces in the event of a general battle; and he covered the neighbouring hills with numerous fortified positions. This disposition would have been acceptable if his chosen line of operation had protected our army's only home base – the River Niemen and Russia itself – and had also provided a defence for the warehouses and supply points between the Niemen and ourselves. But there were none of the latter in that area, for Bennigsen had removed them from that location and concentrated them in Königsberg, on our right flank and almost beyond reach of the present action. Thus any wagon trains sent to supply our army would be irretrievably lost in the event we were forced to abandon Heilsberg and move to the right bank of the Alle.

This lack of foresight could not escape the sharp, all-encompassing scrutiny of a commander of Napoleon's stature. He decided to take advantage of this situation not only because any military leader must pounce upon his opponent's errors, but also for reasons of sheer necessity. The resources of the region occupied by his troops had been exhausted after they had settled in their winter quarters during the previous two months. We, too, had formerly occupied it for the same period and it had nothing more left to offer. We had to rely on warehouses set up beforehand and, as I have said, those were only to be found in Königsberg.

It is only natural that Napoleon should have been quick to settle on that city as his primary objective, whereas we had neglected even to leave a token garrison to protect it against the smallest party of enemy hussars.

In order to capture Königsberg, however, and to avoid the same dangers that Bennigsen had faced during the winter campaign, he had to dislodge the Russian army from the Heilsberg heights and force it to retreat to the right bank of the Alle; he now sought the means to achieve this. After crossing the Passarge, the French army was closing in on Heilsberg, its left wing sweeping our right flank. Only then did Bennigsen remember about Königsberg. There were three ways to safeguard the city, at least temporarily. One was to fend off Napoleon from the fortified heights of Heilsberg, to defeat his army and pursue it beyond the Passarge and farther towards the Vistula. The second was to move our whole army towards the Bay of Danzig and to avoid giving battle at Heilsberg – a risky venture which, even if it succeeded, would engender the same dangers that faced us during the winter campaign.

The third way was to direct part of the army towards Königsberg; and that is the course that Bennigsen chose to follow, especially as the military situation favoured it. The Prussian corps of L'Estocq, which was in action on the lower Passarge, was cut off from our army by the left flank of the French army moving towards Guttstadt. Much the same had happened to the Russian detachment under Count Kamenskoy returning from an unsuccessful attempt to break into the fortress of Danzig before it fell under French control. Bennigsen exploited both these circumstances. L'Estocq, reinforced by Kamenskoy's detachment, now numbering about 20,000 men, made all speed for Königsberg.

In the meantime, Napoleon attacked our army defending the Heilsberg fortifications, and after incredible efforts that lasted well into the night, was repulsed with heavy losses.

We had won a defensive action, but won nevertheless; so we could have turned this to advantage and attacked the enemy on the following day. But Bennigsen spent that whole day on his fortified positions, and on the third day, with an army encouraged by success, having sustained small losses and still in good order, crossed over to the right bank of the Alle and followed the river towards the Pregel. In this manner Napoleon achieved his objective not through victory, but through a setback. There are no examples of this in recorded history. It would be hard to find a commander of a fortress who would be so unenterprising as to fail to make a sortie of some kind after repelling an assault, let alone give up after a victorious outcome.

Bennigsen's belief in Napoleon's extraordinary resourcefulness forced him to avoid a general battle; and it was Bennigsen's own lack of resourcefulness that led Napoleon to make some rash moves. He was apparently unwilling to ascribe our evacuation of the Heilsberg heights and subsequent retreat along the Alle towards the Pregel to a deliberate, unilateral decision on our part. He preferred to interpret it as a victory, and failed to realise that nothing had been resolved. The Gordian knot had yet to be unravelled at a future date with the aid of greater military forces. How else can we explain that the great commander dispatched Murat with Soult's corps, Davout and the greater part of the cavalry, numbering about 50,000 men, to pursue L'Estocq, and would seek to resolve a war that had been dragging on for more than half a year with only two-thirds of the army at his disposal?

It would have been a more certain and less dangerous option for Napoleon to leave L'Estocq untouched in Königsberg, to march with all his forces after our army to the lower Alle, and to divert other corps from his main body of troops only after victory had been achieved. This would have accomplished another purpose. Königsberg could have been captured without a shot being fired and L'Estocq's corps doomed with no chance of escape.

On the 4th [16 June] L'Estocq heard about Bennigsen's defeat at Friedland and our retreat towards Tilsit. He immediately abandoned Königsberg and made for Labiao, in order to reach the road that led to Tilsit. Realising the full danger of his situation, he did not march; he raced there without taking a breather.

Murat captured our warehouses in Königsberg, left Soult's corps to guard them and, sending back Davout through Labiao to rejoin Napoleon's main army, went chasing after L'Estocq with only his cavalry. He caught up with him, but only after L'Estocq had crossed the open ground and entered the woods and marshes outside Labiao where cavalry was useless. In the meantime, on the 3rd, Napoleon directed Ney's corps from Friedland towards Insterburg and followed him with the main body of his troops.

Unaware that Soult had been left in Königsberg and that Davout had joined up with Napoleon; and convinced that the least delay in the Russian retreat would enable Ney and Murat, together with Davout and Soult, to intersect the road to Tilsit and cut him off from it, Bennigsen reasoned that the greatest threat to our army was an attack from the rear by Ney and Murat, rather than a push from Velau by the main French army. This thinking was to some extent justified and almost led to the entire Russian army hastening to occupy the intersection of the roads from Insterburg and Labiao with the Tilsit highway. But this would have led to new dangers: the French troops, not meeting with any obstacles or defences from our rearguard, now combined with our main force, would have been free to overwhelm us in one mad assault and, keeping up the pressure, would have completed our destruction before we could reach the right bank of the Niemen.

In order somehow to slow down Napoleon's impetuous move from Velau and avoid the barriers that Murat and Ney would erect while we fell back on Tilsit, we had to sacrifice our rearguard. Bagration was left at Taplaken with orders to fend off Napoleon's onslaught and to retreat as slowly as possible behind our army which would speed up its crossings.

Something similar had taken place a year and a half earlier when Kutuzov, in the same dire straits and for the same reasons, had left Bagration under Hollabrun and Schoengraben to face the enormous forces of Lannes, Soult and Murat. But, just as before, a lucky star was watching over Suvorov's protégé. It seemed that Providence was saving him for the day of Borodino and his great sacrifice!

During the course of 3 June, the pursuit was conducted without the notable enthusiasm and confidence that the French normally displayed at the least success. On the 4th, however, we noticed that the numbers of the forces pursuing our troops had multiplied, reflecting the iron will of their commander-in-chief. Our rearguard was mercilessly set upon at Klein-Schirau, Bitemen and Popelken. We were still far from the intersection of the roads with the

Tilsit highway, and even farther from the Russian main army. We had received no news from L'Estocq's corps, nor any intelligence from the parties that had been dispatched to keep an eye on Ney's movements and direction. It was enough to make us despair!

On that day, as if to offer us a distraction from dire events, several Bashkir regiments arrived to join our rearguard. Armed with bows and arrows, wearing caps with long ear-flaps and dressed in weird-looking caftans, riding on short, bulky mounts that lacked any elegance, they seemed to represent caricatures of bold Circassian horsemen. We were supposed to believe that their appearance was intended to impress Napoleon with the notion that all the peoples and nations under Russia's rule were ready to rise up against him and give him real cause for worry.

What might have given him reason for concern was not the spectacle of a handful of barbarous tribesmen, but the prospect of 300,000 reserve soldiers of the regular army standing in battle-readiness at the frontiers of the empire, under the command of a determined general well-versed in the art of warfare. As it was, Napoleon was hardly likely to be deluded with such fantasies. Had the situation been reversed and our victorious army invaded a European nation, it is just possible that a multitude of natives from the Urals, Kalmyks and Bashkirs, sent as a diversion in the enemy's rear, might have induced a state of panic. Their numbers, their appearance, their wild behaviour, might perhaps have stirred the imagination and conjured up visions of the hordes of Attila the Hun – as effective in its way as the capture of military supplies and provisions. But after the defeat at Friedland and our retreat to the Niemen, when our own infantry, artillery and cavalry could barely contain the onslaught of victorious Napoleonic forces approaching the frontiers of Russia that lay open and unprepared to repel an invasion, how could anyone hope for success by opposing fifteenth-century weapons to nineteenth-century cannon balls, shells, grapeshot and bullets – even if the warriors with their bows and arrows had presented themselves in unthinkable numbers!

Be that as it may, French and Russians alike who came across these Bashkir horsemen were unanimous in greeting them with laughter. That evening, stories were circulated of adventures with Bashkirs during the course of the day; and I myself was witness to one rather amusing episode.

During the course of an exchange of fire, we took prisoner a French lieutenant colonel whose name I have now forgotten. To this officer's ill-fortune, nature had bestowed on him a nose of extraordinary size, and to make matters worse, this nose had been shot through with an arrow which was embedded to half its length. We helped the lieutenant-colonel down from his horse and set him on the ground so that we could free him of this distressing adornment.

A few Bashkirs were among the curious people who gathered around the sufferer. Our medic grabbed a saw and prepared to cut the arrow in two, so as to remove it painlessly from either side of the enormous pierced nose, when one of the Bashkirs recognised the weapon as one of his own and seized the medic by both hands.

'No,' said he, 'my good sir, I won't let you cut my arrow. Don't offend me, sir. Please don't. It is my arrow. I'll take it out myself.'

'Are you raving?' we said to the fellow. 'How will you get it out?'

'Well, sir, I'll take one end and pull it out, and the arrow will stay in one piece.'

'And the nose?' we enquired.

'And the nose,' he answered, 'the devil take it!'

You can imagine the roar of laughter that greeted his words. Meanwhile, the French officer, not understanding a word of Russian, was trying to guess what was going on. He begged us to chase the Bashkir away, which we did; the affair was settled, and in the end the French nose triumphed over the Bashkir arrow.

On 5 June our situation did not improve. There was still no news about L'Estocq and Ney, we were unable to shake off the vanguard pursuing us, and no amount of effort and dedication on the part of our troops seemed enough to resist enemy pressure. While discussing the outlook with one of my then closest friends, second captain Baron Diebitsch of the Semenovsky Guard Regiment, we happened to glance to our right and sighted 50 or so Prussian hussars galloping in our direction. I set off briskly on my horse, cossack style, joined up with the Prussians and rode over with them to meet Bagration. They informed him that L'Estocq had successfully got through the Gross Baumwald forest, that the French had fallen a good way behind, and that they would be delayed even further on account of a narrow dike that bisected the woods for more than two miles (which they had damaged and dug up in several places to slow down the enemy).

This gave us a new lease of life. And fate had more to offer us. At that very moment, another dispatch arrived with no less happy news: our look-outs sent towards Insterburg to keep an eye on Ney reported that he was no longer aiming for the road to Tilsit, but had changed direction instead towards Gumbinen. So here, too, the skies were clearing. Matters were taking a new turn and our salvation was now assured.

Finally, towards evening of the same day, our armies reached both Tilsit and the Niemen, those objectives that we had been determined to attain, even at the cost of sacrificing our rearguard. The various units that constituted our army were arrayed in battle order near the Dranghof church to safeguard the crossing of our heavy equipment.

These events, so important to us, freed Bagration's hands and released him of the obligation to hold back Napoleon's forces, ten times superior in numbers to his own. Ney and Murat no longer menaced his rear and he could confine his efforts to fending off routine attacks against his front line originating from Velau.

This was the state of affairs when I was sent to see Bennigsen on the morning of the 6th to inform him that our rearguard was no longer threatened, that our troops were safeguarded and in good spirits, that Murat had joined up with the main body of the French army, and that Ney's corps had veered off towards Gumbinen.

When I arrived at the Dranghof church, I was unable to catch up with our troops. Having sent its heavy equipment across the Niemen, the army had also crossed, and the main headquarters were now located in Tilsit. Beyond the church, I ran into the mayor, Ernest Sheping, a witty friend and brilliant conversationalist.

'What's new, Sheping?' I enquired.

'What's new is that I am carrying a letter from Bennigsen. He instructs him to use me to contact the French and offer them an armistice, until we enter into peace negotiations. There's news for you, lad. Goodbye!'

I cannot express how this news affected me! It was not that the notion of armistice and peace were repugnant to me. Indeed, the endless retreats, even after successes, the constant occupation and subsequent abandonment of positions considered impregnable and vacated the moment the enemy showed up, and the absence of offensive actions – all this drove me to despair.

I was well aware of the glaring inequality of talent between Bennigsen and Napoleon, the disparity in numbers between our army and the enemy forces, the conviction among most of our soldiers that Napoleon was invincible. Then, too, there was the material chaos that plagued us after the defeat at Friedland, the lack of reserves, the enormous distance between ourselves and the militias still in the formative stage, and a host of other equally important circumstances.

I recognised all this, but I dismissed it completely from my mind when I heard the casual words uttered by Sheping. I felt nothing except the shame of entering peace talks without avenging Friedland, and was quite beside myself with indignation, as if the duty of answering to our country for the grave wrongs to its glory and honour had fallen upon me alone.

In my madness, I rushed off to see Bennigsen, to assure him of the excellent state of our rearguard and the possibility of our still continuing to fight bravely, whatever military actions he considered necessary. As if everything depended on the rearguard! As if a handful of troops would be enough to engage a commander against whom an entire army was deemed insufficient! Such is youth.

I galloped over to headquarters. There were crowds of people there: Englishmen, Swedes, Prussians, French Royalists, Russian military and civil servants who knew nothing of either military or civil service, men of intrigue and without employment. It resembled a market-place for political and military speculators whose previous hopes, plans and actions had already thrown them into bankruptcy.

Entering the house occupied by Bennigsen, I learned that he was still resting, but was expected shortly to make his appearance. Having nothing better to do, I went back into the street to watch the troops moving towards the crossing and preparing to burn the bridge. At that moment, as luck would have it, I ran into an acquaintance, whose sad aspect and bearing alone contradicted the measures that were running through my head. This pale and trembling apparition, learning of my intentions, got the idea that Bennigsen might listen to me and agree to the suggestions of a twenty-year-old madcap. Panic seized him. He began to lecture me about how reprehensible it was for a man of my rank of staff squadron leader in the Life Guard Hussars, so young and so inexperienced, to proffer advice to a high personage such as the commander-in-chief. Besides, everything had already been settled anyway; I would simply become the butt of jokes and ridicule and accomplish nothing. His remarks were absolutely justified and left me shaken.

It gave me food for serious thought. I looked around at the fashionable crowd that had gathered, reflecting that these were the very people who were recently so confident that Napoleon could be easily defeated. They were enough to ensure that my lips would remain sealed. With hangers-on such as these, how could we even think of continuing our struggle with the enemy? I had stumbled into the midst of what was to me a new world – people who lived under a real roof, never giving a thought to what might be happening on the battlefield. How different from the world I had left a couple of hours ago, where men spent their time under open skies, facing bullets and cannonballs, geared up for endless fighting.

At general headquarters everything was in a state of alert, as if the world was a half-hour from coming to an end. Only Bennigsen seemed unchanged. He was clearly in agony, but he suffered in silence, a manly, Roman-style distress. As soon as he entered the hall, I went over to him and told him I had been sent by Bagration, without mentioning a word of the stupid thoughts provoked by my talk with Sheping. Indeed, I was soon brought down to earth by reflecting on the good sense of that panicky officer and the petrified atmosphere at headquarters, which sooner or later was bound to filter down to the troops under their command. The news that I had brought concerning the safety of the rearguard appeared to be a welcome present for Bennigsen, because his face suddenly cleared. After a few questions and answers, my audience was over and I returned to my station.

In the meantime, throughout the day of the 6th and part of the 7th, our army went on crossing to the right bank of the Niemen under the protection of the rearguard which, regardless of Bennigsen's offer to Napoleon, continued to fight as it was hard-pressed by the French vanguard. Finally, all the troops had crossed the Niemen with the exception of a few dozen cossacks who kept exchanging fire with enemy skirmishers. Orders for them to hurry and join up with the rest of the troops had been dispatched. At that very moment, French *chasseurs à cheval* and dragoons burst into the town. The cossacks galloped off, not realising that the foremost pursuer with sword drawn was Murat himself. They got safely over to the right bank just as he reached the bridge, which immediately burst into flames under the very muzzle of his beautiful horse!

The hapless general reined in his animal and returned slowly to town. The Niemen now separated the opposing sides. During the subsequent armistice, Murat bragged about his hot pursuit and assured his audience that he was all set to gallop over the bridge to the opposite bank.

'Too bad that didn't happen, Your Highness,' answered one of our officers. 'We would have had one more prisoner!'

Our army had been positioned as follows: main headquarters at Amt-Baublen; infantry and regular cavalry between Pogegen and Vilkishken; the guard at Benigkeiten; L'Estocq's Prussian corps at Amt-Vinge; the 14th Russian infantry division opposite Ragnit (where Ney's corps had arrived) as far as Jurburg; and the entire cossack army on the flood plain of the Niemen, opposite the burned bridge.

The advance guard and Bagration's headquarters initially settled in the village of Shaaken, on the road leading from Amt-Baublen to Vilkishken, on the shore of one of the Niemen's bays. But a few days before peace was concluded, the vanguard was disbanded and Bagration's headquarters moved to Pogegen.

This is how the war of 1806 and 1807 ended. What an astonishing turnaround in less than two years!

In August of 1805, France, which neighboured other countries of comparable resources and power, had been content to remain within its borders behind the Rhine. By early June of 1807 there no longer existed a single independent state between France and Russia; all had bowed before one will, that of the conqueror who gazed ever more hungrily from the banks of the Niemen at the land of Russia, which appeared as a blue line on the horizon.

On the morning of 8 June (20 June new style), I was at general headquarters in Amt-Baublen. While I was there, an answer was received to Bennigsen's offer of an armistice, brought by an adjutant of Marshal Berthier by the name of Louis Périgord (a nephew of Talleyrand). I had met him three years before in St Petersburg when he was with the French embassy there. But then he was a mere lad dressed in formal costume; now I saw him as an adult and in hussar uniform. He appeared more handsome in a black pelisse ablaze with gold braid, red wide trousers and a bearskin cap that the French call a colback.

Périgord was received quite politely, as was to be expected, but unfortunately he received no rebuke for his insolent manner. In the hall where General Bennigsen and a host of other generals and officials were all bareheaded, Périgord appeared with his fur cap and kept it on, even at Bennigsen's dinner table, and remained covered until he left. All this was done under the pretext that French military code forbids officers to remove their hats and helmets while they are wearing cartridge boxes to signify that they are on duty. Even so, what prevented Périgord from unbuckling his cartridge box after completing his mission and then removing his hat? He would thereby have observed his army's military code and adhered to the rules of polite society, which are much older and which have always been observed by the French, before and since. Presumably this impertinence was not his idea, but had been suggested to him by his superiors, to test our tolerance and perhaps to gauge what demands we might make when the peace talks got under way.

Would we ever know? It is just possible that if someone had knocked off Périgord's hat, Napoleon might have omitted to include several paragraphs of the peace treaty. But we did not dare to force the issue and take the chance to find out. All of us felt the deliberate snub to our commander-in-chief in the presence of an important gathering, but no one even hinted at it, even in jest, to Périgord.

My God! What a feeling of anger and indignation swelled in the hearts of our young officers who had witnessed this scene! Not one of us pretended to be cosmopolitan. We were all brought up in the spirit of the old school, Russian Orthodox men for whom an insult to the honour of our country was an offence to our personal honour. Our imagination, stirred to boiling point, envisaged Périgord as some kind of Tartar envoy coming to the camp of a great Russian princess to claim payment of tribute. His action was just the first insult to our dignity which was later affronted so frequently by envoys such as Lauriston, Caulaincourt (whose insolence was especially damnable) and Savary; but on the day of our victorious entry into Paris you should have seen how all these people were humbly beseeching favours of our magnanimous Emperor.

Looking back on this difficult five-year period and observing Russia today, one realises that everything she accomplished was done without the help of admirers or allies, and that she alone, through her own efforts, overcame the odds. Then one can speak of Austerlitz and Friedland without blushing, and see Napoleon's henchmen for what they were, insignificant drops in the ocean of events of 1812. And then, with head proudly lifted, one can say, 'I am a Russian!'

On the same day, at 6 o'clock in the evening, Lieutenant General Prince Lobanov-Rostovsky travelled to Tilsit for the armistice talks that were

concluded on 9 June and ratified by Napoleon on the 10th. The most important articles of the agreement concerned the demarcation lines between the
opposing armies through the middle of the River Niemen; the resumption
of hostilities (in the event of no accord between the negotiating parties) which
was not to take place for a month, starting on the day when the truce was
to be called off; the conclusion of an armistice with the Prussian army separate from that concluded with the Russian military; and the adoption of all
possible measures to ensure a speedy conclusion of the final peace treaty.

The last article was indispensable for Napoleon. Despite his victory at
Friedland and his menacing position on the Niemen, his circumstances were
actually not as favourable as they appeared. Ahead of him lay Russia with
its countless resources, but offering little or nothing to the enemy – limit-
less and unfathomable. Behind him was Prussia, a country without an army,
but with a people whose national pride had been humiliated, driven to despair
by the violence and coercion of its conquerors, not putting up any resistance
because there was no rallying point, but anxiously awaiting an imminent
uprising in Austria. For its part, Austria, shaken by the disasters at Ulm and
Austerlitz, still had at its disposal an army numbering 340,000 men, ready
for action and whose 80,000-strong vanguard had already been moved to the
northern borders of Bohemia and the area adjoining the lines of communication between Napoleon and France.

This is the situation that troubled the great army commander at Tilsit and
which required a speedy conclusion to the peace talks. Emperor Alexander
was then not very far from the general headquarters of his army.

On the 11th, at 3 o'clock in the afternoon, Napoleon sent his marshal of
the palace, Duroc, to His Majesty with congratulations and the official ratifi-
cation of the armistice declaration. The Emperor received Duroc very gra-
ciously and in turn ratified the document that he had handed him. Apparently
this was the occasion when the famous meeting of the Emperors was agreed
upon – a meeting which Napoleon seized upon for publicity reasons. It was
to prove of benefit to Alexander, and was also to provoke the first of a series
of mistakes which led to Napoleon's downfall, namely the uprising that began
in Spain.

The 13th was a solemn occasion and also a very curious day. Because the
demarcation line ran down the middle of the Niemen near the burned-down
bridge, that is precisely where two pavilions were set up, very much like
bathing platforms, square in shape and girded with white canvas. The larger
one, more spacious and attractive, was intended for the two Emperors; the
smaller one was to house their retinues. They had been erected at Napoleon's
order by General Lariboissière, who commanded his artillery. On the front of
the larger pavilion facing us was an enormous letter 'A' and on the side facing Tilsit, a letter 'N' of the same size, neatly painted in green. Two large

rowing boats were moored on opposite shores, ready to transport both monarchs and their retinue to these pavilions.

The right bank of the Niemen, occupied by us, was a sloping meadow that was dominated by the hilly left bank in the hands of the French. This gave them an unimpeded view of our bank from the town to the surrounding hills where the villages of Amt-Baublen, Pogegen and others stood, whereas we were unable to see anything except Tilsit, situated on the opposite ridge. But we had a good view of its occupants. We could identify the uniforms of the various units and admire on either side of the main street the Old Guard drawn up in several rows facing us and all the way down to the bank of the Niemen. They were eagerly awaiting the appearance of their invincible leader, the all-powerful demigod, ready to greet him the moment he galloped down to the pier.

On our side, there were no preparations made except for the rowing boat with the oarsmen, half a squadron of Chevalier Guards and half a squadron of Prussian mounted guards to provide an escort for our Emperor. These troops were arrayed on the bank of the river with their right flank abutting the burned bridge and their left adjoining a once-prosperous farmhouse called Ober-Mamelshen Krug, which stood right on the shore at the point where the road from Tilsit to Amt-Baublen makes a turn. This farmhouse was chosen as a temporary shelter for Emperor Alexander so that he could get to the boat and and head for the pavilion on the river no sooner and no later than Napoleon.

There was no prettier building on the shore – everything else had been dismantled for bivouac fires – and even this farmhouse was not much to look at; instead of a roof, there were only beams left because the straw covering had been stripped by the troops to feed their horses who were in need of both hay and straw.

In the morning, some of the high-ranking generals rode over to Amt-Baublen where the Emperor had already arrived. Prince Bagration went there too, and because I was his adjutant and keen to witness such an extraordinary spectacle, I followed him, decked out in a rich-looking pelisse of the Lifeguard Regiment.

Almost everyone was in parade uniform. The Emperor was wearing the Preobrazhensky Regiment's uniform of the style of that period. On either side of the collar were embroidered two small gold knots (very much like those they have nowadays, except much smaller, and without the present-day epaulets). He had on white pantaloons and short boots. His hairstyle was different from that which is in vogue today – his hair was powdered white. He wore a high hat with cockade and a black plume. A sword at his side, a sash tied around his waist and the blue ribbon of the order of St Andrew over his right shoulder completed Alexander's dress.

Today this outfit would seem a little odd, but at the time it was much admired, especially on a handsome, slender and agile 30-year-old man, as the late Emperor then was.

Around 11 o'clock in the morning, the Emperor, the King of Prussia, the Grand Duke Constantine Pavlovitch (Alexander's brother) and several generals designated to accompany the Emperor on the boat got into carriages and headed for the shore along the Tilsit road. The other generals and their adjutants rode on either side. This procession was undoubtedly visible from Tilsit. At Ober-Mamelshen Krug the carriages stopped and we all entered the large main room of the farmhouse. The Emperor sat near the window facing the door. He put down his hat and gloves on a nearby table. The room filled up with generals who had followed his carriage. We adjutants came in after them and remained in the background near the door.

My eyes did not leave the Emperor. I felt that he was concealing, with an artificial calm and relaxed attitude, the true feelings that lay beneath the surface of his open, benevolent features. He was about to meet the greatest man of the time – military leader, politician, lawgiver and administrator – a man with a dazzling aura as a result of his astounding, almost legendary career. This was also the man who had conquered the whole of Europe in the last two years and defeated our army twice, and who now stood on the very borders of Russia. He was coming face to face with a man renowned for captivating people, endowed with an extraordinary ability to size up and take measure of the character, feelings and thoughts of his opponents. It was more than just an interview; through this meeting Alexander had to charm the charmer, seduce the seducer, and outwit an acknowledged genius.

It was paramount to divert Napoleon's attention and direct his military activities towards some other enterprise – so remote as to provide Europe with additional time to clear away the suffocating rubble of war. It would also give Russia the opportunity to prepare the means to repel any future attempts against her independence, which as our Emperor foresaw, would, sooner or later, loom ahead.

These were the concerns that occupied Alexander, mind and soul, and these are the goals that he achieved despite public opinion, ever swayed by appearances. No matter how you look at it, victory in this instance was squarely on his side. This is shown by the fact that Napoleon came to his senses only towards the end of 1809, when the obstinacy of the spirited Spaniards diverted a sizeable portion of his forces away from the rest of Europe, and when we refused joint action with him against Austria in order to preserve the ties of friendship that would serve us well at the time of the Russian campaign.

Barely half-an-hour had elapsed when someone came into the room and announced: 'He is coming, Your Majesty.'

An electric spark of curiosity coursed through us all. The Emperor rose nonchalantly and without haste, picked up his hat and gloves and went outside with a calm face and measured step. We burst pell-mell from the room and dashed down to the shore to see Napoleon galloping at full speed between two ranks of his Old Guard. His escort and suite consisted of at least 400 men on horseback. The roar of enthusiastic greetings and shouts was deafening, even on the opposite bank of the Niemen.

Almost simultaneously, both Emperors boarded their boats. The Tsar was accompanied by Grand-Duke Constantine, Bennigsen, Count Lieven, Prince Lobanov-Rostovsky, Uvarov and Budberg (Minister of Foreign Affairs).

Accompanying Napoleon were Murat, Bessières, Berthier, Duroc and Caulaincourt. On that day, the King of Prussia did not come to the meeting; he remained on the right bank with us. Now both imperial boats left shore and got underway. At that moment, the enormity of the spectacle triumphed over every other feeling. All eyes were turned and fixed on the opposite shore, to the boat carrying this remarkable man, this commander whose likes had never been seen since the days of Alexander the Great and Julius Caesar, both of whom he greatly surpassed by the variety of his talents and his glorious conquests of civilised and cultured peoples.

I looked at him through my spyglass, even though the distance separating us from the opposite shore was not great and was dwindling as the boat got closer to the pavilion set up in midstream.

I saw Napoleon, standing in front of the government officials who composed his suite, apart and silent. Time has erased from my memory the type of uniform he wore, and in my diaries, written hurriedly, I cannot find reference to it. But I do seem to remember that he wore not the usual *chasseur* uniform but instead that of the Old Imperial Guard. I do recall that he wore the Legion of Honour ribbon over his shoulder and had on his head that little cocked hat familiar to the whole world.

I was struck by the resemblance of his figure to all the images that were then sold by print-makers. He even stood with arms crossed over his chest exactly like in those pictures. Unfortunately, from lack of support, the spyglass wavered in my hands and I could not see his features as clearly as I would have wished.

Both boats reached the pavilion almost simultaneously. However, Napoleon's arrived a little sooner, so he had a few seconds in which to jump out and cross smartly through the pavilion to greet our Emperor as he disembarked; then together they entered the pavilion. As I recall, the members of either entourage did not go in, but remained on the raft, getting acquainted and conversing.

After an hour or so, they were called inside to join the Emperors. That is when Napoleon, having greeted and addressed each one in turn, spoke at greater length with Bennigsen. He said, among other things, 'You were wicked at Eylau', commenting on the obstinacy and fury with which our armies had fought in this battle. And he concluded his conversation with the words: 'I have always admired your talents, your prudence even more.'

The respected old warrior proudly construed this semi-epigram as a full-blown eulogy, because great commanders usually consider circumspection to be the least of military qualities, far beneath enterprise and bravery. This anecdote was told me by Bennigsen several times, and each time with new pleasure!

Because Napoleon had greeted Emperor Alexander when he alighted from his boat, etiquette required that Alexander duly accompany Napoleon to the boat on which he had arrived. And thus the first meeting was concluded.

The French were exultant!

The meetings of the Emperors on the raft continued in the same vein, the only difference being that the Prussian King was invited to the last meeting and some members of the imperial suites yielded their place to other officials. Eventually, both the Tsar and the King of Prussia were invited to set up residence in Tilsit, and their meetings with Napoleon continued there. At the same time, Napoleon arranged to move part of his guard out of Tilsit and to prepare that part of the town to accommodate our guard. He set aside two of the best houses for the use of the other two monarchs.

Around 6 o'clock in the evening, when Tsar Alexander moved to Tilsit, Napoleon met him at the shore as he alighted from the rowing boat. The whole Imperial Guard, mounted and on foot, stood on parade on either side of the main street, all the way from the jetty to Napoleon's residence where the Tsar arrived on horseback together with his host. A table was laid for dinner, to which both the Grand Duke and Murat had been invited.

The house reserved for the Tsar was located on the main street and was about 200 yards from the one occupied by Napoleon. It was a two-storey structure, but not very large, with a narrow main entrance adorned by four columns. The door on this side was directly off the street, with three or four steps between the two central columns leading through a fairly spacious hallway to the downstairs rooms on either side of an attractive flight of stairs that ascended to the upper floor occupied by our Emperor. Here there was a salon on the right, a connecting room in the middle and the Tsar's bedroom on the left. The connecting room opened on a balcony supported by the external columns.

Other than the Russian Imperial Guard that was quartered in Tilsit under the command of Vorontsov, Levashov and Reytern, no one from the regular Russian or Prussian armies was allowed to come to Tilsit. This excluded adjutants who went back and forth on business between the army and Imperial Headquarters, and I, of course, did not fail to take advantage of this privilege. However, the desire to gawk at Napoleon overcame all these obstacles. Many of our generals, staff officers and others dressed themselves in civilian clothes and managed to stay in Tilsit for several days. After a long and arduous campaign, the town seemed to them like a sort of earthly paradise. To be candid, however, although both sides wanted to display harmony and an eagerness to please that fell just short of friendship, it was an uneasy relationship in which neither was really prepared to modify its normal habits.

Day followed day monotonously. At 12 or 1 o'clock there was lunch; at 6 o'clock Emperor Alexander rode on his horse to see Napoleon with a small escort, or Napoleon would come to visit him with an enormous entourage and a huge escort. Then they would go and watch manoeuvres of some French troops or the Imperial Guard and its components of Davout's corps. It is worth noting that despite the small distance to Tilsit, the corps under the command of Marshal Lannes was never presented to and reviewed by Emperor Alexander because it consisted only of fragments that were left after the losses incurred at Heilsberg and Friedland.

After the manoeuvres, Napoleon usually invited Alexander over to his house where they had dinner together. Later that night, at 10 or 11, Napoleon would almost always call on Alexander, simply as a friend, on foot and without entourage or escort, in that famous hat and grey overcoat, at the sight of which the earth trembled. Both hat and overcoat seemed to have battle smoke clinging to them, even on friendly occasions. Napoleon would then have a cup of tea there and remain chatting with our Emperor until 1 or sometimes 2 o'clock in the morning.

The Prussian King moved to Tilsit on the 16th, and from then on often spent time with Napoleon and Alexander, except for the late-night chats. The Queen of Prussia arrived on the 25th, only two days before peace was concluded.

Everything that took place openly was obviously witnessed by many apart from myself and it must be hoped that someone else will fill in the gaps and correct what I forgot or reported incorrectly. Regrettably, no one can describe much more important events, such as the conversations of the two Emperors in their first private meetings in the pavilion on the raft and their subsequent late-night chats. All this took place without witnesses, so that there was no historian to record it. What a terrible loss![5]

Having some right to visit Tilsit, I begged Prince Bagration for permission to go there as often as possible. The prince, such a strict and exacting superior in everything that concerned military service, was quite indulgent

---

[5] The two conversed in French. At the initial meeting on the raft that lasted one hour and 50 minutes, no notes were taken, Napoleon declaring with his usual panache, 'I'll be your secretary and you'll be mine.' He also preferred one-to-one meetings, explaining, 'The two of us shall accomplish more in an hour than our intermediaries could in several days.'

and helpful to his subordinates in other circumstances. He agreed to my request and sent me almost daily with errands for various people living in Tilsit. This gave me the opportunity to see Napoleon almost on a daily basis, often standing a couple of steps away from him.

To avoid repetition, I will only describe my first meeting with Napoleon. The others that followed were quite similar and do not merit special mention.

I don't remember the exact date, but only recall that shortly after the Emperor moved to Tilsit, Prince Bagration sent me with a message to one of the officials at Imperial Headquarters. I put on my parade uniform of the Life Guard Hussars and crossed the Niemen by rowing boat. The person I was supposed to see was in an upstairs salon of the Emperor's house. There I found Prince Kourakin and Prince Lobanov-Rostovsky, who were the official representatives at the peace talks, as well as the Prussian Field Marshal Kalkreuth, fresh from the spirited defence of Danzig, and a multitude of ministers and other government officials. While I was there, Caulaincourt came in with a courtly, yet haughty and insolent air. He had been sent by Napoleon to invite our Emperor to attend manoeuvres at 6 o'clock and dinner afterwards. Thereafter, when he was French ambassador in St Petersburg, his pomposity and aloofness became even more intolerable; but God, you should have seen him eight years later in Paris on the morning of our triumphal entrance into that capital!

Shortly after 5 p.m. I was already at the main entrance of the Tsar's residence. Within less than a half-hour we heard the clatter of a large group of cavalry, and I saw a crowd of horsemen galloping down the main street towards the house of His Majesty. It was Napoleon surrounded by his retinue and escort.

The crowd that accompanied him must have numbered at least 300 people. At their head galloped *chasseurs à cheval*; after them came other officers adorned with gold braid crosses, followed by staff officers mingled with court officials richly attired in various outfits. Behind this cavalcade came dozens of *chasseurs* from another military unit.

In the middle of this long column, surrounded by marshals, rode Napoleon himself.

Now they had reached the house entrance. One of the two pages who always attended him was named Marescault, the son of a general in the Engineer Corps, a handsome youngster of seventeen, dressed in a hussar brown dolman and tricorn hat. He dismounted, grabbed Napoleon's horse, and ran so quickly up the entrance steps and past me up the stairs leading to the Emperor's private quarters that I barely had time to spot him.

He was followed by the marshals and staff officers, but the rest of the official retinue and escort remained in the saddle outside. Murat, who was following Napoleon, met the Grand Duke, engaged him in conversation and stayed behind. I gazed for a long time at this Murat, undoubtedly one of the most brilliant and brave cavalry leaders in Europe. His handsome stature and features, his carnival costume, worn with the coquetry and deliberation of a stylish beauty, captured every eye. He was known to dress up even more elaborately and magnificently when engaged in more dangerous activities. But for all his chivalrous spirit and showy appearance, his talents were displayed mainly in the fury of battle, commanding and handling masses of cavalry under Napoleon's orders.

Marescault came to the door and stopped near me, entrusting Napoleon's horse to a colourfully dressed stable official by the entrance steps. I remember that it was a small bay horse, but of pure Arabian stock, with a long tail. The saddle was of crimson velvet, the bit and stirrups were of solid gold.

Suddenly, there was a commotion at the top of the stairs. The marshals and adjutants came down quickly to get to their horses. But Marescault headed them off. He rushed to retrieve Napoleon's horse from the stable official and grabbed it by the bridle as before. The proud courtier (and former Republican) Caulaincourt, dressed in rich palace finery with two stars on his breast, was holding the stirrup with one hand, the whip in the other, awaiting the arrival of his lord and master.

Napoleon emerged from the hall and paused at the entrance next to Emperor Alexander. The doorway was so narrow and he was so close to me that I had to back away for fear of jostling him accidentally. He was busy telling the Tsar something in a jovial, impulsive manner. I heard nothing. I was all eyes, devouring him visually, trying to memorise all the features, all his changes of expression, all his mannerisms. By good fortune, as if to indulge me, he became even more talkative and paused near me for more than two minutes. I was content, but not entirely. I had to get a closer look at the colour of his eyes and, as if on purpose, he suddenly looked right at me. His glance was so direct that in any other circumstance I would have lowered my eyes; but my curiosity overcame everything. His eyes met mine in a hard, unwavering gaze. Then he turned to the Tsar again, replying to some question that had been asked, put on his hat, mounted his horse, spurred it on and galloped off at full speed the way he had come. All this happened in a flash, without pause. At the same instant, everything behind, around and ahead of him erupted, and this incredible prodigy, like a brilliant, exploding meteor, vanished from view.

I have already remarked on how much I was struck by the overall resemblance of Napoleon to the prints on sale everywhere. But the same was not true of his facial features. None of the portraits that I had seen bore the least resemblance to him. Believing them, I had supposed that Napoleon sported a rather large hooked nose, dark eyes and dark hair – in a word, the true Italian facial type. In fact, his face was slightly swarthy, with regular features. His nose was not very large, but straight, with a very slight, hardly noticeable bend. The hair on his head was not black, but dark reddish-blond;[6] his eyebrows and eyelashes were much darker than the colour of his hair, and his blue eyes, set off by the almost black lashes, gave him a most pleasing expression. Finally, no matter how many times I had occasion to see him, I never noticed those frowning eyebrows with which the portrait-pamphleteers endowed him.

The man I saw was of short stature, just over five feet tall, rather heavy although he was only 37 years old and despite the fact that the lifestyle he followed should not, on the face of it, have let him put on much weight. He held himself erect without the least effort, as is common with all short people. But what was peculiar to him alone was a nobility of bearing and an urbane, martial air, which undoubtedly was derived from the habit of commanding men and a consciousness of moral superiority. No less remarkable were the ease and frankness of his approach, his natural dexterity and the quickness of his movements.

On that day, and those that followed, he wore the dark green *chasseur* uniform with gold epaulets of a colonel, without stars. He also wore a star and a small cross of the Legion of Honour. His linen was dazzling white, and he sported jack-boots that came above the knee, with small gold spurs and a dress-sword at this side. He held his hat in his hand and did not put it on until he mounted his horse.

On 25 June the peace was finally concluded. Our troops headed back to Russia. Prince Bagration made for St Petersburg, and I accompanied him. Our rest period did not last long. The following January, we joined the troops fighting in Finland. I am reminded here of the words of my friend and military comrade, the unforgettable General Kulnev: 'Our mother Russia is wonderful because there is always some corner of the empire where people are fighting.' And there was to be another corner that witnessed hostilities – Turkey – where the prince and I were called upon to appear after military action came to a close in Finland.

---

[6] Davidov is probably the only memoirist to describe the colour of Napoleon's hair accurately. This has been defined most appropriately as 'Venetian blond' or dark blond with a reddish tinge. It became an important issue when authenticated samples of Napoleon's hair were analysed by the FBI laboratory in 1995 and the results were found to be consistent with arsenic poisoning. For further data, consult *Assassination on St Helena Revisited* by Ben Weider and Sten Forshufvud (John Wiley & Sons Inc., 1995).

Tsar Alexander I remains an enigmatic figure to this day – a man of immense personal charm, yet rather secretive and somewhat aloof in his private life. He knew how to cajole and appear quite seductive! Napoleon was taken in by his open and friendly manner and later complained that Alexander had tricked him into believing that he shared his enmity towards England – 'a Byzantine Greek of the later empire'.

His liberal inclinations later gave way to rigid conservatism. He felt it was his mission to save Europe by forging a holy alliance between former enemies of Napoleon. Later he came under the influence of a mystic and died in the Crimea under mysterious circumstances in 1825. When his coffin was opened by the Soviets in 1926, it was found to be empty, thus reinforcing the belief that he did not die, but instead had gone to live in Siberia as a holy man under the pseudonym of Fedor Kuzmich. Apparently, he had always harboured guilty feelings about his father's assassination, which propelled him to the throne of Russia in 1801. The court figures who carried out the assassination of the demented Emperor Paul I were never punished or brought to trial.

A grim memento of Paul's murder is presently on display at the Hermitage Museum in St Petersburg – a plain-looking gold snuff box with a big dent which had been used by Bennigsen to hit the Tsar on the head. In his anecdotes about various people, Denis Davidov reports that Bennigsen is supposed to have said to the other accomplices: 'We have come too far to back down. When you want to make an omelette, you must start by breaking the eggs.' The other accomplices were Count Zubov, Prince Yashwil, Tatarinov and Skaretin, who brought the scarf with which they finally strangled Tsar Paul.

CHAPTER 5

Recollections of Kulnev in Finland, 1808

The war in Finland, even at its height, did not attract the attention of either civilians or military men. General curiosity was fixed on the tremendous events in Moravia and East Prussia and nobody could be bothered with another war in which the number of participants alone hardly equalled the number of killed and wounded in a single battle of the preceding campaigns. Moreover, the first half of this new war involved our armies in little more than a stroll almost to the borders of Lapland and the surrender of a well-defended fortress after a weak cannonade and raids by several hundred cossacks.

It must be agreed that the means by which we achieved such successes hardly merited general attention. Unfortunately, we were so over-confident of an easy conquest in this region that when the enemy massed its forces against our scattered troops, initiated a people's war in which the local inhabitants intercepted our supply trains carrying food and ammunition, and lit forest fires which blazed out of control over vast areas and cost us many lives as we tried to escape – then our compatriots refused to believe the ensuing rumours and, in their ignorance, even sent us written invitations to family functions and to join them for festivities in the capital.

Yet all the while the blood of brave men was being spilled in the Finnish tundras and staining the rocks of those boundless plains. And we were spending most of our time shivering in the northern frosts, patrolling the ancient forests and the shores of deserted lakes, pursuing glory which evoked no responding echoes from home!

Once a peace treaty was concluded with Sweden, new threats, new calamities and new triumphs brought about renewed activity and effort in different directions; and thus the Finnish war was swallowed up by much greater events and perished in oblivion.

Since I am not recording history, I am under no obligation to make claims for that war to take its place in immortality. As a horseman and a writer, I shall be happy if my notes help to remind my comrades of the magical moments of our youth, our dreams and hopes of honour and glory, the dangers we braved, our travels and our poetic campfire conversations under the overcast skies.

Over the whole vast area of Finland and on the eastern shore of the Gulf of Bothnia, there are no man-made fortresses. But the northern shore of the Gulf of Finland is defended by the powerful fortified town of Sveaborg, with a harbour that can accommodate up to 60 ships, the fort of Svartholm and the fortified capes of Perkelaut and Hanhout, and by oar-propelled flotillas which control inshore navigation.

The coastal sections of this land differ from the inland areas because of their prosperity and cleanliness, and the civilised and cultivated manners of their inhabitants. There is a European look to them; commerce brings communities closer together and gives a certain similarity to customs and living conditions; but as you progress farther inland you find very different usages and ways of life that are undoubtedly influenced by the severe and gloomy surroundings.

At least that is how it appeared to us in 1808.

The Finnish military forces numbered up to 15,000 regular troops and 4,000 militiamen scattered all over the country. Some 6,000 men were located in the fortified towns of Sveaborg and Svartholm; the remaining 13,000 were concentrated among other designated points at the first news of our offensive movements.

Tavasthust was to be the rallying point for the troops located in the south; Vasa and Karlebi for those farther north; Kuopio for those in Savalak province, and Uleaborg for the forces located in Tavasthust, Kuopio and Karlebi.

Moreover, Field Marshal Klingspor, who was designated commander-in-chief of the Swedish and Finnish armies, had received strict instructions to avoid any military engagement until the Finnish army had gathered together in Uleabor.

By the end of April, our army was positioned between Friedrichsham and Neyschlot. It encompassed three divisions – the 5th, the 17th and the 21st. The first was under the command of Lieutenant General Tuchkov (I), the second under Lieutenant General Prince Gorchakov (I), and the last under Lieutenant General Bagration. To these divisions were added three squadrons of Life Guard Cossacks and the following regiments: Finnish Dragoons, Grodno Hussars and a Don Cossack regiment under Loshlin.

The whole army numbered about 20,000 men made up of infantry and cavalry units and was entrusted to Infantry General Count Buxhoevden.

There was much discussion as to the best time to begin military operations. Some urged that we cross the border immediately, others counselled a delay until spring.

The advantages of a winter campaign were mainly that Sweden was not yet in a state of readiness, its regiments not yet near to the theatre of operations; and the Finnish regiments were still scattered all over the country and had not begun to come together. Once the snow and ice receded, Finnish territory was devoid of natural obstacles. The Sveaborg fortress was not completely armed for regular defence nor supplied with military and food supplies. Moreover, it was located on islands and thus more accessible in winter than when the ice cover broke, especially since some of its defences needed a final build-up. Those that were completed faced the harbour and the sea, and were not directed inland to the points from which our siege and assault would be coming. The other fortifications of the northern shore of the Gulf of Finland were not in any better shape.

Indisputably, by delaying matters until spring, we would have sufficient time to join up with other military units on the march from central Russia and commence action with larger forces; we would also be able to cut off the Finnish armies from Sweden by moving towards Vasa or Uleaborg, come spring when winter crossings through Kvarken and Aland were no longer possible. But would these advantages compare favourably with those of a winter campaign, and indeed be outweighed by greater inconveniences?

Our government gave preference to a winter campaign over a spring offensive. As a result, Gorchakov's division was assigned to direct its efforts at Sveaborg, Bagration's division at Tavasthust, and Tuchkov's division at Vasa by way of Kuopio.

Military actions began on 8 February.

When our armies entered enemy territory, I was on leave. Moscow's pleasures were truly captivating and my head was kept in a spin. At the age of 23, already a company commander in the Hussar Life Guard Regiment, with two crosses around my neck and two other decorations on my gold-braided red jacket, I was drowning in delights and, as is customary, was in love up to my ears.

The first rumour of a war with Sweden and troop movements beyond our borders spelt an end to Moscow balls and romance, and sent me off to my posting with the army on the move into Swedish Finland.

On my way to Helsingfors[7] at the station of Esbo, I met a fellow who like me was on his way to join his regiment, the Archangel Infantry Regiment – Lieutenant Zakrevsky, adjutant of Count Kamenskoy. This chance acquaintance blossomed into a sincere friendship of 30 years which has never wavered under any circumstances.

Helsingfors was the location of the main headquarters of Count Buxhoevden and the troops who had been assigned to besiege Sveaborg under the command of Count Kamenskoy. This was the first time I met Lieutenant Neidgart, then adjutant to Count Buxhoevden, attached to the Nevsky Infantry Regiment and today a full general and commandant of the VI Infantry Corps.

---

[7] Now Helsinki, capital of Finland.

The daily bombardment directed at the fortress was sparse and only teased the enemy, but their return fire against our batteries was truly devastating. What kept me in Helsingfors, however, was the delay in preparing the ladders and other equipment needed for the assault that had been declared imminent by the commander-in-chief. I decided to stay because I knew Prince Bagration's line of thinking and personal feelings. In the event of an attack, he would be delighted to hear that his adjutant had taken part in such a brave exploit. Another consideration was that in the direction taken by the 21st Division from Tavasthust to Abo, there was no enemy force in the vicinity and therefore no possibility of a battle.

At that time, an amusing incident took place, which is probably not known to anyone or perhaps long forgotten. During the war in East Prussia, eight months previously, the Grodno Hussar Regiment formed part of the vanguard under the command of Prince Bagration, and so I was known to all the officers in that outfit.

When I was in Helsingfors with the vanguard, there was a quartermaster of this regiment, Lieutenant Malevsky or Mayekovsky (I don't recall his exact name) who, while I had been with the vanguard, had heard me talk at some length about army operations and had seen me poring over a map – enough, in his opinion, to make me an expert in military matters. Assuming that I was better informed than anyone, he came to ask me the best way to reach the regimental headquarters, as he was bringing dispatches from St Petersburg. Delighted by his show of confidence in me and knowing that the headquarters of the Grodno Hussar Regiment must be with the 21st Division, I unrolled the map and, having noted the date on which the division had set out from Tavasthust, gravely calculated the number of stages, each 20–25 miles, needed to cover the distance between Tavasthust to Abo. I told him positively that the division was now headquartered in Abo. There was only one thing I failed to take into account: I forgot that the map did not show the presence of snow, which was now especially deep, and that the wide roads appearing on it had now narrowed to trails that allowed cavalry to proceed single file and the infantry, too, in one line. The artillery and baggage could barely advance, so that instead of 25 miles a day, the 21st Division progressed no more than eight or ten miles a day.

The quartermaster gave me a deep bow in thanks for my help and, supremely confident of the accuracy of the directions given to him by a 23-year-old madcap strategist, set off at full speed on a stagecoach and rode into Abo as if into St Petersburg or Moscow.

In Abo, no one had heard anything about our troops and it was empty of enemy troops as well; but the quartermaster did run into a mob of students who were keen to take on any group that comprised fewer numbers than themselves. Fortunately no harm came to the terrified fellow; before news of his arrival had a chance to spread, he took refuge in the home of the town's governor. There he laid low, half-petrified, until finally one of the units of the 21st Division entered the city. But that was not the end of the story. In fact, it heralded the quartermaster's greatest moment.

No sooner had our troops arrived than the Abo town officials were seized with panic of their own. They appealed to him to take the town under his personal protection and to inform his commander that Abo had made its submission to Russian forces immediately when the first Russian officer, Mr Malevsky, had turned up. Malevsky, in turn, puffed up with self-importance, donned his dress uniform, saddled the governor's horse and set off to meet the detachment, accompanied by town officials.

Meanwhile, the commander of the unit, seeing from a distance the approaching uniformed crowd with a hussar officer at its head, mistook them for an enemy party out to reconnoitre the troops of the vanguard. Orders were given, the men formed a battle line, got the cannons ready and prepared to open fire. Fortunately, the timely arrival of the quartermaster, waving a white handkerchief, changed their minds. All that remained was to arrange for a peaceful and triumphant entry into the city, and to compose a report relating what had happened – rather more difficult to explain than the capture of the Finnish capital with its castles, containing 280 and 323 cannons, respectively.

I did not stay long in Helsingfors. As soon as negotiations began for the surrender of Sveaborg, I was urging my horse along the road to Abo. Reporting for duty there, I was caught up in a social whirl of balls and celebrations. Prince Bagration told us that there was nothing else for the 21st Division to do except to enjoy ourselves, since military action in southern Finland had ended and would probably not resume again, at least in the foreseeable future, now that Sveaborg, Svartholm and the capes of Hanhout and Perkelaut had been conquered.

I figured that if I had to concentrate on social distractions, my needs might be better served by riding back to Moscow where the same pleasures were on offer, but more to the Russian taste – promising excitement, colour and romance. In fact, the main reason was the young lady with whom I was so in love. It was all very well watching Lapp lasses throwing themselves about, but hardly worth the sporadic musket shots for which I had sacrificed my amorous dreams. This thought prompted me to ask the prince to let me travel north to join Generals Rayevsky and Kulnev, who were pursuing the Finnish troops towards Uleaborg. The smell of gunpowder was still there, and that was where my place ought to be. As ever, Bagration responded positively and approvingly to my request. The impulsive nature of youth, and the hunger for military adventure, found a ready echo in his heart.

After two days in Abo, I hired a long Finnish sledge to carry me at speed through the empty snow-covered Finnish landscape of lakes, hills and forests, towards Vasa.

At first the people had been indifferent and peaceably disposed to us. They went about their business as calmly as if they had been Russians. But with the dispersal of the 50,000 Finnish troops who had surrendered at Sveaborg and had been released by our high command to return home, and our simultaneous setbacks in the north, everything changed entirely.

General Rayevsky was stationed in Vasa. I would have remained with this gifted and fearless leader, whom I had admired since childhood, if Kulnev had not been in command of the vanguard, and therefore in advance of Rayevsky and much closer to the enemy. So I decided to join Kulnev at Gamle-Karlebi, and did not leave his side until Finland was completely won.

Much had been said, written and printed about Kulnev, each account offering a different interpretation, based on what had been heard or seen. Some felt he was an extraordinary man, worthy of the highest praise and deserving to be put in charge of large military units; others admitted he was brave, but condemned him for his lack of education, labelling him an ill-bred, coarse hussar.

Before I say a few words about him, let me set out my credentials and explain why I am confident of my opinion of Kulnev.

I met him in 1804 while travelling through the town of Soum, where he was a major of a hussar regiment of the same name which was stationed there. He was exactly 21 years older than me, and we became friends in the course of the 1807 war in Prussia. I was then a company commander in the Hussar Life Guard Regiment into which he had been transferred. But it was during 1808–9 in Finland, and 1810 in Turkey, that our friendship reached the depth of intimacy that continued unabated until his spectacular and enviable death.[8] In the Finnish and Turkish wars we were inseparable; we lived together, as occasion had it, in the same room or tent, or beside the same campfire under the open sky; we ate from the same pot and drank from the same flask. That was our relationship to each other.

Kulnev was born in 1763 and received his education in the cadet corps under the famous director Betzky,[9] during the most brilliant period of this military academy. Kulnev was quite well versed in artillery science and had a thorough theoretical and practical knowledge of field fortification. He could

---

[8] Kulnev met his end on 31 July 1812 while in command of the Russian rearguard, during a two-day engagement with Marshal Oudinot. He was famous for his reckless bravery, often getting carried away in battle and foolishly placing his life and that of others in deadly danger.

[9] Ivan Ivanovich Betzky was the illegitimate son of Ivan Yourievich Troubetskoy, born in 1704 in Stockholm, where his father was being held prisoner. He became one of Catherine the Great's assistants, and created the Foundling Children's Home and other institutions, including the Imperial Corps of Cadets.

express himself fairly well in both French and German, although he often made mistakes in writing them. But his knowledge of Roman and Russian history were really remarkable. A simple hussar and military man, he equalled any professor in recounting and correlating events in chronological sequence. He drew his own conclusions on the basis of common sense and acumen, and enjoyed offering the exploits of Roman and Russian heroes as examples to the young officers who served under him. The wording of his orders and official reports, the enforced quick-marching of troops entrusted to him, and certain oddities and mannerisms in both his private and official life were regarded as imitations of the great Suvorov. This was quite unnecessary. Having served under the great man during the Polish campaign of 1794, Kulnev, along with many other Russians, simply paid him due tribute. He revered him and always spoke of him with tears of admiration, but he never tried to ape any of his quirks. He was much too clever to attempt to copy Suvorov's eccentricities, which could be justified only by innate genius and enduring achievement.

Kulnev's odd behaviour was merely a result of his mischievous disposition. He was never downhearted and remained a truly original character, preferring to lead the simple, severe life of a soldier rather than to bask in luxury. In truth, he couldn't afford any other lifestyle on his meagre pay, but to the end of his life he assigned one-third of it to the upkeep of his elderly, poverty-stricken mother (as is attested by all the inhabitants of the town of Liutsin where she lived). Another third of his salary was earmarked for the necessities of army life – his uniforms and the maintenance of his horses and their harnesses. The remaining third was spent on himself and his food, which consisted of simple fare, mainly soup, buckwheat gruel and beef or ham. All this food was prepared daily in sufficient quantity for several people. 'Welcome to my table,' he would say in his loud, gruff voice. 'You are welcome, but each guest must bring his setting with him because I have only one.'

As regards drinking, he was no different from many hussars of that day, and did not get carried away: a glass of tea with milk in the morning and with a dash of rum in the evening; a shot of vodka before lunch and one before dinner; a small glass of fruit brandy with an acquaintance; and to slake the thirst, water or home-brewed beer. He was fond of vodka, and prepared and flavoured it himself in very ingenious ways. He also loved to prepare various appetisers with it, marinating fish, mushrooms and similar delicacies; and he managed to do all this, too, in wartime, during the wars, between battles and marches. 'Poor folk are very resourceful,' he used to say while entertaining his guests. 'I, gentlemen, am like Don Quixote, a sad, wandering knight with nowhere to hang my hat; so I offer you my own concoctions and whatever the good Lord has provided.'

This avoidance of luxury and choice of a humble way of life gave him opportunities to help poor people, which the rich neglect because they are too busy pursuing pleasures and spending on themselves.

Kulnev always found ways to assist his family, beginning with his own military career. When he received the news once that his mother was in dire financial straits, and was obliged to send her 5,000 roubles, he wrote to Count Kamenskoy asking for this money in lieu of promotion to major general, which had been awarded to him after a brilliant victory. The count agreed and this sum was dispatched to him. Kulnev immediately sent it on to his beloved mother. On another occasion, during the Turkish war, he received one of the highest awards – a thousand roubles a year for twelve years – but he assigned the right to this money to a very young niece to whom he was godfather, so that these funds would be forwarded to the wardship council and kept for her until she got married.

But that is not all. His good deeds extended beyond his relations, although taking a different form. He consistently sponsored officers from his units who had been demoted to the status of rank and file. During the Turkish wars, they numbered up to twenty men in his vanguard. They all enjoyed friendly, almost fatherly treatment from him and were eventually promoted to officer status in the course of a single campaign. To enemy prisoners he was both a protector and a comforter. The French general, St Geniex, whom he took prisoner in 1812 near Drouya, burst into tears when he heard of Kulnev's death. Levenhelm, Klerfelt and all other officers and soldiers, both Finnish and Swedish, who were taken captive during the Finland war, spoke of his chivalrous behaviour and were all grateful to him for their treatment. The civilian population in the area where Kulnev campaigned did not suffer insults or ruin at the hands of his soldiers; they continued to live in substantially the same way as they had in peacetime.

His fame had spread far and wide. When, after the conquest of northern Finland, Kulnev arrived in Abo and made his appearance at a ball given by Prince Bagration, all the locals of both sexes rose from their seats. The dancers stopped dancing and came over to express their gratitude for his having preserved order and respected the private property of those in the area of military operations, and to thank him, too, for favours he had extended to their relatives who had been taken prisoner. I had been an eye-witness to these things.

Yet what a strange contrast! The soldier who had such compassion for every suffering creature that he would refrain from eating meat for a day or more on hearing the pitiful cries of animals being slaughtered in his camp – this same soldier remained unmoved by the carnage on the battlefield and would fly into a rage at his subordinates when they showed the slightest fault in carrying out their military duties. He would extend them no mercy. Threatening orders, sarcastic reproofs inspired by his caustic and biting wit frequently made it unpleasant, even unbearable, to serve under him. Anyone who showed reluctance in battle or who exploited peaceful civilians could expect his severest reprimands, and displays of such rage that true friends had to take him aside after his outbursts and restrain him from dealing with the culprits in cruel and inhuman ways.

On the other hand, he would show more than ordinary concern for the feeding and wellbeing of his soldiers, whether in war or peacetime. 'A soldier's honour and reputation should be impeccable,' he would say, 'and since we have the duty to restrain him from looting, we must see to it that he lacks for nothing, because a hungry stomach has no ears.'

As a commander of the vanguard, Kulnev was tireless in keeping a sharp eye on the enemy. 'I don't sleep and rest so that the army can sleep and rest.' And it was true. He hardly ever relaxed. He almost literally put on his uniform when the war broke out and would not take it off until peace was concluded. At night, the only thing he removed before falling asleep was his sword, which he placed by the head of the bed. Only if had returned from a long expedition, having been told that the enemy was far away and inactive, would he agree to bathe and change his underwear; then he would dress again and spend the night in that fashion, keeping his horse saddled up nearby, just in case.

At the first news from the front line of enemy movement, Kulnev would appear with only an adjutant or aide at the spot where a shot had been heard or where the appearance of enemy troops had been noted. There, on that very spot, he would ascertain with his own eyes if the whole vanguard or only a section of it should be alerted, and if there was any need to awaken and warn the entire army or corps to which the vanguard under his command was assigned. Sometimes he was woken from sleep seven or eight times in the course of one night. And since I was in the same tent or bivouac, the patrol riders, not being sure in which corner each of us slept, would sometimes shake and wake me up instead of Kulnev, and for several nights I was denied any sleep, which was truly intolerable.

I have already mentioned the ruthless severity with which Kulnev always dealt with pillage perpetrated by the lower ranks; he was equally harsh when it came to their steadfastness in battle. He was extremely strict with soldiers who dodged enemy bullets and left their post under the pretext of getting a fresh supply of cartridges to replace those that had been spent. To put a stop to this abuse, he detached small commands whose assignment was to carry ammunition from the depot, stay behind the firing line and keep supplying cartridges to the men who needed them. The same was prescribed for the artillery. Kulnev made sure that skirmishers and artillery personnel did not leave the firing line and move their pieces on the excuse of having run short of ammunition.

Those who had fired their last shot were required to stay at their post without firing until the necessary supplies had been brought to them by the commands assigned for this purpose. This was essential in Finland where most of the fighting involved firearms and took place in wooded or rocky terrain. It was also dictated by the fact that our regiments were full of raw recruits, having lost a lot of regular army men in the battles that took place in Austria and East Prussia. These new men were not accustomed to fighting and would often discard their ammunition after the first few shots, taking advantage of the lack of supervision in a wooded area, and head for the supply depot under the pretext of getting more cartridges. Kulnev's new arrangements put a stop to these wiles of recruits determined to avoid danger, forcing them to be more careful and not to squander their ammunition, and to improve their marksmanship.

It was among Kulnev's detachments that I first took note of a new way to reinforce the lines of skirmishers. I had long realised the disadvantages of reinforcing them from the rear. It merely overcrowded their ranks to such an extent that they were transformed into a shapeless mob of soldiers, sometimes shooting at one another. Kulnev's reserves were positioned further back behind the flanks of the skirmishers and not directly to their rear; so that when they fell back before the enemy, the reserves could attack on the flanks. The enemy were no longer able to charge a disorderly line, confronted as they were instead by flank attacks, and were themselves repelled and pursued. I don't know whether this procedure is a fundamental rule in Jäger formations when on peacetime manoeuvres, but in actual fighting in a wooded area, such as Finland, it was extremely valuable. Indeed, it proved decisive in the Durovai victory which was due to Kulnev's dedication, and for which he was decorated with the Order of St George 3rd Class at the recommendation of Count Kamenskoy.

To complete the portrait of Kulnev, I have resorted to some passages from his various letters and orders. After serving for ten years in the rank of major, without any hope of promotion, and in his 42nd year, Kulnev had decided to leave the service. He wrote to his brother at the beginning of 1805:

> I confess to you that this war will be my last endeavour. I won't let this opportunity pass me by and will serve in it as a true son of the fatherland. Afterwards, I shall retire to our village of Boldyrev. I am weary of not seeing any change to my service duties.

But then, military fervour got the upper hand and he hastened to add:

> However, war has its advantages and disadvantages as well, and we must put all our trust in the Almighty. For the sake of Russia's honour and glory, as well as to be of help to my family, I will not spare my own skin.

That year again, he wrote to the same brother:

> I trust you will not forsake our poor mother and I assure you that for my part, wherever I may be she will receive one-third of my salary. If I am killed there will be enough horses and household goods of mine to keep her going for three years, because these things cost more than 1,000 roubles. This is all I possess and have accumulated over 20 years of service. Goodbye. Give me your blessing to defeat the enemy. I beseech you again not to abandon our dear mother, especially if I am gone.

From an order to an officer occupying a post near Vasa in 1808, comes the following:

> Even if you have only two men left, your honour requires that you keep the enemy in sight at all times and keep me informed. In any case, try to defend the post that was entrusted to you until the last extremity; there is always time to beat a retreat, but seldom to obtain victory.

And from another order of that year:

> We must banish all kinds of unmanly rumours with a firm spirit. We weren't sent here to plough fields. The Tsar has peasants for that purpose. Honour and glory is what we are here to reap; the more numerous the enemy, the more glory there is to gain. You must keep in mind at all times the words I have repeated to you over and over: an honourable death is preferable to a life of dishonour.

To his brother, that same year, he wrote:

> Be patient and don't become depressed. Prayer to God and service to the Tsar are never wasted. What service life was less happy than mine? But all has changed and I am the happiest of mortals with my present fate. (He had received the rank of colonel and the Order of St George 3rd Class.) It is better to be rewarded for real deeds than to be rewarded for nothing special. How can my Vladimir 4th Class with military ribbon ever be compared to a Vladimir 1st Class worn by some court grandee?

Order of 9 June 1808:

> Be ready to march. Don't allow the men to wander off under any pretext. Fortify them with thick, boiled gruel. A lot of supply wagons have arrived. Ask them for all you need and report to me if they can't satisfy your demands. A well-fed soldier is worth ten hungry ones; we can't determine beforehand how far we can march. We'll set out on a 25-mile stretch and we may end up covering 80.

In a letter dated 1810 to the Byelorussian Hussar Regiment of which he was the colonel, Kulnev wrote:

> Soldiers should be trained as set forth by the commander-in-chief, no more than three hours a day, but make sure you know what they'll be taught and question closely the officers in charge to see if they really know their trade, otherwise it will not be a lesson, but a torment of an exercise.

From an order at the outset of the conquest of the Aland Islands in the Gulf of Finland in 1809:

> Be energetic and cheerful on the march; only old ladies are miserable. As soon as we get to Kumlinger – a shot of vodka, gruel with meat and a litter of pine branches. A good night!

In 1812, while on the Dvina and therefore not far from Liutsen where his brother lived (after their mother had passed away), he wrote to him:

> I haven't been able to locate my carriage all this time. I have only the uniform which I am wearing and I have nothing to drink or eat. Please, brother, fetch me a little vodka and a loaf of bread to fortify my guts, because from the beginning of this war I have not had my fill of sleep or food.

And, to the same:

> If I am to fall by the enemy's sword I will have perished bravely. I consider it a great joy to offer the last drop of my blood while defending my country.

Kulnev was as good as his word. A few days after this letter, on 31 July, in the battle near Kliastitsy, a cannonball tore off both his legs. He fell, and ripping the Cross of St George from his neck, threw it to those near him, saying:

> Keep it! When the enemy finds my corpse let them take it for the body of a simple soldier and not pride themselves that they killed a Russian general.

Having portrayed Kulnev as he was, with his qualities and faults, I shall end by saying that he was less remarkable for his military spirit and exploits than for his truly Russian feelings and attitudes. We can say with confidence that he was the last genuinely Russian warrior, just as Brutus was the last Roman.

Others, no less brave or enterprising or eager for military adventure, and some even more brilliant, fought alongside Kulnev, but their thoughts and feelings owed as much to a foreign sky as they did to Russia. Kulnev was

truly our very own – our Russian star, immutable as the pole star. He typi-
fied the Russian of that era who would seal all deals, promises and oaths by
adding, 'May shame befall me', and who kept his word not for fear of the
law, but for fear of the reproach of his own conscience. His unwavering love
of throne and country came from the heart. His respectful love for his par-
ents, and his good deeds, hidden and mute towards his enemies, were always
modest and natural. His memory for us, his contemporaries and service
friends, is sacred and everlasting. I return now to the military action.

While I was on my way from Helsingfors to Abo, and from Abo through
Vasa to Hamle-Karlebi, the fortress of Sveaborg surrendered to our arms. The
Swedish troops who defended it and constituted one-seventh of the garrison
were conveyed as prisoners to Viborg. But about 6,000 Finnish troops were
released and sent home with safe-conduct papers. This was a mistake that
caused us no end of harm during the summer campaign and even during the
first retreat of our troops from northern Finland.

In the meantime, our commander-in-chief, Count Buxhoevden, not tak-
ing into account the weakness of our detachments engaged in the north, kept
sending them order after order to step up their pursuit and pressure on
Klingspor, whose troops became increasingly concentrated as they fell back
towards Uleaborg and were further reinforced by troops arriving from
Sweden. This situation signalled a setback for us, because our whole 21st
Division remained at a standstill in Abo and its immediate neighbourhood.
The troops of the 17th Division, which had surrounded Svartholm and
Sveaborg, entered these fortresses for garrison duty, and the reserves that had
arrived from Russia were deployed to protect the shores from enemy land-
ings, which lay far in the future. As a result of this situation, the small bunch
of troops seeing action in the north was separated from the main army in
the south by a gap of over 50 miles of empty land and had no reserve to fall
back upon. I don't mean this as a criticism, but just to show the disposition
of the troops.

On 1 April Kulnev occupied Kalayoki. On the 3rd, two hours before daybreak, he marched off to attack at Ipperi at the same moment as the vanguard of the enemy army had taken the offensive against him. Our infantry,
consisting of three battalions and six guns under the command of Lieutenant
Colonel Karpenko and Majors Vrede and Konsky, took the main road while
two squadrons of hussars and 200 cossacks under Major Silin made up our
left flank, riding over the ice of the Gulf of Bothnia not far from shore.

Hostilities got under way at sunrise and musket fire became intense on
the main road and the adjoining woods. At that moment the Swedish dragoons of the Nieland Regiment rode from the shore and appeared on the ice
to cut off our cavalry and moved against a small number of cossacks scattered ahead of them. The cossack skirmishers pulled back and began to entice

the enemy cavalry in their direction as it began to lose battle order. Seeing this, Kulnev and I galloped together to muster our cavalry, but by that time it had charged and dispersed the Swedish dragoons. We just had time to enjoy seeing the cossack lances going to work and our horsemen chasing the enemy over the flat, snowy wastes of the Gulf of Bothnia. It was a marvellous, spectacular sight!

Many dragoons had been run through and many captured. But amid this confusion we caught sight of a group of horsemen surrounded by a crowd of cossacks who were still putting up resistance. Racing there at full speed, we heard cries in French of 'Koulnev, Koulnev, save our lives!'

It was General Levenhelm, adjutant to the King of Sweden, who had just arrived from Stockholm to join the Swedish army to take up the duties of Chief of the General Staff; and his personal adjutant, Captain Klerfelt, a young man who had visited us the previous day as a messenger under a flag of truce. They had several dragoons with them. Kulnev pushed back the lances directed at them, jumped off his horse and rushed to embrace the officials, now our prisoners. The Swedish general had been wounded in the throat by a lance and his blood ran down Kulnev's moustaches and sideburns. Luckily for him, though, it was not as dangerous a wound as we first thought.

Our pursuit of the enemy continued to the village of Pigayok. Levenhelm's wound was immediately bandaged by our own surgeon; afterwards he and his adjutant, encouraged by our welcome and Kulnev's hospitality, were sent under escort to General Rayevsky, who had already left Vasa to come to our assistance.

The following day we proceeded further. We occupied Bregestadt almost without opposition, but we met unexpected resistance at Olkioki, which did not continue for very long.

It would have been useless to warn Kulnev about making sure that the vanguard kept an eye open for a possible surprise attack on our detachment. In this respect he was a byword for vigilance and perseverance. But he needed to be reminded that his confidence that Klingspor would retreat indefinitely might be unfounded, and that the latter was falling back for strategic reasons, in order to link up with the Swedish and Finnish troops near Uleaborg, and not by reason of panic induced by our rash and overstretched pursuit. I took it upon myself to put him straight on this, arguing with him until I was worn out and on the point of quarrelling with him, but it was all in vain. He could not see that as the Finnish troops fell back towards Uleaborg – this junction of main roads – all the Finnish troops on the march would eventually converge there. He did not take into account that his detachment and that of General Rayevsky, cut off from our main forces and trapped on the northern shore of the Gulf of Finland, were advancing towards the same centre without support or hope of reinforcement by fresh troops. Giving not a thought for all of this, he kept going without looking back, carried along on the cloud of his previous successes.

On 6 April, our detachment ran into the enemy again. It was near the Siganok church. They occupied a position that they appeared unlikely to give up without a fight. We attacked them fiercely. Our initial engagements were successful and the Finnish rearguard seemed ready to fall back from their position and join up with the main forces who were retreating. But suddenly, Klingspor had a change of heart. He halted the retreat and sent back half of his army to support the rearguard. The fire was renewed with the greatest fury. The Finnish troops, supported by ten of their cannons, arranged themselves in columns, lowered their bayonets and charged at us. Our forces, encouraged by Kulnev's thus-far uninterrupted successes, and in good spirits, greeted the enemy in grand style. Gunfire gave way to slaughter by cold steel. The Finns and the Swedes were worthy opponents in this kind of combat. The contest was bravely conducted, but the superior numbers of the enemy turned the tables and brought them victory that day. We yielded the field of battle. Losses on both sides exceeded a thousand men. We lost Major Konsky of the 24th Jäger Regiment; on the enemy's side, Colonel Fleming was killed. Kulnev was saved by divine providence – a cannon ball came so close to him that it burned his leg.

On the following day, Klingspor quit the battlefield and concentrated his forces between Limingo and Lumioki. We immediately fell back on Sigayoki. In the meantime, Rayevsky kept marching in our wake and stopped at Pigayoki where he joined up with the 5th Division which came from Kuopio but comprised no more than 3,000 men. One of the brigades with 2,000 men was left on the road leading from Kuopio to Uleaborg to pursue the enemy brigade of Kronstedt which was heading that way.

Lieutenant-General Tuchkov was in charge of the 5th Division, and because he was senior to Rayevsky assumed command over all the troops engaged in northern Finland who did not exceed 7,000 men in total.

Kulnev, who had been punished at Sigayoki for his lack of foresight, became more reasonable. We remained there, observing the utmost military caution, but not undertaking any armed action and awaiting the arrival of Bulatov, who had been directed by Tuchkov to leave the Kuopiyoki highway and head for Revolaks, a village about seven miles away.

But because Kulnev could not remain inactive for long, he sent me on 12 April with a squadron of hussars and a hundred cossacks to the island of Karlo. This island is ten miles from the shore, almost opposite Uleaborg. I was instructed to rid the place of its occupants, but to do nothing except attract the attention of the enemy vanguard. The island was situated on their flank and almost behind their position. I got there at daybreak and found only a few foragers with a small escort. The fighting did not last very long.

We beat down a few horsemen and took some prisoners, while the others fled for safety as soon as they spotted us coming. During the course of the day, I returned safely to the unit from which I had been sent.

On the same day, 12 April, Bulatov entered Revolaks and at about the same time Tuchkov and Rayevsky moved towards Bregestadt.

The enemy army stayed put at Limingo and Lumioki. Their combined forces now numbered 14,000 men. We expected a quick resolution of the conflict, and not in our favour, because our main forces were so far away and we were now outnumbered by about two to one. On 15 April, that is exactly what happened.

Here ends Davidov's account of the war against Finland and Sweden in 1808. Apparently, he did not care to continue his description of the hostilities and we do not know when or how he subsequently got back to Russia.

It must be acknowledged that Tsar Alexander had started this war at the behest of Napoleon, to punish them for their alliance with England. Hostilities ended to the disadvantage of the Swedes because when peace was concluded, Finland was actually wrested from Sweden and incorporated into the Russian Empire. The acquisition of Finland also constituted one more argument used by Alexander at home to keep the peace with Napoleon, since a renewed falling out would have been dangerous and disadvantageous to Russia at that time. For these and other reasons, Russia remained at peace with France after the celebrated interview of the two monarchs at Erfurt on 27 September 1808.

CHAPTER 6

Diary of Partisan Warfare, 1812

In 1814, Denis Davidov organised his diary of partisan warfare which spans the period from August to December 1812 – from the battle of Borodino (7 September) to the time when the last remnants of Napoleon's Grande Armée recrossed the borders of the Russian Empire.

What had started out as a 450,000-strong main army six months before had melted down to about 1,000 effective troops and a few stragglers. This was due not only to losses on the battlefield prior to the fall of Moscow, but also to severe weather, lack of food and the actions of the cossacks. The war which had started with engagements between regular troops had now become a sad contest between disorganised remains of men who hailed from France, Belgium, Holland, Italy, Germany and even Switzerland, and the Russians who now had fresh troops at their disposal, together with cossacks, irregulars and partisans who relentlessly pursued the luckless invaders, weighed down by booty and plagued by absence of discipline.

The mounted regular and irregular troops were particularly effective. Most of the French cavalry were on foot as a result of the disastrous casualties among horses during the early part of the war, and were now suffering from the bad climate, lack of fodder and the loss of portable forges. The surviving horses slipped and fell on the ice and could not be reshod in time for winter, properly fed or rested.

The cossacks, on the other hand, were mounted on small native horses that were well adapted to the climate and better able to endure with the help of the local peasantry. Flying columns of cossacks kept on the move, hiding in the woods during the day, attacking at dawn, relentlessly pursuing small enemy units, transports, couriers, stragglers and foragers, and appearing out of nowhere, taking even larger units by surprise and spreading panic everywhere. The circumstances were ideal for partisan warfare.

From 1807 to 1812, I was an adjutant in the service of the late Prince Peter Ivanovich Bagration. In Prussia, in Finland and in Turkey I was in constant attendance of this brilliant commander. When circumstances interrupted his active service, he left me, at my request, with the army; thus I completed the course in advance tactical formations under General Kulnev in 1808 in northern Finland, and again with him in Turkey in 1810, under the leadership of Count Kamenskoy.

By 1812, the days of learning were over. As crisis gripped the motherland, each of her sons had to contribute his own particular expertise and talents. I begged the prince for permission to join the ranks of the Akhtyrka Hussar Regiment. He commended my fervour and wrote to the Minister of War.

On 8 April, I was reassigned as a lieutenant colonel to that regiment, which was then deployed to the town of Lutzk. On 18 May, we marched off to Brest-Litovsk, and on 17 June our regiment was stationed near Bialystok. On that day, the retreat commenced and until I was assigned to become a partisan, I remained with the regiment, commanding the 1st Battalion which participated in the engagements near Mir, Romanovo and Dashkova, and in all the advance skirmishes right up to Gzhatsk.

Realising that I was no more useful to our country than a simple rank-and-file hussar, I decided to ask for a separate command in disregard of the much repeated and generally observed rule: never ask for an assignment nor refuse one! On the contrary, I was convinced that in our profession the only way to fulfil one's duty is to step forward from the ranks and volunteer for assignments rather than merely remain in line with the others.

With these thoughts in mind, I wrote a letter to Prince Bagration in the following terms:

> Your Excellency! You are aware that when I left the position of being your adjutant, so flattering to my pride, and joined the Hussar Regiment, I had in mind partisan warfare which is better suited to my age and experience, and if I may say so, to my daring. Circumstances at this time find me in the ranks of my comrades where I have no will of my own, and therefore am unable to undertake or carry out anything remarkable.
>
> Prince! You are my only benefactor; allow me to appear before you and outline my intentions. If they should find favour in your eyes, please put me to use according to my wishes and rest assured that the person who was called adjutant to Bagration five years in a row will assuredly uphold this proud title with all the fervour that the calamitous state of our country calls for.
>
> Denis Davidov

On 21 August, the prince called me, and when I appeared before him I explained to him the advantages of partisan warfare in the present circumstances. 'The enemy is marching along in one direction,' I said to him. 'This extended advance has lost all sense of proportion; the enemy's transports of food and military supplies are stretched over an area from Gzhatsk to Smolensk and beyond. In the meantime, the vast extent of that part of Russia which lies south of the road to Moscow suits not only the twists and turns of individual units, but of our entire army. What are the crowds of cossacks doing in the vanguard? Leaving enough of them to man the posts, we should divide the rest into detachments and send them to strike at the heart of the cavalcade following Napoleon.

'Should strong forces be sent against them? They have enough space to avoid destruction. What if they are left alone? The enemy army's sources of strength and sustenance will be destroyed. Where will it find ammunition and food? The country to either side of the road is not sufficiently fertile to sustain 200,000 troops; nor are the ordnance and gunpowder factories situated anywhere near the old Smolensk road.

'Moreover, the reappearance of our troops among the peasants who have been displaced by hostilities will encourage them and transform the military conflict into a people's war.

'Prince! I will speak frankly. I am disheartened by this strategy based upon parallel positions. Surely we must realise that these will not protect the vital heartlands of Russia. Everyone knows that the best method of defence against this direct attack is not to dispose our army in a parallel line but at right angles, or at least an oblique angle, to the enemy advance. If we persist in the pattern of retreat chosen by Barclay de Tolly and continued by Prince Kutuzov, Moscow will fall, peace will be signed there, and we shall all march off to India to fight for the French!'

I continued, as if speaking to myself: 'If I have to die, let it rather be here! In India I'll disappear with 100,000 other Russians, unknown and useless to the motherland. At least here I can lay down my life under the flags of freedom which will rally the people, oppressed by the godless enemy. But who knows? Maybe our army is destined to fight in India!'

Here the prince interrupted my flight of my fancy, shook hands with me and said: 'I will go today without fail to see the commander-in-chief and present him with your ideas.'

On this particular day, Kutuzov was busy and so the prince postponed his talk until the next day. Meanwhile, we reached Borodino. These fields, this village, were more familiar to me than to others. Here I had spent the carefree years of my childhood and felt the first stirrings of my heart for love and glory. But in what condition did I find the home of my youth! My father's house was hidden by the smoke of bivouacs, rows of bayonets glistened in the fields about to be harvested, and masses of troops swarmed over the hills and valleys where I had grown up. Everything had changed. Bundled up in a military coat, a pipe between my teeth, I lay down under a clump of trees behind Semenovskoe, denied a corner in my own house or even in one of the barns now occupied by staff officers.

In the evening, the prince sent his adjutant to fetch me and told me: 'The commander-in-chief has agreed to send one detachment round to the rear of the French army, but since he judges the outcome of this undertaking to be doubtful, he has assigned only 50 hussars and 150 cossacks; he wants you to take charge of this affair.'

I answered him: 'I'd be ashamed, Prince, to propose a risky venture and let someone else carry it out. But to do any good, it is really too few men!'

'He won't spare any more.'

'Well, I'll take that number; maybe we can pave the way for larger detachments.'

'That's exactly what I expect of you,' said the prince. 'On the other hand, I can't imagine what the commander-in-chief is so afraid of. Is it worth economising with a few hundred men, when, if all goes well, he could smash the enemy's essential supplies and transports, and if not, risk losing only a handful of soldiers? What's to be done? War's not waged so that we can all kiss and make up!'

'Believe me, Prince, upon my honour, the detachment will be safe; all we need for these raids is daring, determination if the going gets rough, and vigilance whenever we stop or rest; I'll make sure of that. But, seriously, this is too few men. Give me a thousand cossacks and you'd see wonders!'

'I would have given you 3,000 to start with, because I don't like messing about, but there's no use talking. The field marshal himself has fixed on the number to go. We have to obey.'

Then the prince sat down and wrote my instructions in his own hand, as well as letters to Generals Vassilchikov and Karpov, the former to assign to me the best hussars, and the other the best cossacks. He asked if I had a map of the Smolensk region. I had none. He gave me his own and blessed me, saying, 'Go with God. I rely on you!' These words I have always remembered.

Having received 50 hussars and 80 cossacks (in lieu of the 150 promised) and five other officers, I marched off through the villages of Sivkovo, Boris and Egorievskoe, and from there to Medyn, Azarovo and Skugorevo. This last village was situated on a hill which overlooked the neighbouring area, so that on a clear day one could see out to a distance of seven or eight miles.

This hill adjoins a forest which stretches almost to Medyn and could easily conceal the troop movements of my party or offer a hiding place in case of defeat. I chose Skugorevo as my first base of operations. In the meantime, the enemy army was streaming towards the capital. Innumerable carts, transports, convoys and marauding bands followed behind them on both sides of the road for a distance of 30–40 miles.

This multitude, subject to no form of discipline, committed all manner of violent excesses. A broad band of territory had been laid waste, consumed by fire, and whole communities were fleeing from the onslaught with their remaining possessions, headed nobody knew where. As for my party, it is important to stress that our progress was becoming increasingly dangerous as we put more distance between us and the army. Even places left untouched by the enemy posed many difficulties for us.

Local volunteer militia groups habitually barred the way. In every village the gates were closed: young and old manned them with pitchforks, pikes, hatchets and sometimes firearms. As we approached each settlement, one of us had to ride up and parley with the inhabitants, telling them that we were Russians, that we were coming to help them and to protect the orthodox churches. Often the reply came in the form of a shot or an axe thrown at us. Providence saved us from these missiles!

We could have skirted the villages, but I wanted to spread the word that troops were returning, strengthen the determination of the peasants to defend themselves and persuade them to inform us of approaching enemy troops. Once we had explained matters to the villagers, we were free to enter the streets. There the atmosphere changed and as soon as doubt gave way to realisation that we were Russians, bread, beer and cakes were offered to the soldiers.

After peace was concluded, I often asked these villagers: 'Why did you suppose we were French?' They invariably answered: 'Well, you see, my dear sir,' pointing to my uniform, 'they tell us this resembles their outfits.'

'But don't I speak the Russian language?'

'Well, you know, sir, they have all kinds of people in their ranks.'

Only then did I learn by experience that in a people's war one must not only speak the local language, but also adopt their ways and their clothes. I put on a peasant smock, let my beard grow and, instead of the Order of St Anne, I hung an icon of St Nicholas around my neck and began talking to the people in their own dialect.

Yet these dangers were insignificant compared to those lurking in the areas occupied by enemy units and transports. Our party was inevitably outnumbered by the convoys guarding the transports and even by marauding bands. At the first rumour of our arrival in the Viazma area, strong detachments were sent out to hunt us down. The villagers, disarmed and petrified of the French, were therefore not inclined to wait and see. Disaster loomed everywhere.

To be on the safe side, we spent the day in the heights near Skugorevo, hidden and on the alert; towards evening, not far from the village, we laid out campfires. Farther out, but opposite the place where we planned to bed for the night, we prepared other campfires and finally, having entered the forest, we spent the night without fires.

If we happened to meet a passer-by, we detained him and kept him under guard until we went out on an expedition. If he managed to disappear, we changed our base again. Depending on the distance to the place that we planned to attack, we would start our search one to three hours before sunrise and, having intercepted and destroyed the enemy transport, which we could cope with, we would find another target; after this attack we would return to the safety of our forest, using circuitous roads which would gradually bring us on a round-about route back to Skugorevo.

Thus we fought and moved from place to place from 29 August to 8 September. Learning that the village of Tokarevo had been invaded by a band of marauders, we attacked it at sunrise on 2 September and took 90 prisoners together with their convoy of pillaged possessions. The cossacks and the peasants had hardly divided the spoils among themselves when sentries established secretly outside the village signalled the approach of another band of marauders.

This village lies on the slope of a hill near the shore of a small river, Vory, and that is why the enemy failed to spot us as they marched towards Tokarevo without the least precaution. We mounted our horses, hid behind the wooden huts, attacked from all sides, with much shouting and shooting, broke into the middle of the convoy and took 70 more prisoners.

Then I called the villagers together and announced to them the expected arrival of a great number of our troops to help the Ukhnovsky and Viazemsky townships. I distributed among the peasants the muskets and ammunition seized from the enemy, convincing them to defend their property and instructing them how to deal with the bands of marauders who, for the time being, outnumbered them.

'Receive them in a friendly way,' I told them. 'Do plenty of bowing (because not knowing Russian, bows will be better understood) and bring out all you have in the way of food, and especially drink. Put them to bed drunk and when you see that they are properly asleep, grab all their weapons, which are usually stacked in the corner of the hut or outside in the street, and do what God has ordained against enemies of Christ's church and your motherland.

'Once you have wiped them out, bury their bodies in the animal barn or in some inaccessible place in the woods. In any case, take care that the spot where they are buried will not stand out because of recently dug-up earth. Cover it with a pile of stones, logs, ashes or whatever. As for all the military booty, such as uniforms, helmets, belts and so forth, either burn it or bury it in the same type of place where you bury the bodies. Take this precaution because otherwise another band of robbers will be sure to dig in the freshly moved earth, naturally hoping to find their money or valuables. But when they uncover instead the corpses of their comrades and their belongings, they will be sure to turn on you and burn down the village.

'And you, the village elder, keep an eye on everything and see that there are always three or four lads in the square who, when they spot a force of Frenchmen, will be ready to mount horses and gallop in different directions to find me, so that I can come to your aid. God wills that orthodox Christians should live peacefully among themselves and not betray one another to the enemy, especially to the sons of the Antichrist who do not spare even the Lord's churches. All that I have told you, repeat to your neighbours.'

I did not dare to issue these instructions in writing, fearing that they might fall into the hands of the enemy and inform them about the methods I had suggested to the villagers on how to exterminate foragers.

After this, having rebound the prisoners, I put them in charge of a non-commissioned officer, nine Cossacks and twenty or so villagers. The whole convoy was sent to Ukhnov to be handed over to the town's administrators against signed receipt. I ordered these cossacks to await our party in Ukhnov. Although I knew that with such small numbers, I dared not remain for long in an area swarming with the enemy, I was eager to tempt fate once more with a handful of comrades and challenge the impossible. I felt that my duty was not to defeat vagabonds, but to destroy the French army transports of food and military equipment.

Therefore, having broadcast the instructions given to the Tokarevo peasants in all the villages through which we marched, I veered off in the direction of Tsarevo-Zaymische which lay on the old Smolensk highway (one day's march from Borodino). It was a clear, cold evening. The heavy rain of the previous night had beaten down the dust of the trail we were following and made the ground firm. Six miles from the village we came upon an enemy unit, which did not spot us as we rode through a valley near a woodland area, and continued on their way without a worry.

Had I not urgently required fresh intelligence about the village, I would have let this detachment proceed unmolested for fear of allowing one of them to escape and giving the alarm to the troops or the convoy stationed there. But I needed an informant and so I sent ten riders to intercept them and ten more to cut them off. Seeing themselves surrounded, they gave up without a fight. They numbered ten men and a non-commissioned officer from whom we learned that the village was harbouring a transport with munitions, together with a convoy of 250 horsemen.

In order to take this force completely by surprise, we left the road and cut across fields, taking cover in clumps of woods and small valleys. Three miles short of the village, however, as we reached open space, we encountered some 40 enemy foragers. Seeing us, they fled immediately towards their unit. We had no time for tactical manoeuvres, and leaving 30 hussars to guard the prisoners and who could in an emergency serve as our reserve, we gave chase to the enemy with the remaining 20 hussars and 70 cossacks. We galloped into the village on the heels of the fleeing enemy, taking everyone by surprise. Fear has big eyes, and fear goes hand-in-hand with disorder. On our appearance, everyone scattered. We took some Frenchmen prisoner without weapons or even clothes, others we dragged out of barns. Only one group of about 30 soldiers tried to put up a fight, but they were routed and quickly cut down.

This raid resulted in the capture of 119 men, two officers, ten wagons with food supplies and one with ammunition. The rest fled for their lives. Our booty was placed under guard and promptly evacuated by way of Klimovo and Kozhino and on to Skugorevo, where we arrived on 3 September at midday.

My party, having been on the move and in action without stop for 30 hours, needed rest and so we remained there until the evening of the 4th. To rest the horses, I employed the method which I had noted before when serving in the vanguard under General Yurkovsky back in 1807. Detailing four cossacks for two sentry posts and 20 for reserve (ready for action at the first shot from the sentries), the other 96 men were divided into two groups and were told to remove the saddles from two horses for an hour, to wash and tend to their sores and allow them to rest. After an hour, these horses were saddled anew and two others followed suit, so that in 24 hours, 96 horses had been refreshed.

On the same day, I also gave permission to the reserve to unsaddle one horse at a time for one hour. On the 5th we entered the village of Andreyevskoe, but on the way nobody was captured except some 30 marauders.

On the 6th, we turned off to the village of Fedorovskoe, on the old Smolensk highway, still spreading the instructions that I had given to the Tokarevo villagers. On the way, we met a soldier from the Moscow Infantry Regiment who had escaped from a transport of Russian prisoners. He informed us that this transport, numbering 200 soldiers of the line, had stopped for the night in Fedorovskoe and that its convoy consisted of 50 Frenchmen. We put on speed and had barely reached the village when it became clear that the transport had altered its aspect without our assistance. The prisoners were now the convoy guards and the soldiers of the original convoy were prisoners themselves!

Shortly afterwards, I was informed that members of two depleted cossack regiments were wandering about in the area. I also made contact with several officials from Ukhnov, and reached that town on the 8th, by way of Sudeyki, Lukovo and Pavlovskoe. There I set about the formation of local militia forces and the incorporation of these cossack regiments into my party.

The man who gave me a helping hand in the former project was a local dignitary, Semen Yakovlevich Khrapovitsky. A true patriot, despite his advanced age, he not only set a shining example of determination by remaining with his family at this outpost of the Kaluga region, but also displayed willpower and severity in overseeing the supply of arms to the local population, an enterprise in which he was joined by 22 local landowners. The 120 muskets which my group had captured, as well as a large cart filled with ammunition, were turned over to the first militia group organised and stationed in the village of Znamenskoe on the River Ugra.

The second matter required a certain amount of cunning on my part: the cossack regiments in question had been placed under the authority of the commander of the Kaluga militia, retired Lieutenant General Shepelev. I knew well his good-natured disposition and noble character, but I also counted upon the flattery to his self-esteem were he suddenly to be put in charge of a military outfit. Being certain that a request to incorporate the two cossack regiments into my party would not find any favour were it to become an independent force, I made it appear as if I was placing myself voluntarily under Shepelev's command.

I dispatched Lieutenant Beketov to him with an official report from the village of Pavlovsk. In it I outlined the scope of my operations within the district adjacent to the province supervised by His Excellency; and as far as military operations were concerned, I said that I felt it my duty to serve under his command and make a full report about all that was going on. From Ukhnov I sent him another courier describing my modest successes and requesting that he intercede on behalf of those who had distinguished them-selves. My true reports were sent directly to the official in charge of all Russian armies, General Konovnitsyn. My friend Shepelev was overcome with rapture. He was convinced that I was acting according to his plan and that he was dealing a decisive blow against the enemy!

On 9 July I dispatched him another courier, rhapsodising about the advan-tages of concerted action, and concluding my report by humbly begging that my group be reinforced with the cossack regiments under his command. In the meantime, from among the 200 prisoners whom we had freed, I chose 60 or so volunteers of medium height; and in the absence of Russian uniforms, I dressed them in French outfits and armed them with captured muskets, leaving them with Russian caps instead of shakos.

We were still unaware of the fate of the capital when on the 9th, Major Stepan Khrapovitsky of the Volyn Regiment, a son of the leader of the local gentry, arrived in Ukhnov and informed us that Moscow had been occupied by the enemy.

Although I had been expecting this event and had argued that it was inevitable as long as we continued our retreat along the Smolensk highway, nevertheless the news shook me to the core, and my comrades, too, were equally affected. However, since there was no point in becoming despondent, we questioned Major Khrapovitsky, seeking further details. He told us that he had left the army at Krasnaya Pokhra, that it had continued moving to protect the Kaluga road, that Moscow had been abandoned to the flames, but that no one in the army was giving any thought to peace.

I trembled with relief and assured the local landowners and villagers that our country would be saved if Napoleon were to leave our army alone, between Moscow and Kaluga, until it was reinforced by reserve armies and Don cossacks. Provided the commander-in-chief adopted this policy, the outcome must surely be apparent to anyone with the least understanding of military science. I felt it as pointless to lecture the Ukhnov landowners about strategy any more than Columbus would have tried to explain astronomy to the American savages when he predicted to them the coming of a lunar eclipse. That evening I received a letter from the civil governor of Kaluga, dated 8 September, containing the following passage:

> Everything has come to pass! Moscow is no longer ours: it is being consumed by flames! I received on the 6th assurances from the commander-in-chief at Podolsk that while protecting the Kaluga road he will concentrate his efforts on the Smolensk highway. Don't fool around, Denis Vasilievich! You have a great obligation! By covering Ukhnov you will save the heart of our province; but don't stray too far, hang on to Medyn and Masalsk. It is my sincere wish that you hold to this course of action so as not to bring the enemy's forces down on yourself.

I was flattered by his reliance on me, but as for his timid advice not to draw the enemy's attention on myself (that is to say on Kaluga and its reluctant governor), that I disregarded.

On the evening of the 10th, I received an order from the commander of the Kaluga militia to take under my command the cossack regiments I had requested earlier, and also Major Khrapovitsky, who had already joined my group.

On the 11th, we went to a church service attended by a multitude of people and civil servants and set off on our campaign accompanied by the blessings of all the inhabitants. We were joined by retired midshipman Nicolas Khrapovitsky, the 60-year-old private counsellor Tatarinov, and the surveyor Makarevich. The other landowners stayed behind, content to parade their hunting clothes, and sporting sabres and pistols tucked into their belts. Towards nightfall we reached Znamenskoe and joined up with elements of the 1st Bug and Teptyarsky Regiments, the first numbering 60 and the second 110 men. Through an unexpected turn of events we had graduated from what might be called a gang of bandits to a well-organised raiding party.

On 12 September I decided to extend our operations as far as the town of Viazma. My heart leapt at the sight of my 'regiments' stretched out on the march. With 130 horsemen I had previously been able to capture 370 men with two officers and free 200 of our men who had been taken prisoner, seize one wagon filled with munitions and ten others with provisions. But here I was, in command of 300 horsemen; what a difference! What prospects! Moreover, I was immeasurably heartened by the enthusiasm of the townsfolk and the activity of the head of the local gentry who urged everyone to join the new militia, promised to supply my unit with provisions and undertook to supervise the organisation of a field hospital in Ukhnov. Not least, I was jubilant at the army's life-saving move towards the Smolensk highway.

At sunrise, we attacked an enemy unit in sight of the town which was escorting a transport of food supplies and artillery shells. Their resistance did not match our impetuosity and our success exceeded all expectations: six officers and 270 men laid down their arms and up to a hundred of the enemy were finished off on the spot; twenty transports with provisions and twelve more containing gun carriages with artillery shells fell into our hands. Right there and then two carriages with munitions and 340 muskets were turned over to retired captain Belsky, in charge of recruiting and training new militiamen, so that from the very outset I already had enough to equip almost 500 men in the village of Znamensky.

On the 14th, we arrived at the village of Teplukha, situated on the Smolensk highway, and, with all due caution, settled there for the night. Here a peasant from the town of Tsarevo came to me and offered to serve in my party. This courageous fellow, named Theodore, left behind his wife and children who took refuge in the woods, stayed with me until the last of the enemy was expelled from Smolensk province and only then went home. After I returned from Paris in 1814, I stopped on purpose in Tsarevo to visit my brave comrade-in-arms only to be told he was no longer alive. He had died from contagion along with many other people who had sought refuge in the woods during the hostilities. What a lesson to us all! Those who seek to avoid death and those who face it bravely often share the same fate: each is allotted a certain amount of time; what is the point of trying to hide and court disgrace?

That evening we encountered marauders, and because we were so carefully hidden we were able to grab them without any resistance, almost one after another. By 10 o'clock we had taken 70 men and two officers, one of whom had his pockets filled with looted seals, penknives and other stuff. It has to be said, however, that this officer was not French, but from Westphalia.

On the morning of the 15th, around 8 o'clock, our sentries on duty spotted a large number of carriages with white covers on their way from the village of Tarbeyev. Some of us jumped on horseback and saw them as they moved along like a sailing fleet. In the blink of an eye, hussars and cossacks galloped to cut them off. The first in line attacked those escorting the convoy, and after a few pistol shots they scattered in flight; then, when cornered by the Bug Regiment, they laid down their arms. Two hundred and sixty men from different regiments with their horses, two officers and twenty carriages filled with bread and oats and harnesses fell into our hands.

Up to now, all my operations had taken place between Gzhatsk and Viazma. Their success prompted the French governor to take action. He gathered all available mounted units, organised a strong force (composed of 2,000 men, eight officers and one staff officer) with instructions to clear the area between these two towns, to destroy my group and bring me back to Viazma dead or alive. I had already been informed of this 'disrespectful' step on the 13th, and when we captured the enemy transport on the 15th, I was told by a peasant horseman that this force had already reached Fedorovsk. I did all I could to avoid it by adopting evasive manoeuvres. My unit set out from Teplukha and followed the road to Shuyski. After a while the road follows a wooded valley and veers sharply to the right, crosses the highway out of sight of Teplukha and continues to Rumyantsevo and Andreyvskoe. There, after spending the night in great secrecy, we proceeded at a quickened pace to the village of Pokrovskoe, which was some five versts from the highway. [About three miles: a verst equals approximately two-thirds of a mile.]

My moving around was based on three suppositions: either the detachment assigned to take action against me, and having lost contact, would resume their march towards Moscow; or, by chasing me from Dorogobuzh to Gzhatsk and back again they would exhaust their horses and give me the opportunity to defeat them with less trouble; or perhaps, by splitting their forces in an effort to surround me, this would enable me to defeat them piecemeal.

On the evening of the 18th, as we arrived at the village of Pokrovskoe, a peasant having come from the main highway told me that he had seen a foot soldier running from a transport of Russian prisoners who had spent the night in the village of Yourenev and had now settled for the night at Nikolskoe, between Yourenev and Pokrovskoe. I asked the man if he could possibly bring this soldier to me. He answered that he could, but because he was afraid to go there alone, he requested one of my cossacks to accompany him. I gave him orderly Kruchkov, and they set off together.

A couple of hours before daybreak on the 19th, the two of them came back with the soldier in question. He reported to me that a thousand Russian prisoners had stopped in Yourenev, that some of them were locked up in the church and that the rest were spending the night in various huts in the village where up to 300 men of their French escort were also quartered. I ordered my men to saddle up and as our party got under way, Kruchkov told me how, as the three of them approached Nikolskoe, they had met a passer-by who told them he had seen a band of vandals enter the village and did not dare go near it. Kruchkov, having questioned him closely as to where the soldiers were being kept, therefore put on peasant clothing and entered the village that was full of French soldiers, located the hut where the soldier was spending the night, woke him up and brought him back. This brave deed increased our respect for Kruchkov and placed me under the pleasant obligation of reporting the incident to our commander-in-chief.

We skirted Nikolskoe and stopped a short distance from Yourenev. There was still about an hour left before sunrise. Unfortunately, while our party was on the march, the prisoner transport had been rounded up and had proceeded further down the Smolensk highway, making way for three battalions of Polish infantry who were en route from Smolensk to Moscow. One of them settled in the village and two others in a bivouac behind the church. These troops were in complete confusion, which goes to prove the lack of planning in their disposition.

Having relied on the report from the soldier and assuming that there was only half of the escort in the village itself, and that the other half was around the church which held some of our prisoners, I had reviewed the situation and given orders to 60 foot soldiers who sneaked through the hollow leading to the village and broke into the main street, shouting, 'Hurrah, our men, this way!', ready to rush the enemy with a bayonet charge. This infantry unit was under the command of ex-midshipman Khrapovitsky.

At the same time, the Bug Regiment was supposed to skirt the village from the other side and to occupy the open space between the village and the church so as to cut off any possibility of retreat to the survivors. My original detachment and the Teptyarsky Regiment had been left in reserve and deployed half-hidden near the woods, under instruction to keep the highway to Viazma open by constant patrols.

My operation was carried out with great punctuality but not with the success I had expected. Our infantrymen, having burst into the village after their silent approach, found, instead of our prisoners and a small escort, a strong enemy battalion which quickly recovered from its initial surprise. A lively exchange of gunfire ensued in the street and from the surrounding windows. Our heroic lads held fast and managed to charge at bayonet point to the arranged meeting place with the Bug Regiment. But in five minutes, out of the original 60 men, 35 lay dead or mortally wounded.

In the meantime, the Chechensky and Bug Regiments completely cut off the enemy battalion which was awaiting reinforcements in the hope of hanging on to its position in the village by keeping up its fire from the huts and orchards. Thirsting for revenge, I asked for volunteers to set fire to the village buildings still occupied by the enemy. My call was immediately answered by the 25 brave survivors of the original group. The peasant huts caught fire quickly and over 200 men were engulfed by flames. A terrible cry went up, but it was too late! Facing certain death, the soldiers began to run out in every direction. The Chechensky Regiment hit them hard, capturing 119 men and one captain. The remains of the battalion regrouped, were attacked several times and managed to retreat in good order towards the other two battalions, which were streaming from the church to their aid. As soon as they showed up, I ordered a gradual retreat, realising that there was nothing else we could do. The musket fire directed at us did not cause us much harm and, picking up our wounded, we were able to move beyond enemy range.

At that moment, one of the patrols we had sent towards Viazma came back and reported the presence of an artillery park located about three versts from the scene of the fighting, beyond the highway. After conveying our wounded to Pokrovskoe under the escort of the Teptyarsky Regiment, I made for the park at all speed with the remaining troops and captured it without any resistance. It consisted of 24 carriages, 144 draught oxen and 23 drivers; the rest escaped into the woods. Having returned from my half-successful expedition to Pokrovskoe, I was at least consoled by the fact that the raids we had carried out on the Smolensk highway, and the experience gathered there, drew the commander-in-chief's attention to my original proposal and that light detachments of troops were set aside to conduct diversionary operations on the enemy's lines of communication.

We had hardly time to settle down in Pokrovskoe when I received news that a fresh transport of about 400 Russian prisoners had stopped not far away from us. Having already been punished once for daring to storm a village occupied by infantry, I sent forward orderly Kruchkov, with six hand-picked men and directed them to approach the village, fire a few pistol shots and disappear quickly so as to alarm the convoy and force it to seek a quieter spot to settle in. The rest of our group followed Kruchkov in secrecy and remained in ambush, awaiting the exit of the convoy from the village.

Complete success crowned our enterprise. Hardly had the shots been fired by Kruchkov and his cossacks before their hasty retreat, than the whole convoy began to pull away from the village. After giving the enemy time to proceed about 500 yards, my party climbed the hill and charged down on the hapless convoy. The prisoners gave a helping hand to the attackers and the entire escort of 166 men and four officers was quickly disarmed. We returned to Pokrovskoe with our prize and settled in for the night.

On the morning of the 20th we moved to Gorodistche where we could rest and also inspect the levies of the new militia formed at Znamensky. Besides, I was now laden with spoils. I found I had 908 men, 15 officers, 36 gun carriages, 40 supply wagons, 144 draught oxen, which I distributed, and about 200 horses from which I chose the best to replace the poor mounts of the cossacks. The rest I apportioned out among the peasants. Since Gorodistche was fifteen versts away from the Smolensk highway and therefore not under direct threat from enemy attack, my unit split into two groups. The Bug Regiment occupied the village of Lougy, five versts further on from Gorodistche; where I remained with the rest of my party. Observation posts were set up on the two main roads and patrols were sent out twice a day to a distance of three or four versts.

In the meantime, I selected 250 men from the 400 prisoners we had freed

Denis Davidov. A watercolour, c.1810, by an unknown artist.

Denis Davidov the partisan. An engraving by M. Dubourg from a painting by A. Orlovsky (1814).

Far left: Alexander Suvorov. An engraving by J. Neidl from a portrait by I. Kreizinger (1799).

Left: Tsar Alexander I, aged 28, wearing the uniform of an officer in the Preobrazhensky Guard Regiment. A portrait by George Dawe (1806).

Above right: The two emperors embrace at Tilsit. A contemporary British cartoon.

Below: The meeting of Napoleon and Alexander I on the Niemen in 1807. An engraving by Lamo and Misbach.

General Kulnev, Davidov's dashing commanding officer during the Russian campaign in Finland. An engraving by F. Vandramini.

Prince P. I. Bagration commanded the Russian Second Army in 1812 and was mortally wounded at Borodino. An engraving by S. Kardelli.

General Kutuzov commanded Russian forces at Borodino and during the French retreat from Moscow. He died in 1813. A portrait by R. Volnov (1813).

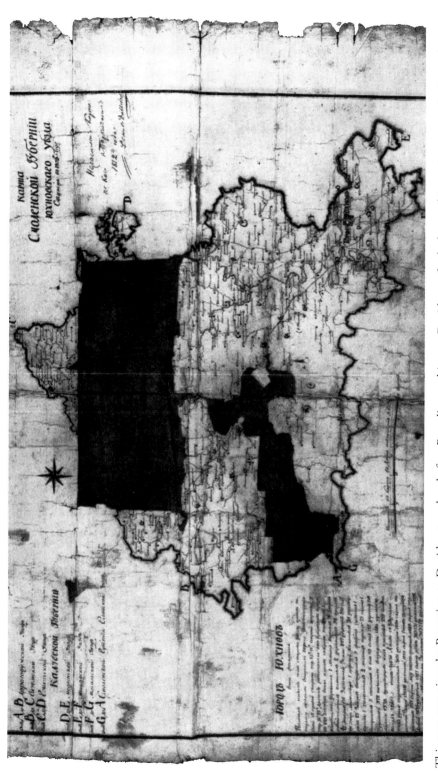

This map was given by Bagration to Davidov two days before Borodino and just as Davidov embarked upon his partisan career. It shows the area around Smolensk, and the Ukhnov province in particular, Davidov's first base of operations.

A letter from Bagration to Vorontsov, written hastily during the Russian retreat before Napoleon's army in the summer of 1812. It reads '... tell Vassiltchikov that he should keep himself closer to you, and Platov will be behind. Thus you will form the rearguard in 3 lines – Platov, Vassiltchikov and your excellency'.

Above: Denis Davidov and his officers on campaign.

Opposite: Napoleon observing the battle of Borodino by V. Vereshchagin. The emperor's preoccupied expression reveals something about the nature of the struggle.

Russian partisans prepare for a raid. A painting by an unknown artist.

'Don't get them yet – let them come closer.' The figure in the centre of these armed peasants is Semen Arhipovitch, a village elder from one of the localities in the Mozhaisk district. A painting by V. Vereshchagin.

Cossacks pursue the retreating French army. This painting is by A. Desarnaud and the artist himself is pictured in the centre, receiving a wound from a cossack lance.

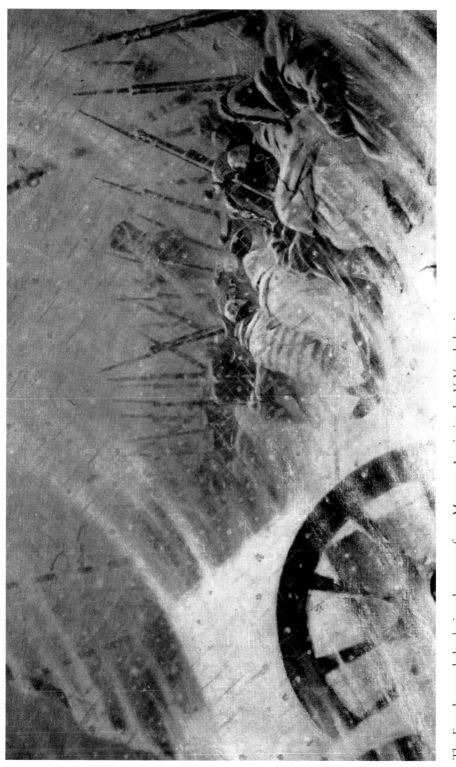

The French army halts during the retreat from Moscow. A painting by V. Vereshchagin.

Above: Hetman Platov. A painting by V. Tropinin (1812).

Opposite: The Russian army crosses the Niemen, under the gaze of General Kutuzov, in December 1812. A painting by P. Demidov (1958).

Above: Denis Davidov in 1828. A
drawing by P. L. Iakovlev.

Above right: Denis Davidov.
A lithograph, c.1830, by an
unknown artist.

Right: The memorial to Denis
Davidov in the cemetery of the
Novodevitchy monastery. The
inscription reads 'DENIS
DAVIDOV, HERO OF THE
PATRIOTIC WAR OF 1812'.

and added the remains of my infantry to these, which I baptised the 'Heroes' Half-Battalion'. Men were transferred to it only if they had distinguished themselves and in this way the outfit gradually grew to two battalions. The remaining 150 men were sent on to Znamenskoe and named 'The Honorary Half-Company', urging the new militia to emulate them.

On the 21st, early in the day, I visited Znamenskoe where I already found about 500 men under arms. Belsky explained to me that the other 1,500, also armed with captured muskets, were quartered in several neighbouring villages and were ready to gather in Znamenskoe at the first notice. He assured me that the villagers were so keen that in case of need we could rapidly muster up to 6,000 men; but these could only be armed with picks and axes instead of muskets. Shock seemed to have inspired people with renewed impetus, and there was a fresh sense of purpose – as if the whole world were threatening us! I wanted to do even more, but had to be content with what had been achieved.

It is to our people's credit that in this whole region the only traitors to be found were the servants of retired Major Semen Vishner and two peasants, Efim Nikiforov and Sergei Martynov. The servants joined up with French marauders and killed their master. Nikiforov also enlisted the French to help kill retired lieutenant Danilo Ivanov; and Martynov pointed out wealthy citizens to the enemy, who killed the governor of Gorodistche, plundered the church, dug up the remains of a local female landowner, and opened fire on the cossacks. When my party arrived there, they all took flight and disappeared but we finally apprehended the last rascal on the 14th. This captive was more important to me than 200 Frenchmen! I immediately reported the matter to the commander of the militia and prepared to carry out exemplary punishment.

On the 21st, the order came for me to execute this criminal by firing squad, and within the hour I sent out a notice to all the villages within ten versts for the locals to gather at Gorodistche. Four priests from neighbouring villages were invited to attend. On the morning of the 22nd, the condemned man made his confession, was dressed in a white blouse and led under guard to that very church that he had plundered with our enemies. The priests stood in front of the church, in line with the firing squad, and behind them stood the populace and our whole group under arms. The criminal was placed on his knees facing the priests. A memorial service was sung while he was still alive. Did he hope for forgiveness? Was he hardened by evil or had despair driven all feelings from him? During the service he did not cross himself even once. When it was over, I ordered him to bow in all four directions and he did so. I directed the people and my unit to make way. He looked at me without any comprehension, but finally, when I had him taken aside and gave the order to place a hood over his eyes, he began to tremble. The squad came to attention and fired all at once. Afterwards my group surrounded the spectators; there were no other traitors or plunderers, but some who had disobeyed the authorities. I had a list of these, called out their names and had them whipped. After the punishment had been carried out, Stepan Khrapovitsky read out an announcement:

Thus will be punished all godless people, traitors to our country and those who disobey our authorities. Remember that the army may be away for a time, but our Tsar, our orthodox lord, will find out where evil has been perpetrated and at the least infringement or disorder we will be back to punish all godless people and traitors as we have done today with this scoundrel; there is no room for him in consecrated ground. Bury him in the 'Robber Hollow'.

Then Father John, raising the cross, said, 'Let any man who disobeys the constituted authorities be cursed. An enemy of God and a traitor to the Tsar and fatherland, let him be cursed!'

After that I read to the assembly the same instructions I had given to the Tokarevo villagers and dismissed them. In the evening I sent a courier with the report about the success of my search and the punishment of the above criminal.

On the 23rd, in the morning, I learned of the death of my benefactor, the heroic Prince Peter Ivanovich Bagration. Fate enriched me with his special protection and also allowed me the satisfaction to honour him by defeating the enemy at the moment this news arrived. A lookout posted on the country road linking Dorogobuzh to Gorodistche let me know that two large enemy columns were on the march towards Gorodistche. I ordered the cavalry to saddle up quickly and gave the same order to the Chechensky Regiment at Lugui. Then I advanced with the infantry along the Dorogobuzh road to the gates of Gorodistche. My intention was to delay the enemy's entry into the village and allow the cavalry enough time to get ready, skirt the place and attack the enemy in the rear. We had to cover almost a mile. Although I was riding at full trot, I swear the infantry not only kept up with me, but several of them actually got ahead of me – such was their hunger for a fight. When we reached the outermost huts, I halted the troops and dispersed about 50 sharpshooters between the huts and the orchards. I disposed the remaining 225 men into two columns, but revealed only the heads of the columns, concealing the tails behind the buildings.

Having organised the defence of the village, I rode out to satisfy myself that the enemy was worthy of such a sophisticated plan. Soon I spotted a crowd of about 400 foot soldiers. At first they appeared to be aiming for Gorodistche, but when our sharpshooters let off several shots and they sighted my columns, they decided to pass by. At that point I realised that this mob had no evil designs on us. And, in fact, it turned out that they were none other than a large band of marauders. I ordered the sharpshooters to press on and for the infantry to follow them. At this moment we saw Major Khrapovitsky charging at full speed with his cavalry. The enemy made for the nearest grove and my men after them. The roar of firing and shouts of 'Hurrah' fused together. The grove adjoined the River Ugra, where there are shallows, and beyond the river there stretched dense woods all the way to Masalsk. It appeared that our prey was about to escape. But Khrapovitsky, who was born and bred in Gorodistche, on this occasion combined an intimate knowledge of local topography with his great military talents. He immediately skirted the trees and positioned himself between them and the river, just as our infantry rushed into the grove.

The enemy, seeing inevitable disaster, began to throw down their weapons and surrender. I ordered them to be given quarter, convinced that the greatest tribute I could show to the memory of my heroic benefactor was to be merciful. Then we saw Chechensky galloping towards us with his regiment to offer help. He had been told that we had been defeated and hemmed in with our backs to the river. His surprise was only equalled by joy to see that we were victorious. This unexpected engagement yielded 330 men and five officers. The man in charge of our infantry, ex-midshipman Nicolas Khrapovitsky, really distinguished himself in this affair. Upon our return to Gorodistche we held a brief service in memory of Prince Bagration and proceeded to march towards the village of Andreyani.

At this same time, I received the order to detach the Teptyarsky Regiment from my forces and send it to Roslavl and Briansk for joint operations with a detachment of militia from Kaluga, which was entrusted to protect the government centre of Orlov. Although it was painful for me to carry out this order, I realised the importance of Roslavl, which was threatened by units advancing from Smolensk along the road to Orlov. So, without any objections, I ordered Major Temirov to march towards Roslavl.

On the 24th we learned that the enemy detachment detailed for action against us, having spent several days without success between Viazma and Gzhatsk, had appeared in the village of Monin, between Semlev and Viazma. Without departing from my intended course of action, I continued towards Fedorovsk and arrived in the evening at Slukino.

The next day, leaving Fedorovsk, we veered right along the highway towards Viazma. I wanted to attract the enemy detachment in this direction with heavy musket fire, and then make for Semlev, which was a much more suitable theatre of action for a weakened force.

My vanguard opened fire outside Viazma itself and I split the party, as usual, into three groups, with only the heads of the columns visible. We soon heard the beating of drums and spotted the enemy infantry which began to answer our musket fire, but did not venture out of the city. This suited me, and remaining where we were until evening, we lit our bivouac fires and retreated under cover during the night to Losmino. On the 26th we reached Andreyani, and I sent two peasants into Pokrovskoe to get information on the enemy detachment. Within four hours two lads galloped over from Losmino with the news that the French were on their way from Viazma, marching in the direction of Gzhatsk. My wishes were being granted.

Our party immediately headed for Monin. Towards evening we reached this village and captured 42 wagons loaded with food, ten artillery carriages under the protection of 126 light infantrymen, and one officer. This group was part of the detachment sent at the double to overtake us. The captured officer told me that my opposite number, frustrated at his lack of success, hoped to catch us up at Gzhatsk, but failing that was determined to pursue the search along the River Ugra so as to cut me off from Ukhnov and Kaluga.

I have noticed that partisans in charge of a separate unit sometimes tend to get the notion that they are military leaders in command of an entire army. Hence their overriding thought is how to cut off the opposition from the rest of the army and to occupy positions favoured by Austrian tacticians. It cannot be emphasised too strongly, however; the best strategy for a group of partisans is to be continually on the move, leaving the enemy in the dark as to its true location and keeping their sentries constantly on the alert. Meanwhile, patrols must be active in guarding the group to ensure it is never cut off or surrounded, operating in accordance with the maxim of 'live to fight another day'. My opponent was clearly unaware of this essential truth of partisan warfare, and that is why I was able to cope with him so easily. Having sent our captives and booty into town, as previously, we continued towards the highway and lingered there uneventfully for a couple of days.

On the 29th we arrived in Andreyani where I was met by the courier who had returned from army headquarters. He brought me various papers and informed me that we would soon be reinforced by the cossacks of the 13th Regiment under Popov, which indeed joined us in Andreyani on 1 October.

This regiment, despite forced marches all the way from the Don, appeared to me in the best possible shape; and now that my group was strengthened by 500 well-mounted cossacks, I stopped worrying about the detachment in pursuit of us and decided to attack it myself.

Before that, however, I wanted to retrain and sharpen these new troops who now constituted the better half of my unit. Whereas it had been possible to operate with a small party as if they were a band of outlaws, without strict discipline, and relying mostly on rough informality, this could no longer be continued with 700 men. And so, for the next few days, I had to spend time on internal reorganisation and preparing the group for battle. I gave them practical examples of how best to attack, pursue and withdraw; and for the first time I tried out the scattered retreat, so essential for a party composed solely of cossacks in the event of an attack by a superior force. At my first signal the men had to scatter over the whole field of action; at the next signal everyone had to gallop out of sight of the enemy; and finally, after each man had ridden a few versts in a particular direction, he would have to find his way to a rendezvous, chosen in advance, sometimes ten or even twenty versts from the battlefield.

On 3 October, we marched out and came to the village of Pokrovskoe. On the 4th I made a general reconnaissance probe and divided our party into three sections so that each contained a portion of Popov's regiment. Two hundred of these and various cossacks of my old command, under Popov's leadership, were assigned to the woods alongside the River Viazma, between the highway and the village of Luzintsov. I was there with them.

The 1st Bug Regiment and a hundred men from Popov's outfit, under company commander Chechensky, crossed the highway to the villages of Stepankovo and Vopka. Another 200 men from Popov's regiment, together with the Akhtyrka Hussars under Major Khrapovitsky, headed for Semlev, but the infantry remained in Pokrovskoe. Two hours before daybreak, all detachments were on the move. The first body of men halted in the woods, a few yards from the bridge over the River Viazma. Two cossacks climbed trees to serve as observers.

Hardly an hour had gone by when they gave a whistled signal, having spotted an officer walking on foot with a musket and a dog. Ten men jumped on horseback to intercept him, surrounded him and brought him back. This was Regimental Commander Goethals, from the 4th Illyrian Regiment, a keen hunter who loved to track and shoot, and had got ahead of his battalion, which was probably headed for Smolensk for refitting. He had a small dog with him and a bag containing a grouse he had killed. The colonel's despair, far from exciting sympathy, simply made us laugh. After we questioned him about everything that we needed to know, he wandered off and paced up and down in deep thought; but each time he noticed his dog, lying on a cossack's coat, he assumed the stance of the famous actor Talma in the play *Oedipus*, and exclaimed aloud, 'Fatal Passion!' He went on repeating these words whenever his eyes rested on his musket, now in cossack hands, or the grouse that we had hung from a lance as a reminder of his misadventure, and continued pacing back and forth.

At this point we caught sight of his battalion. We got ready and when it came within range the whole party pounced on it – the first cossacks in loose formation and the reserve in a column with six horses abreast. Resistance did not last long. Most of the soldiers on foot threw down their weapons, but many, taking advantage of the nearby woods, scattered and saved themselves by fleeing.

We captured two officers and 200 men of lower rank. At the same time, Company Commander Chechensky came upon a wagon train with provisions which was passing the night in the woods on the way from Vopka to Viazma. When the enemy spotted our cossacks, they tried to form the carriages into a semicircle and put up a defence. But Chechensky did not give them time to carry out this move and captured the transport.

Then the escort of infantry headed for the centre of the wood and kept up a heavy fire. Chechensky, enraged, ordered his men to dismount, pursued the enemy and charged them with fixed bayonets. This brave action completed the defeat, but cost us fifteen of the best Bug Regiment cossacks, badly wounded or dead.

Meanwhile, Major Khrapovitsky reached the highway and proceeded towards Semlev. He ordered the Akhtyrka Hussars, riding ahead, to fix pennons to their lances, and the cossacks to hide behind them with bayonets at the ready. Thus disposed, the force resembled elements of the Polish cavalry associated with the main enemy forces advancing on Smolensk. He did not meet anyone for some time, but near Semlev he spotted a sizeable convoy transporting enormous barrels coming to meet him without the least apprehension, assuming his force to be a Polish unit. Our troops allowed the enemy to come within a pistol shot and all at once, lowering their lances and yelling 'Hurrah!', attacked at top speed. Most of the convoy scattered, but Lieutenant Tiling, with a handful of men, continued to fight until he was wounded, at which point he was deserted by his last comrades.

This transport carried new uniforms and footwear for the whole first Westphalian Hussar Regiment (according to the waybill found on Tiling), and cost 17,000 francs in Warsaw. Returning with his booty to the village of Pokrovskoe, he was attacked by a strong band of plunderers occupying the woods that he intended to cross. Realising that it was impossible to break through the enemy position, he bypassed the woods and in the evening arrived safely in Pokrovskoe, where he joined up with detachments of Popov's 13th Regiment and Chechensky's force.

In this complex raid, Popov's regiment proved the equal of the troops that comprised my group. The regiment's best officer, indeed one of the finest officers of the entire Don army, was Ensign Biriukov, commanding one squadron, and after him Ensigns Alexandrov and Persianov.

The prisoners, consisting of 496 men, one staff officer and four second lieutenants, were immediately conveyed to Ukhnov, together with the 41 carriages captured by Chechensky. The horses belonging to the escorting soldiers were distributed among cossacks who had lost their mounts and also the neighbouring villagers. On that same day, I dispatched a courier to the main headquarters. I described this last raid to the general on duty and requested promotions for all who had distinguished themselves, as well as for

Stepan Khrapovitsky from Ukhnov, thanks to whom we had suffered no shortage of supplies and who had arranged for the wounded to be cared for.

From historical events, I must now turn briefly to affairs of the heart. Lieutenant Tiling came to see me, and said that the cossacks had taken his watch and money. Knowing the customs of war, he was not complaining, but he begged that they would return to him his sweetheart's ring.

Heaven knows, alas, how sensible I was to the feelings that raged in Mr Tiling's soul. I could have kept my own diary of the heart through every campaign I experienced, quite independently of the military events. Strange to admit, but love and war had an equal share in my career, so that even to this day I check the chronology of my life by equating stretches of military service with simultaneous love affairs that stand out like milestones in the wasteland of my youth.

At that particular time I was consumed with passion for a lady whom I believed to be true to me but wasn't. The sentiments of my prisoner found ready echoes in my heart. I promised to try to satisfy his wish. Among our men returning to Ukhnov were the cossacks who had captured him; and I was lucky enough to find not only the ring, but also a portrait, lock of hair and letters that belonged to him. I immediately forwarded them to Tiling with this note in French:

> Receive, sir, the effects which are so dear to you; may they help you remember your beloved and prove to you that courage and adversity are respected in Russia as everywhere else.
>
> Denis Davidov, Partisan

Tiling apparently lived in Orlov until 1814, where he often recalled this incident gratefully, telling people about this adventure as if recounting the magnanimity of a highwayman. I later learned that he gradually tired of changing the objects of his affection, as I had done with each campaign, and that he entered into a legal alliance with his lady when peace was concluded, trading the nomadic life of a hussar for a steadier existence, exchanging fantasy for reality.

On 5 October, our unit went to Andreyani. There I discovered that the enemy detachment had split into two; one part was to be found in a small village towards Krutoy, the other in Losmin, near Viazma. We immediately made for Krutoy. One body of troops numbering 100 men with Ensign Biriukov was dispatched to Belystchino. It was instructed to remain concealed nearby and to send out groups to the right and to the left in order to screen my planned attack on the enemy positioned near Krutoy. Our whole party made for that village, veering to the left so as to keep communications open with Biriukov, and if successful to push the enemy in the opposite direction from where the other part of their detachment was located. Because we were uncertain as to the real distance between Krutoy and Andreyani, instead of arriving two hours before nightfall we got there after dark. We had to decide whether to postpone the attack until morning or to undertake a night foray, which is always uncertain and often fatal to the attackers. Any army group depends upon the cooperation of its constituent parts; and what cooperation can there be when nobody can see anything? What's more, very few people give of their best when there are no spectators around. That goes for soldiers, too. Even Ajax insisted on daylight for a battle.

I knew this to be true, but I also realised the inconvenience of postponing the fight until morning when the neighing of a horse, the barking of a dog or the honking of a goose could interfere with the success of the operation. Therefore, with trust in God, we launched our night attack.

An autumn drizzle had been falling all day and the darkness was total. We struck with our reserve regiment and some infantry. Fortunately, the enemy guards were fast asleep in their huts and refused to wake up!

In the meantime, Khrapovitsky's and Chechensky's men galloped into the village; some of them dismounted and, shouting 'Hurrah!', started to fire at the windows. Reinforcing them with 100 infantrymen and taking 200 cossacks from the reserve, I led them across the Uda stream to prevent the enemy sneaking into Viazma by the side roads. But the night was so black that we lost our way and our guide brought us out at a different spot from the usual crossing. This forced us to descend by fits and starts from a considerable height and get across as best we could. Not knowing the surroundings, I decided to go slowly and keep firing away with pistols and shouting 'Hurrah!' Fortunately the enemy chose not to come this way but turned towards Kikino and fled in disorder along the road from Ukhnov to Gzhatsk.

Our whole party chased them for about four versts. Then I detached 100 cossacks to pursue the fleeing French, but to bear left so as to keep closer to our group, and stay in touch with the road between Viazma and Tsarevo where I intended to turn up after our sweep on Losmino.

In this operation we took prisoner one platoon leader, one officer and 376 foot soldiers. And, because it was night, I directed my men not to get involved taking a lot of prisoners. We captured as many of the enemy as we killed. After tying them up and sending them to Ukhnov, as was customary, I let the horses enjoy a well-deserved rest; then, dispatching the infantry to Ermaki, we set off for Losmino. I had to go by way of Belystchino in order to join up with Biriukov and to replace his unit with the 100 cossacks who had been sent to pursue the enemy; also I needed to gather information from him about the enemy located in Losmino; and lastly, by turning towards Derevestchin and Krasnoja Gora, we planned to arrive from the Viazma side in the rear of the enemy and fall on them like snow out of the blue.

All my plans would have been fulfilled to the letter if only enemy foragers had not sighted my party and hurried on to Losmino to warn their commander of my coming. My riders chased this rabble, but because we had been on the march for the preceding 24 hours, including two hours of fighting, the horses had become weary, thus allowing some of the foragers to get away and spread the alarm through the detachment, which was clearly doomed. Meanwhile we continued to advance at full trot along the road from Viazma to Losmino. It was getting light and because of the incessant rain the road had become quite slippery. My opposite number had been careless and had omitted to shoe all his horses, so that about half of them were not properly provided. Nevertheless, upon my arrival at Losmino he met us on firm footing.

As the fighting got under way, the forward elements came to grips and the action teetered back and forth inconclusively. When our whole force was battle-ready, we charged the three lines of the enemy, positioned one behind the other.

At the first clash, the enemy front line tumbled back into the second and the second collided with the third. Then they all fled headlong. You had to have been a witness to this event to believe the confusion that reigned among the French ranks. To make matters worse, half of the detachment came crashing upside-down. The horses that had not been properly shod collapsed as if struck by grapeshot; their riders ran off on foot in every direction without resistance. Two squadrons did form in battle order and attempted to move forward and impede our attack, but when they sighted my hussars at the forefront of my reserve, they immediately turned back for good.

The pursuit continued until noon. We cut and slashed and shot and dragged into captivity officers, soldiers and horses – in a word, the victory was complete. I was overflowing with joy! We came to a halt. There were 403 men and two officers taken, all wounded. The regimental commander, I was told, had fallen on the field of battle and with him another 150 rank-and-file men; the others scattered through fields and woods or were captured by the inhabitants. In all these engagements we lost only four cossacks and fifteen others were wounded together with two hussars; up to 50 horses had also been killed or wounded.

It goes without saying that I was impatient to boast to the field marshal about this, my finest success to date! A courier was immediately dispatched with a report still smoking from the fire of the battlefield. I was utterly confident that this double victory would be received with praise from all quarters. In the meantime new plans, new alarms, new engagements overshadowed the past. I did not inquire from headquarters about this matter, assuming that it could not get lost in all the shuffle and that the only reason they were keeping quiet was that they were too busy.

I received no reply because I did not follow things up, and this mutual silence continued until the armistice of 1813. Only then did everything become clear. I learned that my courier had been seized by scavengers on the way to Ukhnov and had perished along with my report. Through a piece of bad luck this exploit which, I may say without bragging, was marked by superior planning and implementation, remained known only to my party, the enemy governor of Viazma and the remnants of the French forces which survived the engagement. I am pretty sure that it was even concealed from Napoleon himself because they feared his anger if he heard that troops had been used for totally different purposes than those for which they were intended.

That is what fate has in store for individual commanders, whereas the soldier of the line receives strict accounting for every little thing. It happened that several similar affairs sank into oblivion, but for different reasons. On this day and the following two days, my reconnaissance squads were patrolling along the highway between Viazma and Fedorovsk and succeeded in intercepting three couriers. On the 8th, my group came to this last village and joined up with the 100 cossacks who had been sent in pursuit of the enemy in the neighbourhood of Krutoy.

At that very moment, the French army awoke from its lengthy slumbers in Moscow[11] and moved towards Fominskoe. Napoleon's intention was to march around our left flank located near Tarutin, first to occupy Borovsk and Maloyaroslavets, and then, reaching Kaluga before the Russians, to open communications with Smolensk by way of Meschovsk and Yelnya. As a result, when he got to Fominskoe on the 11th, he ordered Junot's corps, which occupied Mozhaisk, to fall back on Viazma, and General Evers's detachment, numbering 4,000 men, to march from Viazma by way of Znamenskoe and Ukhnov. He also ordered Marshal Victor, with Girard's division and light cavalry, to proceed by forced marches from Smolensk in the same direction. By glancing at the map it was easy to see the situation in which I would soon find myself.

Meanwhile, General Dorokhov, occupying with one detachment the village of Kotovo, close to the road leading from Moscow to Borovsk, decided to attack the Viceroy of Italy [Eugène Beauharnais], who arrived on the 9th at Fominskoe and was asking for reinforcements, unaware that the entire French army was following behind this corps.

Prince Kutuzov, having been advised by Dorokhov that a strong enemy column was approaching, dispatched the corps of Dokhturov with Ermolov,

---

[11] In his notes on *The Year 1812* Davidov asserts that if Napoleon's 34-day stay in Moscow had been cut short by two weeks, none of Kutuzov's plans would have come to fruition and the French army could have reached Smolensk in fair weather and largely unmolested!

Chief of the General Staff of the 1st Army. Ermolov gave orders to the partisan leaders Figner and Seslavin to proceed in the direction of Fominskoe in order to gather information about the enemy. Figner failed to get across the River Louzha, heavily guarded by enemy outposts. Seslavin managed to cross this river and approach the Borovsk road. There, leaving his party behind, he sneaked on foot through the woods to the road itself. There he saw enemy columns in depth, following one another to Borovsk; he even spotted Napoleon himself, surrounded by his marshals and Imperial Guard. Daringly, Seslavin managed to grab a second lieutenant from the ranks of the Old Guard, tied him up, swung him over his saddle and quickly headed back to Dokhturov's corps.

In the meantime, both Dokhturov and Ermolov, not suspecting that Napoleon had left Moscow, were heading for Aristov and Fominskoe. Persistent autumn rain had ruined the road surface and the great quantity of artillery that was accompanying the corps was slowing down its progress. Ermolov suggested to Dokhturov to leave the artillery here, within fifteen miles of Aristov. From there, it was not far from Tarutino and Maloyaroslavets; it could easily reach the latter destination, where its presence would be needed, and for now the exhausted horses could get some rest. Dokhturov readily agreed and his corps reached Aristov towards evening, settling in the village for the night while Ermolov, together with other generals, remained in bivouacs. It was already midnight and in a few hours the whole corps was supposed to march out to Fominskoe according to Kutuzov's orders.

Suddenly a horse was heard arriving at the gallop, and Seslavin was shouting, 'Where is Alexei Petrovich?'

Appearing before Ermolov and accompanied by his prisoner, Seslavin gave details to the general of everything he had seen. The prisoner, too, confirmed that Napoleon had left Moscow with his whole army and was now a very short distance from the corps' location. Ermolov considered this news so vital that he had all the troops awoken and armed, and personally went to see Dokhturov. This brave but not very perceptive general, once appraised of the situation, found himself in a quandary. He did not dare continue the advance toward Fominskoe, but feared that by marching away from Aristov he would incur Kutuzov's wrath for not following his assignment.

At this decisive moment, Ermolov, as on many other important occasions, turned out to be the guardian angel of the Russian army. His eagle eye had summed up the entire situation and, in the name of the commander-in-chief, and in his capacity of Chief of the General Staff, he ordered Dokhturov to retrieve the artillery temporarily left behind and to make haste towards Maloyaroslavets. Assuming complete responsibility for not carrying out Kutuzov's orders, he dispatched staff-officer Bolkhovsky, who was to explain personally to the field marshal the reasons that prompted him to change the direction the troops were now taking and to beg him urgently to hurry to Maloyaroslavets with the entire army. Ermolov himself, with the first cavalry corps and the cavalry regiment of Colonel Nikitin, proceeded towards the village of Kotovo where General Dorokhov's detachment was deployed, wishing to ascertain in person that Seslavin's information was well-founded. Learning of an exchange of fire which Dorokhov had initiated with enemy observation posts, he sent him word and asked for it to be stopped immediately. Dorokhov protested, saying, 'If Aleksei Petrovich were here in person, he would act exactly as I am.' But Dorokhov now ran into strong enemy reserves. Ermolov saw this and, fearing he might be defeated by a stronger enemy, moved forward Nikitin's cavalry. Confirming his earlier order to Dorokhov, he proceeded through a small forest and reached a wide clearing which extended from Borovsk to Maloyaroslavets. There he sighted a large encampment of the Italian army and learned from prisoners that Napoleon was expected to dine in Borovsk that very day.

Ermolov promptly ordered a brave officer of the Cossack Regiment, Sysdev, to take the shortest route to Maloyaroslavets, even if he came dangerously close to the enemy, enter the town and collect all possible information concerning the place and the enemy. Sysdev soon reported back to Ermolov that three Italian battalions were already there, but were being held up due to the fact that the inhabitants had dismantled the bridge. The local officials had by now left the town which had recently been visited by Hetman Platov, who had moved on after leaving a force of cossacks there. At daybreak Ermolov reached Maloyaroslavets, in front of which the Viceroy's entire army was already gathered. Dokhturov, encamped behind the town, entrusted Ermolov with the task of relieving Maloyaroslavets and reinforced him with his own infantry. Our forces were driven back from there twice, despite great shows of valour on the part of our officers.

Meanwhile Field Marshal Kutuzov had reached the village of Spaskoe, not far from Maloyaroslavets, with his entire army, and told his men to take a rest. Ermolov sent General Count Orlov-Denisov with an urgent plea for Kutuzov to hurry towards the town, but receiving no reply, dispatched a German prince, who was then with our army, with a renewed request for them to come as quickly as possible.

The field marshal, resentful at this insistence, literally spat with rage. Then General Rayevsky's corps began its march towards Maloyaroslavets and soon the whole army began to follow him. Rayevsky himself, as a mere spectator, remained for some time near the town to observe how the battle was going. Having once more been forced out of the town by superior forces, Ermolov had positioned 40 field-pieces by the main gate and planned to confront the enemy with a heavy bombardment. Lacking sufficient troops, he had prepared to fall back in an orderly retreat. The arrival of the army, however, changed the situation entirely. It was Konovnitsyn who fearlessly drove the enemy out of the town.

Kutuzov, having gained much experience in the war against the Turks, then devised a very strange solution for holding the enemy at bay in the event of renewed attack. He ordered several redoubts to be erected within firing distance of the town. But after a few shots from inside the town, the 1,500 workmen dropped their tools and scattered. Eventually Maloyaroslavets was abandoned and reoccupied by enemy troops.

After the initial battle, Kutuzov had a curious conversation with Ermolov, which I can only summarise here.

The prince: 'My dear man, are we to march on?'

Ermolov: 'Of course, but only towards Medyn.'

The prince: 'How can we move in plain view of the enemy?'

Ermolov: 'There's no danger at all. Hetman Platov captured several field-pieces on the other side of the stream without encountering any resistance. After this battle, which has proved we are ready to repulse all enemy attacks, we have nothing to fear from them.'

When Kutuzov announced his intention to retreat from Maloyaroslavets, Ermolov tried to persuade him to stay for a few more hours when the intentions of the enemy would become clearer. But the prince was adamant and the army retreated. If Napoleon, having reached Borovsk, had made haste to hurl his entire force at Maloyaroslavets, he would have seized the town without any trouble; having forestalled our army here, he would have been able to march to Ukhnov and from there continue his retreat through a part of the country which was fertile and not laid to waste.

Fate dealt Ermolov the enviable opportunity of rendering the greatest service to his country, but this great exploit, distorted by historians, is known only to a few.

At that moment the partisan Prince Kudashev, stationed between Lopasny and Voronov, started to pursue the enemy vanguard which was attempting to screen the movement of the body of troops along the banks of the River Mocha, attempting to link up with the rest of the French army.

Any military man worth his salt can clearly see that the main body of their troops, shadowed by the units of Dorokhov, Seslavin, Figner and Kudashev, could not hope to take a single step in secrecy, although their salvation depended on bypassing our left flank without being detected and showing up unexpectedly in Maloyaroslavets. Through there, Napoleon could have escaped the net drawn up around Tarutino and opened an unimpeded passage towards the River Dnieper and a country yet untouched by war; he could also have made junction with Evers, Junot and Victor, and might even have contemplated offensive action, his flanks and rear being completely free and unimpeded. If we move from effect to cause, it is evident that Seslavin's mission and information decided Russia's fate. Yet to bring about this reversal of fortune it still needed prompt action on the part of Ermolov, and his willingness to assume full responsibility for turning Dokhturov's corps towards Maloyaroslavets, as well as the action of the commander-in-chief who finally realised the strategic importance of this town and directed the whole army to move there eight hours later.

Not knowing anything about what had occurred in this area, on the evening of the 9th we intercepted another courier not far from Fedorovsk and moved on to Spaskoe. When we arrived at that village, our patrols brought back several enemy soldiers who were busy looting nearby settlements. Since they were few in number, I turned them over to the village elder for eventual delivery to Ukhnov. As they were led past us, Beketov noted that one of these prisoners seemed to look more like a Russian than a Frenchman. We stopped him to ask what nation he belonged to, at which he fell on his knees and admitted that he was a former Russian grenadier and had been employed as a second lieutenant in the service of the French for the past three years. 'What?' we exclaimed in horror. 'You, a Russian, are spilling the blood of your brothers?' 'I'm guilty,' he confessed. 'Please take pity on me.'

I sent a few hussars to fetch all the villagers, young and old, and women with children from neighbouring settlements, and had them brought to Spaskoe. When they assembled, I told my group and the villagers about the activities of this traitor and asked them to judge him. With one voice they said, 'Guilty!' Then I asked them what punishment they thought he deserved. A few said, 'Whip him to death.' About ten others said, 'Hang him.' A few said, 'The firing squad.' In a word, all opted for the death penalty. I called for several riflemen and had him blindfolded. He only had time to say, 'Lord, forgive my sin!' The hussars fired and the wretch fell dead.

There was another strange case. A few hours after this execution the peasants from neighbouring villages brought to me six French stragglers. This surprised me no end because until that time they had never brought me any prisoners, always dealing with them on their own. These unfortunates, tied up with ropes and pulled down into a ditch, would not have escaped the fate of their predecessors had the noise of horsemen and the sound of Russian speech not announced our arrival. Killing them would have been useless, so they decided to bring their captives to me and have me decide their fate. I gave orders to include them among the prisoners already in our hands and to send them all to Ukhnov. From there they would be conveyed to remote districts where they would probably either die on the way, become the victims of their corrupt guards or be dealt with by indifferent civilian authorities.

But how amazing are the decrees of Divine Providence! Among these prisoners was a drummer boy from the Young Guard by the name of Vincent

Bode, a fifteen-year-old lad torn away from his family and transported 3,000 versts from home to face Russian steel and Russian frosts! Seeing him, my heart bled for him. I remembered my own family home and my father who handed me over to military service when I was almost his age! How could I consign this lad to the uncertainties of a cold, hungry and shelterless wandering, having the means at hand to save him? I took him aside, told my men to dress him in a cossack coat and hat so that he would come to no unforeseen bodily harm, and in this way, through successes and failures, over hills and vales, from country to country, I carried him on horseback all the way to Paris, in good health, full of optimism, almost grown-up, and delivered him personally to the waiting arms of his elderly father.

What happened next? Two days later, both father and son came to me and asked me for an affidavit. 'With great pleasure,' I told them. 'Here, Vincent, is a paper attesting to your good conduct.' 'No,' replied the father, 'you saved my son, please complete your good deed and give him a document to certify that he was with you and was defeating the enemy.' 'But, the enemy was your countrymen!' 'Doesn't matter,' protested the old man. 'What do you mean? You'll only condemn your son; they'll drag him before a firing squad and for sure. . .' 'Times are different now,' answered the old man. 'Thanks to this certificate he'll wipe out the record of his unwilling service to the usurper of the throne and will receive a reward for having fought against those who served in the ranks of those opposed to the legitimate monarch.' 'If that's so, then may the Lord have pity on your poor France!' I exclaimed. 'Here's the attestation that you insist on.' And truly, I lied in that document and invented things just like those who write about victory in a battle they never took part in. But the old man was right. In a week's time he came again to see me with his son to thank me for his new promotion. Vincent was already sporting in his lapel the order of the *fleur-de-lis*!

On the 10th and the 11th we continued to march to the right of Viazma, between Fedorovsk and Teplukha. Towards evening our patrols let me know that a large transport with convoy had been spotted on its way to Gzhatsk. We immediately went out to meet it, following along both sides of the road, and coming to a hill we spotted the whole caravan and rushed to the attack. Our men broke into its midst and in a short time 70 wagons, 225 men and six officers fell into our hands. Moreover, we recovered 66 of our prisoners and two cuirassier officers who had been wounded. These two, sitting inside a closed carriage, lifted the top and shouted to the cossacks that they were Russian officers. If you have never had occasion to free your men from the enemy's yoke, you've never felt true joy!

On the 12th our party reached Dubravo. We had hardly settled for the night when we spotted a carriage and a cart heading towards us. It was the leader of the Ukhnov gentry, Semen Khrapovitsky, and my own courier returning from the main headquarters. There was a pile of mail, including one letter addressed to me bearing the seal of the commander-in-chief. It contained messages both for myself and for Khrapovitsky, and a special bulletin describing the defeat of the enemy vanguard on 6 October. Although some papers were dated the 10th, there was no positive news about the retreat of the French army from Moscow which had begun on the 7th. There were also many letters from old and new friends which showered me with compliments and such praise that I saw myself as a new Spartacus.

I was soon brought down to earth, however, by the accursed General Evers, who had been sent from Viazma to Ukhnov, and by my own unforgivable lack of vigilance. This is what happened. On the 13th we arrived at Kikino where we celebrated the rewards and promotions brought by the courier and decided, too soon, to rest on our laurels. The sentries followed the example of the rest of the party and the patrols went out only as far as the barrels set up in the middle of the village. On the 14th we sent Khrapovitsky back to Ukhnov and moved on to Losmino in the same frame of mind as before; but we had hardly come to a halt when the enemy made an appearance within sight of the village and with forces four times stronger than ours. If they had been a little more enterprising, we would inevitably have been defeated. But instead of setting their vanguard loose on us in the village where we were wandering around in separate groups, the enemy opened fire with artillery pieces and proceeded to take up a position!

Evers's arrival had caught us napping and served as a corrective to my shameful lack of preparedness. Even though I saw two large columns of the enemy, I remained convinced that in such cases nerve is worth more than discretion (called 'good sense' by cowards). I went into action without further thought. And when prisoners taken by our advance riders assured us that the detachment was only a mixed rabble of every description, the over-enthusiasm of the cossacks was such that they almost caused us more harm than good. My vanguard crushed its enemy counterpart, but was in turn overwhelmed by the assault of two enemy squadrons. Instead of withdrawing in scattered formation towards one of the flanks, which were moving forward (as trained to do) they continued to mix with the enemy and rode back in disarray towards our main body. If I had not veered hard to the right, they would have run into our midst and created total confusion. Luckily, thanks to this quick manoeuvre, we corrected the situation, because we outflanked the enemy chasing our vanguard and quickly put them to flight.

Then, fired with success, wine and the expectation of booty, my regiments were ready to tear after them in pursuit. It took all the efforts and activity of my officers to stem this rush and keep them in check. I realised that the enemy were not in the least upset by the challenge to their vanguard, and learned that after receiving reinforcements from the direction of Viazma, they were moving resolutely forward. I decided, therefore, not to oppose their advance and to fall back in order, or to be more precise, disorder, as I had tested near Andreyani. So I called for a scattered withdrawal and designated the village of Krasnoe, behind the River Ugra, already familiar to my cossacks, as the new rallying point. At a given signal everyone dispersed and disappeared! One hundred cossacks with Ensign Alexandrov were left behind to keep the enemy under observation. They continued exchanging fire and falling back on Ermaki, towards Znamenskoe, so as to draw the enemy in the opposite direction to which my party was heading. By sunrise everyone was in Krasnoe except for the 100 men under Alexandrov, who rejoined my infantry at Ermaki and fell back together on Znamenskoe, which was occupied by militia forces.

During the night of the 16th, I received news from this militia commander, Captain Belsky, that on the same morning, the enemy had reached Znamenskoe, intending to occupy it, but that when they sighted our infantry there, they had fired only a few artillery shots and retreated to Ermaki. It was only then that I found out from the prisoners brought from other villages that the enemy had actually abandoned Moscow; but in what direction and with what plans we did not know.

On the 17th, I marched towards Ermaki and continued to reconnoitre towards Viazma, but always sticking to the road leading to Ukhnov; and it was from here that I received all the news from the army, which was now of paramount importance to us. I figured that in the event our army got the upper hand, the enemy would not avoid the region where I was stationed; and being ahead of them, I could always impede their progress as much as possible. In the event our side suffered defeat, they would undoubtedly retire toward Kaluga and I could then fall back on Ukhnov or Sergeysk.

After crossing the River Ugra, my vanguard let me know that after being attacked near Ermaki they were retreating fast and that a strong force of the enemy was giving confident pursuit. I decided to send 100 cossacks to their aid and ordered my party back across the river.

We had scarcely reached the other bank when I saw smoke from musket fire and a cavalry at full gallop. It was my retreating vanguard, and very soon two dark enemy columns appeared on the horizon. My horsemen reached the river bank, swam across and joined us, while the enemy advance troops stopped on the other side, keeping up their fire with muskets and pistols; some of them tried to find a fording place further upstream. I could see that the river would not stem their advance, and prepared to retreat towards Fedotkovo. To carry this out in the safest manner, I sent out three patrols of ten cossacks each; one towards Kozelsk, the second towards Fedotkovo, and the third to Znamenskoe. Unfortunately, Fedotkovo was already occupied by the enemy, but I was able to contact Belsky in Znamenskoe and order him to leave it immediately with the militia and my infantry and to proceed along the Ukhnov road. Things now did not appear too rosy. I crossed the Ugra at Kobelev and arrived at Voskresensk, a village on the edge of the Medyn district, near the main road from Ukhnov to Gzhatsk.

On the morning of the 20th I received news from headquarters and the duty officer concerning the retreat of the enemy from Maloyaroslavets and their progress towards Gzhatsk and Smolensk. The sudden increase of enemy detachments and supply trains between Viazma and Ukhnov all pointed to the general retreat of the French army. Nevertheless, I would have been unable to budge if the commander-in-chief hadn't dispatched his entire light cavalry to cut off the enemy columns heading for Viazma. The arrival of the greater part of our light army with Hetman Platov and Count Orlov-Denisov in the area where I had been operating for nearly six weeks and which was at the time under enemy control, forced them to fall back partly on Viazma and partly on Dorogobuzh, thereby freeing me from being trapped in Voskresensk. We had to take advantage of the new situation and I immediately sent word to Belsky to move as quickly as possible towards Znamenskoe, where we joined forces that very evening.

On the 21st I left the militia forces behind and adding regular infantry to my group, I marched out at two in the morning along the Dorogobuzh road, made a rest stop at Nikolskoe and proceeded further. Because I took this direction, we found ourselves between detachments led by two generals, one under Count Ozharovsky, the other under Count Orlov-Denisov. The former sent Company Commander Palytsin to feel out if he could perhaps pull me into his unit, and the latter sent an officer to declare that in the event I had not received further orders from the commander-in-chief after 20 October, I should immediately come under his command.

Recognising that being a partisan did not discharge me from obedience to my superiors, but also allowed me to employ a certain amount of cunning, I announced to the first envoy that I was unable to serve under Ozharovsky because I had already received orders from Orlov-Denisov to join his command, and to the second that I had already joined the command of Ozharovsky, whose orders prompted me to proceed along the Smolensk highway.

In the meantime, I felt that it was not out of place, but even a point of honour, to beg General Konovnitsyn to bring to the attention of the commander-in-chief the troubles that threatened me. I wrote to him: 'Being fortunate enough during my six-weeks' activity here to earn special attention from His Serene Highness, it was all the more painful for me to have to serve under the command of one or the other, having gained a certain experience in partisan warfare, especially when I see independent command entrusted to worthy, but totally inexperienced men when it comes to this new method

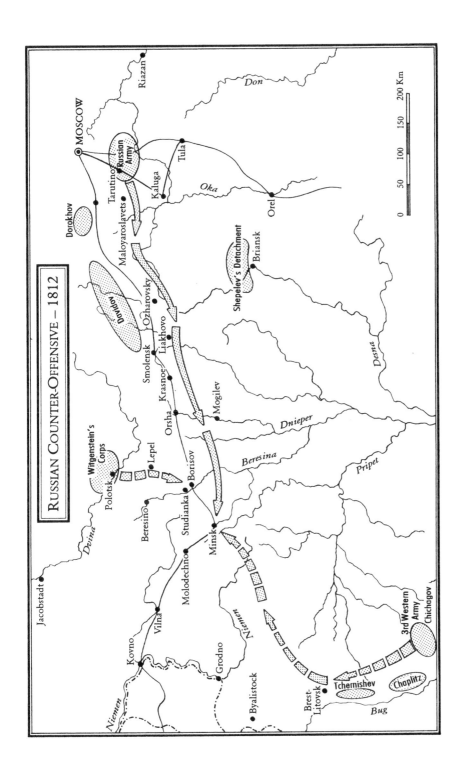

RUSSIAN COUNTER-OFFENSIVE – 1812

Jacobstadt

Dvina

Polotsk

Wittgenstein's Corps

Lepel

Beresino

Studianka

Borisov

Beresina

Pripet

Minsk

Molodechno

Kovno

Vilna

Niemen

Grodno

Byalistock

Brest-Litovsk

Bug

Niemen

Chaplitz

Tchernishev

3rd Western Army
Chichagov

MOSCOW

Riazan

Don

Russian Army

Tarutino

Kaluga

Tula

Oka

Orel

Dorokhov

Maloyaroslavets

Davidov

Ozharovsky

Smolensk

Liakhovo

Krasnoe

Orsha

Mogilev

Dnieper

Desna

Shepelev's Detachment

Briansk

0   50   100   150   200 Km

of fighting.' I ended my letter by calling for more independent partisan commands instead of concentrating their units into one. I dispatched Ensign Kruchkov with five cossacks with my letter to general headquarters, which we reckoned should now be located near Viazma, and told him to look for me on the 23rd near the village of Gavrikov.

On the same day (the 21st) around midnight, my party arrived within nine versts of the Smolensk highway and stopped in the woods secretly without lighting any fires. Two hours before daybreak we began to move towards Lovitva. Three versts short of the main road we began to encounter countless wagon trains and crowds of marauders. We routed them without the slightest resistance. When we reached the village of Rybkov we found total chaos! Carriages, carts, coaches, guns, horsemen and foot soldiers, officers, support personnel and all kinds of riff-raff – they were streaming through in droves. If we had been ten times stronger, we wouldn't have been able to capture even one-tenth of what choked the road.

Having foreseen this, I warned my cossacks about it even before we started out and told them not to bother taking prisoners, but to race down the highway. My Scythians needed no further urging, and you should have seen the terror which suddenly gripped this motley horde! The screams for help, the shouts of encouragement, the sharp cracks of gunshots, the blasts of exploding artillery carriages, and the thunderous 'Hurrahs' of my cossacks – the commotion was unbelievable!

This free-for-all continued until the French cavalry and the Imperial Guard finally showed up. Then, at my signal, our units flooded back from the road and began to regroup. Napoleon's Imperial Guard drew up, with the Emperor himself in their midst. Soon detachments of cavalry left the road and started to line up in battle order, to chase us farther away. I knew very well that it would not be an even contest, but I was dying to put on a riding display, to show off in full view of His Imperial Majesty and to be the first among our commanders to offer him a farewell bow. To tell the truth, this feeling did not last long because the increasing number of enemy cavalry forced me off the road to make way for the masses of troops that were following. However, I did manage to capture 180 men and two officers while engaging the cavalry and defying their Emperor, and we gave a good account of ourselves right up to nightfall.

On the 23rd, we crossed the Osma stream, and made a search towards Slavko, where again we ran into the Old Guard. Some of them were in bivouacs and others stationed in neighbouring villages. Our sudden noisy appearance from a hidden position caused a great deal of confusion among their ranks. They ran to grab their muskets and even honoured us with cannon fire. This exchange of fire continued until evening without causing us much bother.

At nightfall several squadrons of enemy cavalry arrived on the scene, but they were determined not to give battle, because after making a few probes right and left, they sent a few skirmishers and came to a halt. After seizing some of those we fell back on Gavryukov. This foray yielded 146 men comprising skirmishers, foragers, three officers and seven supply wagons loaded with all kinds of junk; this was not important in terms of what we had captured, but important because we forestalled Napoleon's plan to take our vanguard by surprise with the full might of his army. This became evident when we came across an advisory circular which Berthier had sent to all the corps commanders. In fact, such a surprise move would have depended on everyone being in the dark as to the whereabouts of the enemy forces; and this could no longer be achieved because we ourselves had ripped off that veil of secrecy.

On the morning of the 24th I received authorisation from General Konovnitsyn to continue to act independently and to proceed towards Smolensk as quickly as possible. The bearer of this order informed me about the successful engagement which had taken place at Viazma on the 22nd, and that the partisans of Seslavin and Figner were following behind me, while Platov was keeping up the pressure on the enemy's rearguard. This assignment meant that I could no longer drag my brave infantry after me, which still numbered 177 men and two second lieutenants. So I parted company with them on the road leading from Gavryukov and directed them to march to Roslavl and come under the orders of the head of the militia in the Kaluga government.

The disposition of our various detachments on 24 and 25 October, while the French main headquarters was located in Dorogobuzh, was as follows:

Prince Yashvil, commanding the Kaluga militia and having met with the division of Baraguey d'Hilliers, was marching back to Roslavl.

Lieutenant General Shepelev, with the Kaluga militia, six cannon and three cossack regiments, was also in Roslavl.

The detachment of Orlov-Denisov was advancing from Viazma to the Soloviev crossing.

My party, right behind him, was on the march from Gavryukov to Smolensk.

Count Ozharovsky's detachment was marching to Verdebyaki from Ukhnov.

The parties led by Figner and Seslavin were following my group, but actually were closer to the enemy's main forces.

Platov's unit was following the enemy's rearguard near Semlev.

Kutuzov's main forces were between Gzhatsk and Sychevka, advancing towards Dukhovchina.

While I conducted probes in the direction of Slavkovo, Count Orlov-Denisov actually got ahead of me, so that even with forced marches I only caught up with him on the 25th in the village of Bogoroditsk. I went to see the count and report to him. Although he received me cordially, I sensed that he was uneasy to see a lieutenant colonel who had escaped the supervision of a general and was enjoying equal privileges. To overcome this awkward situation, he invited me to join him and march to the Soloviev crossing. But, remembering the woodland area there, and suspecting the futility of such an expedition, I made my excuse, citing my order to march towards Smolensk. Besides, my horses were exhausted and needed a rest of at least four hours. It turned out that I was right, because his enterprise brought no results and he had to resume his march.

While the count was occupied elsewhere, I came across General Augereau's detachment in Liakhovo, and if my party had been stronger I could have accomplished alone what I effectively managed later with the count's help. On the 26th, while marching towards Dubovische, I saw my vanguard starting to chase some French riders. Because of the mist and evening shadows, I could not ascertain their number. I drew up my regiments, and went racing after them with fixed bayonets. But no sooner had we come to a small village, whose name I have forgotten, than I saw some of the vanguard cossacks leading back to me several French élite gendarmes. They declared that the corps of Baraguey d'Hilliers was stationed between Smolensk and Yelnia, and insisted I should take into account that their business was not to fight but to keep order in the army. I told them: 'You are armed, you are French and you are in Russia. Therefore, you must keep quiet and obey!'

Having disarmed them, I placed them under guard and ordered that they be sent to our main headquarters at the first opportunity; but since it was late, we posted lookouts and settled for the night. After a while, I was joined by Seslavin and Figner.

I had often been told that Figner was a barbarian, but I never quite believed that he would go so far as to slaughter unarmed enemies, especially as our country's fortunes were now improving and it seemed to me that there was no room for feelings of revenge when our hearts were so full of overwhelming joy. Yet as soon as he learned about my prisoners, he came running to beg permission to have them shot by some new cossacks of his who had not yet been properly 'blooded'. I can't express what I felt at the apparent contradiction between these words and Figner's handsome face and pleasant expression.

Having reminded him of his remarkable military talents, his bravery and fearless spirit of enterprise – qualities that made him an exceptional leader – I said to him sadly: 'Alexander Samoilovich, do not shatter my illusion. Let me continue to believe that magnanimity is at the heart of your gifts. Without it they bring only harm and no advantage, and as a Russian I always hope that we are better than that.'

He answered me by saying: 'You mean to say, you don't shoot them?' 'Yes,' I replied. 'I did order the shooting of two traitors to the fatherland; one of them had been guilty of looting a church.' 'You must surely have prisoners shot?' 'God forbid! You are welcome to question my cossacks about that.' 'Well, let's march together for a while,' he responded. 'You'll soon abandon all your prejudices.'

'If a soldier's honour and feeling of compassion towards misfortune are prejudice, I prefer them to your reasoning! Listen, Alexander Samoilovich,' I continued. 'I forgive murder that results from the momentary delusion of a passionate heart. And, when I see lofty feelings which prompt a person, some-times unthinkingly and even inhumanly, to brave deeds, I will shake hands with this noble "monster" and be judged by public opinion, or even con-demned by mankind. But I have only contempt for a person who kills for personal gain or the innate pleasure of destruction for its own sake.'

We fell silent. But, fearing that he might order the capture of my prison-ers during the night, I stepped outside the hut on the pretext of giving instructions to my party, quietly doubled the guard and entrusted the safety of the captives to a sergeant who looked after them and had them sent on to headquarters first thing in the morning.

We often discussed Figner – this strange man who hacked a bloody path through his fellow men with all the destructive power of a meteor. I cannot begin to understand the reason for his being so bloodthirsty. It might be understandable if he had only resorted to it in critical circumstances, when cut off or pressed hard by enemy forces, and was unable to convey his pris-oners safely back to headquarters. However, he usually had them put to death not during an emergency, but when all danger had passed. In fact, this absence of human feeling actually nullified his heartless calculations, because it often destroyed all evidence and proof of his accomplishments. We happened to know he was scrupulously exact in his reports and did indeed capture and destroy 300–400 men of lower and higher rank; but others, especially career officials at headquarters, always cast doubt on his reports and remained con-vinced that these were all paper victories and not genuine. Because he per-sisted in this behaviour, he soon lost his best officers who at first had been devoted to him. They recoiled not only from assisting in, but even witness-ing, this pointless bloodshed, and left him with only one officer, a second lieutenant of the Akhtyrka Hussar Regiment by the name of Shianov, a coura-geous but bloodthirsty fellow, who through ignorance believed that he was earning a place in the afterlife by destroying the enemy by all possible means.

During the night my reconnaissance riders sent towards the village of Liakhovo advised me that two strong enemy detachments had occupied it as well as the village of Yazvin. This was confirmed by a prisoner they brought back who assured us that Liakhovo was occupied by General Augereau with 2,000 foot soldiers and part of the cavalry.

We decided to attack that village. But because the three units we had at our disposal comprised only 1,200 men, some cavalry, 800 Jägers and four field-pieces, I suggested we invite Count Orlov-Denisov to join us in this strike, because his detachment consisted of six cossack regiments and the Nezhinsky Dragoon Regiment which was rather weak but still useful, perhaps as a decoration for some hilltop.

I sent a note to invite the count in the following terms: 'When we met and parted, Count, I sensed that you felt I was the sworn enemy of all authority. Who among us does not seek to remain independent? And I myself, with my small abilities, much prefer to be first rather than second and certainly even less to be fourth. But my urge for independent command only extends to the limits of common good. For instance, I have uncovered the enemy at Liakhovo and I have joined forces with Seslavin and Figner. We are ready to fight. But success is a more important issue. We are no more than 1,200 and the French have 2,000 fresh troops. Please hurry and join us at Belkino. Take us under your command and let's go forward!'

On the 27th we were on the march. In the evening, I received this reply from the count: 'I have received your announcement about your move to Belkino. Accordingly I shall also follow in order to attack the enemy, but I do not think this can be assured without the addition of three regiments assigned to me which should arrive in two hours' time; and, therefore, I feel we would be better off to wait for them and act together in concert.'

On the morning of the 28th, Figner, Seslavin and I arrived together in a small village occupied by Chechensky's regiment about two versts from Belkino. Further out we could see Liakhovo surrounded by bivouacs; several soldiers on foot and on horseback were milling around the cabins and the huts, but nothing else could be spotted. After half an hour we saw about 40 enemy foragers riding in the direction of Taraschino without the least precaution. Chechensky sent a hundred of his cossacks after them. The foragers noticed them when it was too late. A few escaped by scattering quickly, but the greater part, together with an officer (who was General Augereau's adjutant) surrendered. They confirmed the news about the corps of Baraguey d'Hilliers and the detachment of General Augereau. But despite the advance of Count Ozharovsky, who passed through Baltutino and crossed the Roslavl road, both forces remained immobile even though Baltutino was not very far from Liakhovo where they were stationed.

My group soon arrived from Belkino in full strength and Count Orlov-Denisov also showed up on a dashing horse accompanied by cossacks who made up his personal guard. He informed us that the three regiments he had requisitioned had arrived. Having determined the direction our attack would follow, he turned to Figner and Seslavin, whose men hadn't yet appeared, and said, 'I hope that you, gentlemen, will give us full support.' I forestalled their answer by declaring, 'I vouch for them, Count, Russians have never yet let other Russians down.' Seslavin heartily agreed, but Figner seemed somewhat reluctant, because he cherished danger as his own preserve and did not enjoy sharing any credit with others. After an hour had elapsed, all parties joined together except for Seslavin's 80 Jägers, and since I was given the honour of leading the advance troops, I ordered the sharpshooters among my cossacks to follow me towards Liakhovo, while the other units followed immediately behind. We aimed our advance so as to cut the Smolensk highway and prevent Augereau from falling back towards Baraguey d'Hilliers, who was occupying Dolgomostye.

As soon as we approached Liakhovo, the general alarm was sounded. We heard the beating of drums as the French detachment came to order and skirmishers ran out of the village huts to meet us. I ordered my cossacks to dismount and the action began in earnest.

I deployed Popov's 13th Regiment and my partisan command to the left of my dismounted cossacks so as to conceal the rest of our advancing troops, and dispatched Chechensky and his regiment along the road to Yelnya to cut communications with Yasmin, where another enemy detachment was stationed. The ensuing results fully supported this move.

Seslavin arrived at the gallop with artillery pieces to support my sharpshooters, opened fire on the enemy columns emerging from Liakhovo and reinforced them further with his hussars. His group, and Figner's as well, drew up behind these elements. Count Orlov-Denisov meanwhile deployed his forces on their right flank and sent reconnaissance units on the road to Dolgomostye.

The enemy, notwithstanding the artillery fire, emerged from the village, reinforcing the sharpshooters in the adjacent woods, and concentrated their main effort against our right flank. Seslavin relieved my dismounted cossacks with his Jägers and ordered the Akhtyrka Hussars to charge the enemy cavalry, which was threatening our sharpshooters. Company Commander Gorsky led this charge, crushed the enemy cavalry and chased it into the woods, now devoid of foliage and unable to afford much cover for the enemy infantry attempting to support this cavalry.

Our sharpshooters followed close on Gorsky's heels and helped him to clear the woods. The enemy skirmishers fell back across open fields towards their own right flank. Crossing from our right to our left flank, I saw one of our Uhlans chasing a French *chasseur* with drawn sword; every time the *chasseur* took aim at him, he rode off and resumed his pursuit each time the Frenchman attempted to get away. Noticing this, I shouted to our rider, 'Shame on you, Uhlan!' Without replying, he turned his horse around and, in the face of the *chasseur*'s fire, rushed him and split open his head with a blow of the sword.

After this he rode up to me and said, 'Now are you satisfied, Your

Excellency?' And, at that moment, a stray bullet shattered his right foot. The remarkable thing about this episode is that after being awarded the Order of St George for this exploit, he was unable to wear it. He was a Jew from Berdichev who had been drafted into the Uhlans. It only goes to show that there is no type of person who is exempt from a sense of honour and therefore unsuitable for military service.

Here on our left flank, they brought me a prisoner taken by Chechensky's men, a one-eyed hussar squadron leader, whose name I can't recall, who had been sent to Yasmino with the news that the Liakhovo detachment was under attack and needed urgent help. In the meantime I got word from Chechensky that he had repulsed the enemy cavalry, cut off completely the road to Yasmino and asked for guidance what should be done to dislodge the 100 men barricaded inside the village barns and firing at him. I ordered the barns to be set alight – a true son of Genghis Khan, prepared to burn both barns and enemy!

In the meantime, Count Orlov-Denisov received word that a column of 2,000 men was hurrying down the road from Dolgomostye towards our rear and that our observation posts were falling back quickly. The count, leaving us, continued his action against General Augereau, turned his detachment against the cuirassiers, attacked and scattered them, and detailed Commander Bykhalov and some of his men to pursue them to Dolgomostye. He returned to join us outside Liakhovo.

It was getting dark. Fires were lit in different parts of Liakhovo and musket fire continued. I am convinced that if General Augereau had bunched his men into one large column, with their heavy equipment in the middle, and had forced his way along the main road from Dolgomostye to Smolensk, we would have been powerless to stop him. We would merely have escorted him until he joined up triumphantly with Baraguey d'Hilliers and waved them both farewell.

Instead of this, we heard a drum beat in front of our line of marksmen and saw a delegation advancing toward us under a flag of truce. At that moment I was setting up the field-pieces that Seslavin had sent me on my left flank and was preparing to open up with grapeshot at a dense enemy column that had come up close. Count Orlov-Denisov sent word that I should desist and advise Chechensky accordingly, because Figner had already departed with the French delegation to Augereau's camp in Liakhovo.

The negotiations lasted no more than an hour. They resulted in the surrender of 2,000 men, 60 officers and one general who became our prisoners.

Night came, the frost increased. Liakhovo was in flames; our men on horseback stood on either side of the road along which the disarmed French troops came out, illuminated by the glow of the fires. The French complained incessantly; they blamed the frost, their general, Russia and us. But Figner silenced them with his 'Filez, filez', ('keep going, keep going'). Finally Liakhovo was cleared, the prisoners were conducted to the next village, the name of which escapes me, and we followed them there.

Here we forgot Caesar's words: 'What has not been completed has not been done.' Instead of marching immediately to Dolgomostye and taking on Baraguey d'Hilliers, dispirited by the defeat of his cuirassiers, or turning against the contingent occupying Yasmin, we all fell asleep. When we awoke four hours later, we decided to write a full report, and this laxness on our part played into the hands of Figner, who volunteered to take the prisoners to general headquarters to persuade the commander-in-chief that he alone was responsible for this feat of arms! As a reward he received permission to carry the news of this victory to the Emperor himself, and lost no time in so doing. You can imagine who reaped all the advantage and glory of this affair, especially as the commander-in-chief added in his own hand: 'This victory is the more remarkable by the fact that for the first time during this campaign an entire enemy corps laid down their arms before us.'

On the 29th, my party arrived at Dolgomostye and the same day marched off towards Smolensk. I reconnoitred the area between the Yelnya and Mstislavsk roads which separated the corps of Junot and Poniatowsky. This netted us six officers, 196 artillery men without their field-pieces and about 200 draught animals which were assigned to move the gun-carriages. Booty, however, was not our main objective. This time I meant to venture beyond strictly partisan activities. My raid was designed to ascertain the disposition of the enemy army and thus decide what future direction I should take. I had the feeling that they would follow the right bank of the River Dnieper toward Katan and not the left bank towards Krasnoe; a single glance at the map will show the advantage of the first approach and the danger of the second, because our army was also moving towards Krasnoe.

Although the corps of Junot and Poniatowsky were both weakened, they would inevitably prove my stumbling blocks; even had I managed to sneak across the Krasnoe highway I would not have gained any more information than I did along the Elnya and Mstislavsk roads, because I found out that the enemy army was still at the Soloviev crossing on the right bank of the Dnieper between Dukhovshina and Smolensk. So far, only the Old and Young Guards had arrived and occupied Smolensk; also, four cavalry corps merged into one beyond the Krasnoe highway had occupied a position near Vilkovich.

Since force of arms could accomplish little, I had recourse to diplomacy and tried to fathom Napoleon's intentions by interrogating the officers we had captured; but they turned out to be merely blind instruments of their master's orders and did not know anything about his real plans.

Something else, however, came to my rescue. I plied them with drink, and glass after glass began to loosen their tongues. As luck would have it, one of them was an adjutant to some general and had just returned from Smolensk where he had gone to fetch orders. On a desk he had noticed all the dispositions being taken by the Imperial Guard to evacuate Krasnoe. There is a saying that what a sober person has on his mind, a drunk has on the tip of his tongue. Soon he was brimming over with candour. Indeed I learned all I wanted to know, and much more besides. He jumbled up this momentous information with a score of tales about his romantic adventures to which I was obliged to listen until in the end he tumbled off his horse!

The news was so important that I made haste to send a dispatch to the commander-in-chief, rushing a courier with sufficient escort along the Mstislavsk road where I expected the headquarters to be located. We duly met oncoming enemy units, returning their fire until their superior numbers finally forced me to retreat along the Mstislavsk road and spend the night within about 15 versts of Smolensk. During these last 24 hours we must have covered at least 50 versts.

The unexpected resistance which I encountered on the way to Smolensk persuaded me to try to reach Krasnoe in a round-about way. I was laden with prisoners and draught animals which I wanted to unload by contacting our army beforehand. Grave error! If I had only continued marching, I could have reached Krasnoe on 1 November, on the same day that Claparède's division had left Smolensk and was marching towards Krasnoe escorting a transport of spoils, the army's treasury and the train of carts belonging to Napoleon's headquarters. True, this information reached me rather late, and even in its weakened state, that division outnumbered my party, and was an infantry outfit, whereas I had only cavalry with me; but this is a lame excuse, and quite counter to partisan principles – namely to keep prodding away, harassing, obstructing and wearing out the enemy, and seizing whatever one can. Prisoners and draught animals should not have diverted me from this aim, although I saved the former and put the latter to good use. I plead guilty!

Having travelled several versts along the Mstislavsk road, I met a squadron of hussars from a life guard regiment, and eight versts further I came across several infantry corps at rest. I gazed on the bivouacs of my comrades as if from the deck of a pirate vessel sighting a friendly shore after a long voyage. I galloped over to General Rayevsky's hut, and his greeting, as ever, was warm and effusive. This was a man I had admired and revered as a hero from my childhood days. But his companions – some of them the very people who had warned me that I was out of my depth and quite unfitted for partisan warfare – accorded me a different welcome. They smiled, threw me half-mocking glances and asked questions that tended to belittle my activities of the past two months. They implied that there was no risk whatever in operating in the enemy's rear, that my reports were dubious. They disparaged my raids by praising partisans of former wars, and criticised the commander-in-chief for allotting too much space in official reports to my activities, which they found offensive, especially since their own names were never mentioned there. Nevertheless, my conscience was clear; I had official receipts for 3,500 men and 43 officers whom I had taken prisoner from 2 September to 23 October. So I laughed off their empty accusations, saying that I wished for Russia's sake that they could all rescue their own names from oblivion by producing similar receipts.

Having handed over the 200 captured heads of cattle to the hungry troops, I spent the night with General Rayevsky in a village whose name I have forgotten, and at sunrise marched off toward Krasnoe.

On 1 November I caught up with General Dokhturov's column which had halted at a landowner's house. Planning to give my group a well-deserved rest, I pointed Major Khrapovitsky to the nearest village and told him to spend a couple of hours there; meanwhile Dokhturov invited me to a light breakfast. But within a quarter of an hour a cossack arrived with word that the commander-in-chief wanted to see me. I never expected to run into the general headquarters in this direction, but there was no time to relax and I jumped on my horse and went to see His Most Serene Highness.

I found him in a log cabin with Semen Khrapovitsky and Prince Kudashev. As soon as he saw me, he called me over and said: 'I am not yet personally acquainted with you but before getting to know you I wanted to express my thanks for your wonderful service.' He embraced me and added: 'Your successful endeavours have proved the benefits of partisan warfare, which has caused and will continue to cause so much damage to the enemy.'

Encouraged by his kind greeting, I asked his forgiveness for having the gall to appear before him dressed as a peasant. He answered me: 'In a people's war this is essential; do, I beg you, carry on as you are, and be guided by your heart as well as your head. I don't care if you wear a cap instead of a shako, and a peasant's overcoat instead of a uniform. There's a time for everything. Some day you'll be back wearing dress shoes and dancing at court balls.'

His Highness talked to me for about a half hour, inquiring as to how we raised peasant militias, about the dangers we had encountered and what I thought about partisan activities and so on. Then Colonel Toll arrived with a map and papers, and we stepped outside. I assumed the interview was over and decided to go and dine with that famous gourmet and glutton, Count Pototsky. But we had hardly joined him when a lackey appeared and announced that the field marshal awaited me at his table. I went off immediately and we sat down for dinner. There were six of us: His Serene Highness, Konovnitsyn, Prince Kudashev, Toll, another general whose name and face I can't recall, and myself.

During dinner the field marshal gave me his full attention, talked about my raids, my poetry and literature in general, mentioned the letter he was sending that day to Madame Stael in St Petersburg, and enquired about my father and mother. He knew my father for his wit and recounted a couple of his jokes that I hadn't even heard. He did not know my mother personally but spoke about her father, General Scherbinin, who had governed three provinces under Catherine the Great. After the meal was over I reminded him of my men and he said: 'The good Lord will forget me if I should forget them', and asked me to submit a list of them. I was striking while the iron was hot and recommended every officer for two awards. His Serene Highness approved everything without objections; and after taking my leave, I headed for a tavern where my men had stopped and where I found my brother Evdokim whom I hadn't seen since Borodino.

Two hours later we marched out to Volkovo. Having been advised, either by me or by other units, about the movement of the whole French army from the Smolensk area towards Krasnoe, the field marshal planned to attack it on the march and made all speed for that town.

Between 1 and 4 November, the partisan units were variously deployed.

On the 2nd Count Orlov-Denisov, having linked up with me, made contact with Rayevsky at Tolstyaki; we continued on to Khilichi where we arrived around nightfall. After resting for three hours, we moved on to Merlin.

On the 3rd the detachment of Count Ozharovsky joined Kutkov's and Seslavin's party and, reinforced by Figner's, reached Zverovich. On that day at sunrise our reconnaissance units reported that enemy infantry was stretched out in marching columns between Nikulino and Stesnam. We made for the highway and covered the entire distance between Anosov and Merlin. Noticing that the enemy had halted to allow the tail of their columns to catch up, Count Orlov-Denisov ordered us to attack them. Such was their disarray that we routed them unopposed and captured Generals Almeras and Burte, about 200 men, four cannon and quantities of supply wagons. Finally, after midday, we sighted the Old Guard, with Napoleon riding in their midst. We mounted our horses and stationed ourselves beside the highway. The enemy troops, sighting our unruly force, got their muskets at the ready and proudly continued on their way without hurrying their step. They resisted almost contemptuously every attempt we made to breach their closed ranks and wrest a single man from their midst. Like blocks of granite, they remained invulnerable.

I shall never forget the unhurried step and awesome resolution of those soldiers, for whom the threat of death was a daily and familiar experience. With their tall bearskin caps, blue uniforms, white belts, red plumes and epaulettes, they looked like poppies on the snow-covered battlefield. If only we had had a few squadrons of horse-drawn artillery and regular cavalry (who,

God knows why, were trailing behind our army), then the enemy's leading and following columns would not have been able to retreat with such small losses as they sustained that day.

Having only cossacks under my command, we bustled in turn around the enemy columns, capturing supply wagons and artillery, and the squads that were over-extended, but failed to make the slightest impression on the columns themselves.

Realising that our Asiatic attacks were unavailing against the closed European ranks, I decided to send the Chechensky Regiment ahead to dismantle the small bridges leading to Krasnoe, obstruct the road and try to block the enemy right and left with an enveloping movement, cutting off the road ahead and engaging the vanguard in a musketry duel.

As if it were now, I see Count Orlov-Denisov prancing about on his light brown mare amidst my Akhtyrka Hussars and orderlies of the Cossack Life Guard Regiment. Colonels, officers, non-coms, plain horsemen threw themselves at the front line, but all was in vain! Column followed upon column, dispersing us with musket fire and ridiculing our useless display of chivalry.

During that day we captured one more general (Martushevich), countless supply wagons and up to 700 prisoners; but the Imperial Guard with Napoleon ploughed through our cossacks like a 100-gun ship through fishing skiffs. Towards nightfall Major Khrapovitsky was almost taken prisoner by enemy cavalry patrolling near the road. Mistaking them for our men, he rode right up to them, so close in fact that, near-sighted as he was, he could make out the one-headed eagles on the brass emblems adorning the shakos of the men and officers who were talking quietly. He fled away at full gallop, and the officers chased him, cocking their pistols, but even though they nicked his horse slightly, he was able to fly over a steep bank and rejoin us. In this exchange Beketov's horse was killed by a cannonball and several cossacks were wounded.

After this raid we fell back on Khilichi where Count Orlov-Denisov handed over his detachment to Major General Borozdin, who had been sent to replace him. From there I marched to Palkino and sent a strong squad to Gorki with orders to make their way to Laninki where my party was headed. On the day of our armed action near Merlin, Seslavin attacked Boyevo and Liady where he captured two large stores and made many prisoners. On the same night, however, Count Ozharovsky was defeated near the village of Kutkov. It was merited punishment for the profitless pleasure of watching the enemy army march by, and then settling for the night one mile away from Krasnoe, practically on stage among the actors! General Roguet, commander of the Young Guard, reached Kutkov during their sleep of the just and woke them up with heavy musket fire from every side.

One can imagine the panic and chaos which followed this unexpected wake-up call. All efforts by Ozharovsky and Colonel Vuitch to bring some semblance of order to this crowd were to no avail. Fortunately, Roguet did not have any cavalry at his disposal, which allowed Ozharovsky to fall back on Kutkov, gathering what was left of his detachment and restoring discipline at the cost of half of his men.

On 4 November, he arrived in Palkino and thereupon I marched out and headed for Liady. Near there my party again ran into the French, this time the corps of the Viceroy of Italy. Thanks to the disorder they had undergone between Smolensk and Krasnoe, we were able to capture a great quantity of carts and 475 prisoners, including several officers. During the night of the 6th, at Boyevo, I received two Russian officers, Major Vanslov and Captain Tarelkin, who had escaped from capture. They told me that they had seen Napoleon entering Dubrovno. I sent them on to headquarters and at 3 o'clock in the morning resumed my progress.

From the time we had left Viazma, our routine had changed completely. We would get up at midnight. At 2 o'clock in the morning we ate the equivalent of a heavy lunch and an hour later we would hit the road. Our party would march together, keeping a vanguard, a rearguard and one more detachment following along the main highway, but all quite close to one another. I rode between both regiments, sometimes on horseback, sometimes in a cart which served as my living and sleeping quarters.

When we encountered no enemy, both regiments would alight from their mounts half-an-hour before dark and settle for the night after feeding their horses. All due precautions taken and lookouts posted, we would fall asleep and, after eating our early morning meal, saddle-up again and continue our pursuit. Camping on a pile of straw under the open skies! Facing death daily! Leading the restless, nomadic life of a partisan! How fondly I remember those days now as I live carefree and peacefully at home, in the midst of my dear family. I am happy – yet I still long for the times when my head buzzed with daring plans and my heart, filled with such enormous hopes, trembled with eager excitement.

After the enemy left Krasnoe, the partisans were stationed as follows: Borozdin's detachment was headed for Orsha; Count Ozharovsky and his men were turning towards Gorki; and Seslavin was marching to Kopys. The last two intended to attack a cavalry depot which I learned about only later, during the night of the 6th when my patrols returned to Palkino from Gorki. They had intercepted a report addressed to Marshal Berthier from the head of the cavalry depot, Major Blancart. Having ascertained the numerical strength under his command, which was detailed in the report, I concluded that whereas our assaults against the main columns of the retreating army could often fail, through no fault of ours, an attack against such an important objective could be undertaken with greater assurance of success. It would also deprive the enemy cavalry and staff of their best mounts and cause them irreparable harm.

Caution nevertheless prompted me first of all to postpone the attack on the depot, which was six times stronger than my party; secondly, to forward immediately the papers we had intercepted to our main headquarters near Romanov, about sixteen versts away; and thirdly, to request from his Serene Highness that he reinforce us with a regiment of infantry and two field-pieces. I would keep a sharp eye on the depot until reinforcements arrived and, should it begin to move towards the Dnieper, would hit it with everything I had at my disposal.

During the night of the 8th, an ambush which I had set up on the road from Orsha to Gorki intercepted first a courier and then, two hours later, a Jew, both sent by Marshal Berthier with orders for Blancart to move beyond the River Dnieper. At the same time, I received word from one of my patrols that they had entered Gorki unopposed and instead of finding the enemy cavalry had met Count Ozharovsky. The villagers told them that the enemy had departed for Kopys, and we set off for that place immediately.

While on the march I learned that the depot had reached their destination and had taken the precaution of dismounting half of their men to provide cover for the horsemen crossing the next day. I was obliged to stop in secrecy within six versts from Kopys at the village of Smetanka. We intended not to undertake our attack until half of the depot had crossed the river and to destroy it piecemeal on both banks of the Dnieper, which had not yet frozen over, only slightly on one side.

On the morning of the 9th, we galloped towards Kopys. Almost half of the cavalry had already reached the other bank; the other half intended at first to put up a fight against my hussars and Popov's cossacks, but as soon as Chechensky arrived with his Bug Regiment and appeared behind them near the crossing, they began to throw down their weapons, slashing the harnesses of the draught animals, and jumping into the river in an attempt to swim across to safety. The river was soon thronged with swimming and drowning men and animals. The banks were littered with piles of wagons, carts and carriages. A hot pursuit and merciless slaughter began in the village and heavy musket fire erupted from the other shore.

Intending to allow my cossacks scattered through the streets enough time to clear Kopys of the enemy, I stopped in the main square near the river bank and gave orders to have the village mayor (appointed by the French) brought before me. I had heard rumours that he had persecuted and even killed our prisoners to placate the Poles. He was a pockmarked fellow of medium height. He asked in the purest Russian for permission to explain himself, while his wife and elderly mother threw themselves at my feet and begged for mercy on his behalf. Bullets kept flying all around us. I insisted that they take cover, gave them my word that no harm would befall Mayor Popov as long as he was found to be innocent, and had him placed under guard until his case was settled.

Soon my horsemen had cleared the streets of enemy soldiers. I gathered my regiments and, disregarding the intense fire from the opposite bank, ordered two large groups to swim across the Dnieper to the left and right of those firing at us and defending the crossing. We hadn't quite reached the far shore when most of the sharpshooters panicked, threw down their weapons and shouted that they were giving up. Once we were across, I detailed 100 cossacks to collect the prisoners and seize those who were fleeing along the Byelorussian highway. My party chased the remains of the detachment, which could be easily followed thanks to the abandoned carts and carriages, and the stragglers, who amounted to no more than 250 men and officers; the rest fled into the woods, perished in the river, slaughtered by the cossacks, or were taken prisoner. Of the last, as I recall, there were some 600 soldiers and about ten officers.

Having completed our pursuit a few versts from the far shore, I sent Second Lieutenant Makarov with 100 cossacks along the road to Tolchin, and Lieutenant Colonel Khrapovitsky with another 150 cossacks to Shklov. I returned with the rest of the party to Kopys, where I discovered not only that Popov hadn't acted as mayor, but had even been hiding in the woods with his family during enemy occupation of this area. Since the innocence of this official was now apparent, I entrusted him with the provisional government of the town and got him to open the town hall as before. We managed to ferret out the real mayor and sent him to general headquarters with a full report about his cruelty towards Russian prisoners and oppression of the local population.

Two hours had not elapsed when a Cossack regiment under Shamshev and 150 hussars under the command of Paul Rjevsky arrived in Kopys. The latter officer informed me that Count Ozharovsky, unable to catch up with the enemy near Gorki, had sent some of his troops towards Kopys and gone off with the rest to Shklov which, rumour had it, was occupied by a strong enemy detachment. Although I knew for a fact that there were no more than 60 enemy soldiers in Shklov, I conveyed through Rjevsky my heartfelt wishes for Count Ozharovsky to achieve the victory he was seeking. Nothing came of this because, when on 10 November his men were getting ready to attack Shklov, Khrapovitsky reported to the count that the village had already been occupied by his own cossacks without any opposition.

A few hours after Rjevsky's arrival, Seslavin also reached Kopys. He crossed the Dnieper immediately and on the 11th continued to follow the French army. Awaiting the arrival of a detachment led by Second Lieutenant Makarov, I was forced to stay in Kopys for one more day. On the 12th I received the order to leave the 11th Jäger Regiment to guard the river crossing, which naturally saddened me. We were approaching the shores of the Beresina, which are covered with woods, and I really could have used an infantry unit.

But they were taking it away from me. What could I do? I appealed to General Miloradovich, who had just arrived, and he lent me temporarily two field-pieces of horse-drawn artillery which improved my situation to a certain extent.

I received another communication: 'Feeling that the forces of Lieutenant General Ozharovsky are too feeble to undertake a reconnaissance towards Mogilev without General Shepelev, please join him immediately and remain under his command until Mogilev is taken. Afterwards proceed by forced marches towards the Beresina, because you will probably manage to intercept a lot there, and to this end you should dispatch parties towards Bobr and Gumny. Signed: Lieutenant General Konovnitsyn, 11 November, on the march to the village of Lestchi.'

This paper completed my dismay! I was always ready to accept service under the command of anyone the authorities had designated. I had voluntarily placed myself under the command of Count Orlov-Denisov at Liakhovo and Merlin because I understood the necessity. But Ozharovsky's detachment was more than adequate to occupy Mogilev, considering that the enemy, numbering 1,200 Polish troops, had abandoned it on the 9th.

I could clearly see that the direction they wanted me to take towards the lower Beresina and the assignment to observe the enemy's movements towards Bobr and Gumny was based on the assumption that the army would veer in this direction and thus render our flanking pursuit – which had brought us such advantages – unnecessary. Of course, I could not bar the road to a whole army with my small detachment if it came to a showdown; but they were in a dire situation and their morale was in disarray. A mere hundred men will often cause more panic among retreating enemy soldiers whose spirits are at a low ebb than will several thousand against troops who are in confident mood, not having been shaken by reverses. Such considerations prompted me to march on Shklov, Golovnino and Belynichi, and I advised both Count Ozharovsky and Konovnitsyn, taking full responsibility for disobeying my orders.

On the 13th, towards nightfall, my party arrived at Golovnino and I learned that Belynichi was occupied by Polish troops who were protecting a hospital which had been moved there from the lower Beresina when under threat from a detachment under Count O'Rourke from Chichagov's southern army.

Early on 14 November, we marched off to Belynichi. On the way we met Second Lieutenant Kazakovich of the Akhtyrka Hussar Regiment who, assuming this region to have been cleared of the enemy, had gone to visit his family and during a secret two-day stay saw their house invaded by robbers from Belynichi. Hearing that we were close by, he had jumped on his horse to inform me of the enemy's presence in that village, with an offer to guide us along roads best known to him.

We moved at a fast trot. The enemy cavalry rode out of Belynichi and was immediately routed by Khrapovitsky and Chechensky and forced to fall back on the village occupied by two strong battalions of their own infantry. Our impetuous pursuit of the cavalry brought us face to face with the infantry battalions, who met us energetically and put up a strong defence. Seeing that we couldn't break through, I thought we might be able to get around them somehow, but soon realised it would be even more difficult because a warm spell had turned the banks of the river into a quagmire. So I continued my frontal attack on the main street and sprayed it with cannon fire. From either side, the enemy column continued to greet us with heavy musket fire from the wooden houses and hedges. I am never one to despair, but in this instance there was ample reason for discouragement. Our men and horses kept falling from the murderous fire, and we were not making any headway. This was my 'Bridge at Arcola'! We could not delay much longer because Count Ozharovsky might arrive from Mogilev any minute, and, thanks to his infantry, grab the prize from my hand. We were extremely enraged. My younger brother, Leo, was the least likely among us to give in. With a few selected cossacks, he dashed down the street under a hail of bullets, struck without hesitation at the enemy reserve standing in the centre of the village and chased them towards the bridge. Yet even this feat accomplished nothing. Having received two bullet wounds, he had to rejoin the main group because our aim was to force the enemy out of the village, not merely to gallop through it, leaving them in charge.

In the meantime, Lieutenant Colonel Khrapovitsky, with a detachment of hussars and cossacks, occupied the hospital and depot located near the village and awaited further instructions. By chance I did not recall him, and when Ozharovsky's detachment of cossacks showed up under Colonel Shamshev and tried to claim from him the buildings which he had already captured, Khrapovitsky chased him away like a predator being deprived of its prey. Shamshev halted his regiment in the middle of a field, refusing to offer us any help with the capture of the village.

The enemy persisted in their defence of the main street. While I gave them their due for the brave resistance they put up, I was equally determined to destroy them before the arrival of Ozharovsky's main forces, and decided to set fire to the village huts by using incendiary cannonballs. At that very moment the enemy began to gather musketeers in a column in the centre of the village, as if preparing to leave. I gave up the idea of setting the village on fire and ordered my men to pepper them with grapeshot to hurry them along, and they began to cross the bridge leading to Esmony.

We allowed them to proceed further, and then rode out to surround them from every side, keeping up our cannon fire. Second Lieutenant Pavlov went on loading some pieces with grapeshot and others with grenades. The tail of the column came to a halt on the road, but the rest kept going, continuing their retreat and returning our fire. In an effort to escape our pursuit, the commander of the column split his forces in two and detailed half of them as sharpshooters to stop our advance. But at that moment my brother Leo, with his hand-picked cossacks, rushed from the woods, put them to flight, captured a lieutenant colonel, two captains and 96 soldiers, cut down half of the remaining men, and chased the rest back into the original group, at the cost of severe wounds.

No matter how painful it was for me to see my brother bleeding profusely on the battlefield, overcoming my personal feelings, I continued to pursue the enemy.

Before all the action of that day, I had dispatched 100 cossacks towards Esmony with instructions to dismantle the bridge on the River Oslik as far as time would allow, and to conceal themselves in ambush at the crossing. I had planned to make a decisive strike at the spot and put an end to the battle which had already cost me dearly. And indeed, when the enemy reached Esmony, they met an obstacle at the crossing and musket fire from my cossacks lying in wait. Their shots were the signal for our concerted attack. Half of the enemy column dropped their weapons, fired back at us from the entrance to the bridge and, gathering some planks that the cossacks had dismantled earlier, scrambled across the river and retreated through the woods towards the lower Beresina.

In this engagement we captured a hospital and a supply depot, quantities of grain, 290 sick and wounded, and fifteen medics. We also took prisoner a lieutenant colonel, four captains and 192 men, and seized the whole wagon train and 180 rifles. To be fair, most of the credit for this feat goes to my brother Leo, the hero of the day.

Returning to the village of Mokrovichi, I immediately sent someone to find two of the best surgeons among the medical personnel we had captured with the hospital and depot in Belynichi. I assigned one to care for my brother and the other for the wounded cossacks, conveying this whole caravan to Shklov on the morning of the 15th.

It was sad for me to part from my suffering brother and to leave him in a region already devastated and occupied by Poles who show no compassion for any person with a Russian name! If Squadron Leader Kruchkov hadn't lent me 25 gold pieces I would not have been able to give financial assistance to my brother, especially since our treasury never contained more than two gold coins throughout our raids, since all booty was equally divided among the men.

That same day I gave orders to turn over to the manager of Count Oginsky's estate the depot, hospital, muskets, supplies and prisoners against official receipt, sent a full report with a courier to general headquarters located in Krugly and gave the signal to march in the direction I had chosen.

Meanwhile, on the shores of the Beresina, momentous events were unfolding. Napoleon, who had experienced reverses for the first time, was facing here what appeared to be unavoidable disaster. As the broken remains of his army, once so awesome, rapidly headed for the Beresina which they had to cross, three Russian armies and various detachments were converging simultaneously from different directions. It seemed that the doom of the French was finally sealed and that Napoleon would either perish here with his army or be taken prisoner. But fate resolved to smile once more on her former favourite, whose presence of mind and determination seemed to increase as the dangers built up around him. Hurrying towards the Beresina from three different directions were Chichagov, Wittgenstein, Kutuzov and detachments headed by Platov, Ermolov, Miloradovich, Rosen and others. Chichagov's army, however, which Kutuzov assumed to be 60,000 strong, had only 31,000 at its disposal due to 27,000 men being diverted against Schwarzenberg.

Chichagov, occupying the high ground on the right bank of the Beresina, was supposed to keep under observation a large section of territory, part of which was quite rugged and swampy. Wittgenstein's army was advancing towards the Beresina, but wary from many successes, it was moving slowly and indecisively.

He was completely fooled by the French General Legrand. In one of his dispatches, Wittgenstein claimed that he was facing a division of skirmishers, whereas in reality they were only sharpshooters drawn from an infantry division. Despite heavy losses, Legrand managed to rejoin Napoleon and conducted a very artful retreat. If Wittgenstein had pressed his attack more energetically, Legrand, with little infantry left, would have been destroyed or at least rendered ineffective. The main objective was to proceed towards the Beresina with all possible speed where the dénouement of the bloody tragedy was supposed to take place. Having arrived quite late with his staff in Borisov, Wittgenstein showed great indecision in face of the troops of Marshal Victor, who, after Napoleon had crossed the Beresina, could and should have been destroyed. Kutuzov, for his part, avoiding any entanglement with Napoleon and his Imperial Guard, not only failed to pursue the enemy, but remained almost stationary in Kopys and its immediate area, although he claimed in his back-dated dispatches to Chichagov that he was close on the heels of the enemy.

In the meantime, Napoleon, reinforced by Victor and Oudinot as well as the remains of Dombrovsky's detachment, reached the Beresina. Although we probably could not have prevented them from crossing the river, it is always within the power of the commander-in-chief to make it as difficult as

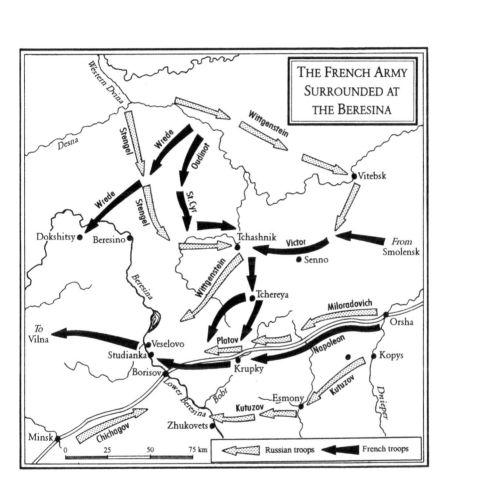

THE FRENCH ARMY
SURROUNDED AT
THE BERESINA

Western Dvina

Desna

Stengel

Wrede

Oudinot

Wittgenstein

Vitebsk

Wrede

Stengel

St.Cyr

Dokshitsy

Beresino

Tchashnik

Victor

From
Smolensk

Senno

Beresina

Wittgenstein

Tchereya

Miloradovich

Orsha

To
Vilna

Veselovo

Platov

Napoleon

Kopys

Studianka

Borisov

Krupky

Dnieper

Lower Beresina

Bobr

Esmony

Kutuzov

Minsk

Chichagov

Zhukovets

Kutuzov

0   25   50   75 km

Russian troops   French troops

possible. Instead of a mistaken move on Igumen, Chichagov should have occupied a central position and should have sent patrols up and down the river to discover the enemy's whereabouts. He is blamed for not having dismantled the pontoon bridges on the far side, but if he had, Napoleon would have been forced to make for Minsk. This would have been disastrous for us as Minsk had ample stores of provisions and could have become a rallying point for the French.

Prince Kutuzov, unwilling to accept unnecessary risks in a campaign that was turning out so favourably for us, would probably not have chosen to attack Napoleon and his guard at the crossing. Although I am in principle opposed to building a golden bridge for the enemy, I can see the validity of the argument as to why we should not have impeded Napoleon's retreat through the marshes of Zembin, unsuitable for the deployment of our cavalry and likely to place us at a general disadvantage against the French. If Chichagov had been rash enough to make a stand alone, he would, in any case, undoubtedly have suffered defeat.

In spite of the fact that Napoleon was retreating with the remnants of his army, once so intimidating, the formidable image of this giant was far from shattered, only slightly impaired by events in Russia, and faith in his invincibility still predominated in Western Europe. Our army, after its valiant efforts and serious losses, was all but exhausted and considerably weakened. Strong reinforcements would be required before it could contemplate the task of liberating Europe, which would fall mostly on its shoulders.

On 16 November I received the first rumoured echoes of the enemy's crossing of the Beresina. I immediately passed on the news to the field marshal, came to a halt and awaited further orders. Although I did not attach much credence to the story, I realised that the enemy had not turned towards the lower Beresina, and appeared to be heading directly for Borisov, rendering my original assignment totally unnecessary. My thinking turned out to be right, because on the evening of the 16th I received a dispatch from general headquarters written by Colonel Toll, in the name of the field marshal, which read in part:

> The whole French army is on the march towards Borisov. You will do well to occupy Ozyatichi quickly and open the road leading to Borisov through the woods. It is desirable that this point be occupied completely and that patrols be sent out along the Borisov highway. Orlov has been dispatched with 150 cossacks towards Chichagov; try to open communications with him. You will thereby earn the favour of the field marshal. All your brave men will be rewarded.
>
> Carl Toll, on the march to Somry, 16 November

Sensing from this dispatch the lack of concert between Wittgenstein and Chichagov, who were separated by the Beresina and the enemy army, which might number up to 80,000, I did not quite believe the news about the crossing but had no doubt that Napoleon would take advantage of Chichagov's numerical weakness and would force a passage across the river by cunning or by force. Once across, I assumed they would march towards Minsk, since this would be the shortest road to Warsaw and there the French army could link up with Schwarzenberg and Reynier, bringing them to a total of 130,000 men and enabling them to avoid the flanking pursuit which had thus far been so fatal to them. Finally they would march through a region less devastated than that of Vilna, through which both French and Russian armies had travelled back and forth since hostilities began. I therefore decided, notwithstanding Colonel Toll's guidelines, to get across the Beresina and to march on Smolevich, which is located between Igumen and Minsk.

For such disobedience I could be punished most severely. A partisan should and is obliged to use his wits, but not to go beyond reason. Of course the junction of Chichagov and Wittgenstein on the right bank of the Beresina would multiply the difficulties for the enemy's crossing; but even alone, Chichagov, with his 30,000 men, could cause them plenty of trouble. The Beresina, bordered by swamps, had not yet frozen over, and its right bank, towering over the opposite shore, could be easily defended. The events that followed proved abundantly that my earlier raid towards distant Smolevich served no purpose, because I ended up in Chichagov's rear instead of that of the enemy!

I soon received another communication from general headquarters stating that since the enemy had no means of effecting a crossing over the Beresina near Borisov, I should immediately carry out my earlier orders. This document was dated the morning of 16 November and made me wonder if I hadn't taken leave of my senses in disobeying my superiors. We were already half-way along the road leading to Ozyatichi when a courier with another letter from Colonel Toll caught up with me. He now informed me about the French army crossing the Beresina and also fully approved the direction I had chosen to march with my party to Smolevich. And so it turned out that I was not at fault after all! However, the march to Smolevich would only make sense if Napoleon chose to march on Minsk. Since he was now turning towards Vilna, my destination should be Borisov instead; but I was now 130 versts away and couldn't hope to catch up with the enemy until they reached Kovno or Vilna at the very least. So I decided to follow my instructions anyway.

About fifteen versts short of Shevernits I learned that general headquarters had arrived there. Leaving my party on the march, I galloped there by the shortest route. His Serene Highness was having lunch at that moment and as I entered the gate I met Sir Robert Wilson, an officer in the English service. He was strolling around the courtyard without daring to enter the field marshal's quarters on account of some recent diplomatic disagreement between them. Having known him well since the 1807 campaign, I asked him what he was up to. 'Dear friend,' he said, 'I'm awaiting news as to the definite direction the army will take after the unhappy event which I had foreseen and which cannot fail to torment every true Russian and English heart!' I was still smiling at this last remark when I entered headquarters. I asked to see Colonel Toll to verify the news of the enemy crossing of the Beresina and to ask whether I should now proceed in a different direction. Toll and Prince Kudashev came out to greet me in the antechamber and asked me to come inside. But unwilling simply to barge in, I made my excuse. They then informed the commander-in-chief that I had arrived and he personally called for me, even made a fuss of me, inviting me to share the meal and showering me with treats.

In his quarters I saw a crowd of exalted officials, covered with multi-coloured decorations – a retinue worthy of the Great Mogul – who vied not only for a greeting and a favour but even a single glance!

After dinner, His Serene Highness questioned me about the action near Kopys and Belynichi, praised my decision and determination to capture the latter village, regretted my excessive severity with Popov whom I mistook for the mayor, and joked: 'How did you summon up enough nerve to scare him? He has such a pretty wife!' I gave him a list of officials who had sworn an oath and co-operated with the enemy. He took it, and after reading it, said: 'Let's not be hasty, let's leave it alone for a while.' I later learned that the archbishop of Mogilev had been demoted to the status of ordinary monk for administering the oath of allegiance to Napoleon and including his name in prayers during the service.

As regards the direction I should now take, I received the order to pursue the French through Borisov, Logoisk, Ilya and Molodechno. We got under way at four in the morning, and managed to cross the river on thin ice. On 20 November we reached the fortifications of Borisov and passed the night there.

That very night, Prince Kudashev, on his way to see Chichagov, spent a couple of hours with me and left under the escort of one of my sergeants and two cossacks, but only one of these returned, the other two being killed by the local villagers. This was best proof as to the true frontiers of Russia and Poland and a reminder to increase our vigilance.

About that time, after a temporary thaw, the frosts increased greatly and did not let up. On the 20th I received instructions to cease my pursuit and to march directly on Kovno and destroy all enemy supplies in that town. The same orders were sent to Seslavin, but neither one of us could carry out this assignment. I was still near the lower Beresina and some 130 versts from the enemy army; as for Seslavin, busy fighting with the enemy vanguard, he did not receive these orders until after Vilna was occupied and he was already wounded.

While I was on the march from the Dnieper to the Beresina, all detachments (except for Count Ozharovsky) and all partisans (except for me) followed the enemy army. On the 11th this army reached Bobry, and on the 12th its vanguard was at Natcha and at Nemenitsa, leaving the rearguard at Loshnitsa. At 8 o'clock on the morning of the 14th, the enemy vanguard began to cross the Beresina at the village of Veselovo. By nightfall on the 16th, all their forces had already reached the opposite bank.

On the 15th, Hetman Platov's detachment had reached the Beresina about fifteen versts above Borisov. That same day, near the village of Kricha, Seslavin successfully attacked the Polish troops of Count Tyshkevich, slew quantities of the enemy soldiers, captured many prisoners and continued on his way to Loshnitsa, where he had another fierce engagement with the enemy.

Next day, this valiant and tireless partisan made contact with Count Wittgenstein and received orders to give a helping hand to Chichagov by way of Borisov. This town was quickly occupied by Seslavin, 3,000 men were captured there and contact re-established with Chichagov.

On the 17th, the French army was approaching Zembin, and Napoleon arrived at Kamen. On the same day General Lanskoy reached Pleshchenitsa. He had the inspired idea to march ahead of the enemy to Vilna and to head off their vanguard at any cost. He could have accomplished this without any trouble, because on that day Pleshchenitsa was occupied only by Napoleon's attendants and the convoy of Marshal Oudinot, who had been wounded.

But in those days the duties of a partisan were poorly appreciated in our army, and when our brave General Lanskoy was attacked by troops approaching Kamen, instead of marching on Molodechno, destroying all stores and supplies and throwing barricades across the road, he simply fell back and joined Chichagov's vanguard which was following the enemy heading for Zembin, contenting himself with the capture of a general, 30 staff officers and about 300 men.

On the 20th, my party overtook Count Ozharovsky's detachment, on the 21st we skirted Uvarov's cavalry, and on the 24th we reached Molodechno where we caught up with the tail of Chichagov's army, made up of hussars and cossacks. Because our orders were to march directly on Kovno, I kept going in that direction without accomplishing much. In the meantime our groups broke into Vilna, encumbered with countless wagon trains, artillery, the sick, the wounded and those simply exhausted or too tired to fight. Seslavin acted differently. To do him justice, I reproduce here, as closely as my memory will allow, his official report about the circumstances which led to the capture of Vilna:

To General Konovnitsyn. With God's help I wanted to attack Vilna, but on the way met the enemy marching there. My field-pieces scattered the column which was swarming round the gates of the city. At that moment the enemy marshalled several squadrons to oppose me. We countered this attack and chased their cavalry through the streets. The infantry came to their support and pushed us back; then I sent a delegation with the offer to accept Vilna's surrender and, receiving a negative reply, I undertook a second attack which netted me six guns and one eagle. In the meantime Major General Lanskoy arrived and we repulsed the enemy right up to the city walls. The French infantry holed up in the houses fired at us from doors and windows and held us up at every turn. I determined to launch a last attack but could not see it through to the end, being severely wounded in the left arm – the bullet shattered the bone and exited. The same happened to Second Lieutenant Orlov. General Lanskoy witnessed the affair. Ask him for details. I do not wish to brag, but I recommend to you and His Serene Highness my whole detachment which, from Moscow to Vilna, displayed fervour for the common cause and did not spare their blood for their country.

Colonel Seslavin, 27 November

Upon arriving at Novy Troki, I received a new summons to appear before the field marshal at Vilna for an interview and set off immediately. From Novy Troki to the village of Ponari the road was clear and smooth. But from Ponari, where the road branches off to Kovno, mountains of dead men and horses, a host of carts, gun-carriages and caissons left barely enough room to get through; piles of enemy soldiers, barely alive, lay in the snow or sought shelter in the carts, awaiting a cold and hungry end. My path was lit up by blazing wooden huts and hovels whose wretched occupants were being burned alive. My sledge kept bumping against heads, legs and arms of men who had frozen to death, or were close to dying. My journey from Ponari to Vilna was accompanied by a strange chorus of moans and cries of human suffering which at times dissolved into something more akin to a joyous hymn of liberation.

I appeared before His Serene Highness on 1 December. What changes in the general headquarters! Whereas previously a ruined village and a smoky hut surrounded by sentries, or a log cabin with folding stools, served as a setting, I now saw a courtyard filled with fancy carriages and a crowd of Polish grandees in dress uniforms, captured generals, and our own generals and staff officers roaming all over the place!

When I entered the hall, my clothes riveted all attention. Among the high-ranking officers in brilliant uniforms covered with gold braid, I sauntered in with my black overcoat and red wide trousers, sporting a curly round beard, and a curved Circassian sword at my hip. The Polish nobles whispered, 'Who is that?' Others replied, 'Partisan Davidov'. A crowd of curious people gathered. Within a couple of minutes I was ushered into the study of His Serene Highness. He told me that Ozharovsky was marching on Lida and that the Austrians had taken over Grodno. He was pleased at their friendly negotiations with Ozharovsky, but, determined to expel all enemies from Russian territory, he was dispatching me to Grodno. I should endeavour to occupy this town and clear the surrounding area if possible through diplomacy rather than armed force. If I found the first insufficient, I could have recourse to the second, but should make sure to send all prisoners immediately to the rear, giving them not only no cause to complain, but indulging them in every way.

Since he was expecting an imminent report from Ozharovsky, he felt that I should await its arrival in Vilna to avoid an unnecessary march to Grodno. Should he be prevented from making a move, then I must proceed with my assignment without delay.

The expected report arrived on the evening of 3 December. Ozharovsky wrote that he had occupied Liady and halted there, while sending two regiments to occupy Belitsy. After reading the report I got into my sledge and rushed back to Novy Troki. I gathered my men quickly, saddled up and the party was half-way to Merecha by sunrise. In this village we captured an enormous depot of food supplies which I turned over against receipts to the commander of the Moscow Dragoon Regiment. I continued to advance along the bank of the River Niemen, entrusting my vanguard to Major Chechensky, and passed on to him the instructions as to how we were to deal with the Austrians.

On the 8th, Chechensky ran into Austrian advance posts near Grodno, took two hussars prisoner and, in accordance with my instructions, returned them to General Freilich commanding the detachment occupying Grodno with 4,000 men and 30 cannon.

Freilich dispatched a delegation to thank Chechensky for this act of indulgence and our man took advantage of the opportunity to open negotiations. To start with, the Austrian general expressed his determination to set fire to all the stores and supplies, which amounted to no less than a million roubles, before surrendering the city. But Chechensky pointed out to him that this would impose hardships on the inhabitants of the area and he would only prove his ill-will towards Russians at a time when every gesture of friendship between us would inflict a mortal wound to the usurper. After some debate, Freilich decided to abandon the city with all its provisions and stores intact, and marched out with his detachment beyond the frontier. Chechensky entered Grodno, stopped in the main square and posted sentries on the streets and security guards in front of the warehouses and hospitals. He did not fail to inform me about the mood of the Polish inhabitants which was very hostile to us. It could not be otherwise; the city of Grodno is the Lithuanian town closest to the border with the Grand-Duchy of Warsaw: and local ties of friendship and family constituted elements bitterly opposed to our forces. The Polish inhabitants of Grodno also had close links with the the inhabitants of the left bank of the Niemen and with Warsaw, the centre of conspiracy and crucible of hatred for Russia – additional factors designed to harm our cause. The Jewish population of Poland, on the other hand, were so devoted to us and prompted by the hope of enriching themselves, that they refused to spy on us, and everywhere, time and again, provided us with the most important information about the enemy.

We had to punish the former and cajole the latter. On the 9th I entered the city with my party. The whole Jewish population turned out to greet me. To express my thanks for their support I listened carefully without smiling to the speech given by their leader, spoke a few friendly words to him and could not resist taking part in a farce by riding into town under a Jewish ritual canopy. Many, I know, would not have risked incurring the wrath of the Polish inhabitants by this display, but I did not fear them and had the means at my command, if necessary, to turn their laughter into tears. Wild with delight, the Jewish crowd, with screams and cries of 'Hurrah!', accompanied me to the town square. Not one Pole was to be seen anywhere, not so much out of national pride, since they threw themselves at my feet that very evening, but from ignorance of the events that had taken place. They had heard that Moscow had been evacuated just before Grodno fell, but they assumed that our army was still in the region of Smolensk and that my party was merely a detachment from Sacken's corps.

I stopped in the square, got off my horse and ordered the city police to beat their drums. When the crowds were big enough, I called a halt to the drumbeats and read aloud, in Russian, a proclamation, prepared in advance, with copies in Polish for distribution throughout the city:

Judging by the reception given to the Russian troops by the Polish inhabitants of Grodno, I can readily see that they have not heard about the events which have taken place: Russia has been freed. All our forces entered Vilna on 1 December. They are now on the other side of the River Niemen. Of the enemy army, half-a-million strong with a thousand cannon, there remain only 15,000 and four cannon which managed to escape across the Niemen. Let the Polish gentry put on mourning clothes! Few among you have not lost a relative or a friend; out of 80,000 of your troops who dared to invade our land, only about 500 are left to run home; the rest lie about on the highway, frozen stiff and covered by Russian snow.

I came here as a result of a peace agreement; we could have achieved the same through armed force, but I renounced my detachment's glory for the sake of sparing this city, which belongs to Russia. You are well aware that street fighting always ends up with houses being looted, and pillage ends up with fires.

And what do I see? I have come to save you and you wish to bring ruin upon yourselves! I see, in the faces of the Poles who have come here, hatred and insidious plans; I see insolence and challenge in their eyes, swords and daggers beneath their belts. And what for, if you honestly wish to return to the obligations you should never have abandoned?

Yet, in spite of yourselves, I must take measures to save you, because if there is one shot the whole town will pay for it. The innocent will perish with the guilty. Everything will turn to dust and ashes!

To avert disaster, not for my troops, who will only profit from it, but for the sake of this city which is threatened with destruction, I propose to change the way it is governed. I order the inhabitants of this city to surrender all firearms in two hours' time and to bring them to the quarters of Lieutenant Colonel Khrapovitsky. Whoever is found in possession of these weapons five minutes after this deadline has expired will be executed by firing squad in the city square. I assure you that I don't like to joke and that I am a man of my word when it comes to rewards as well as punishments.

'What is this pole?' I asked, pointing to a tall pole in the middle of the square. I was told that it was a sort of maypole that had been erected by the Polish people after Moscow had fallen. I quickly called for axes and had it cut down.

'And what are these images I see displayed on the balconies and windows of all these houses?'

'They are transparencies which, like the pole, commemorated the capture of Moscow.'

'Take them down and make a bonfire of them in the square!'

As they carried some of these past me, I noticed various allegorical images which poked ridicule at Russia. But the most remarkable one was on the balcony of a pharmacist. It represented the French eagle and the white Polish eagle tearing apart our double-headed eagle. I had the man summoned immediately and ordered him to have ready by the 12th, our Emperor's birthday, a totally different picture showing these two birds fleeing from the Russian eagle.

I did not spare the other citizens whose houses had exhibited similar images. They were ordered to display, by the same date, new pictures extolling Russia's liberation from the 'enlightened' barbarians. Everyone complied without objections; the pharmacist alone complained that he would not have enough time to execute the complicated picture that had been assigned to him.

Until now I had only made an outward show of cold severity, but I was waiting for a chance to let my anger boil over in order to humiliate the Poles and their haughty attitude. The opportunity had now arisen. My comrades later told me that my nastiness had been transformed into 'ideal beauty'. I bellowed with anger, and an electric spark ran through the Polish crowd. As for the pharmacist, he drew himself up as straight as a thermometer and turned as white as a dose of magnesia. I had him placed under guard with orders that through the whole day of the 12th there should be no fire of any kind in his house, not even in the kitchen, and on the 13th, when there were to be no illuminations, he would light up all his windows and display the commissioned picture on his balcony. And so it was done. To conclude my ravings (as they were referred to by the Poles and with which I agree for once) I summoned a Polish priest who had pronounced words of praise when Napoleon invaded the Russian empire and ordered him to compose and read aloud in the Russian church an address in which he would abuse and curse Napoleon with his troops and allies, praising instead our Emperor, people and army. Since I did not know Polish, he was to submit his text on the evening of the 11th to Khrapovitsky for his approval.

Furthermore, I designated 100 cossacks to be in constant readiness and placed at Khrapovitsky's disposal whenever he felt the need to use force to carry out his orders. These same cossacks were sent on patrols day and night and ensured that there were no gatherings of more than five people.

I gave instructions that warehouses were to be sealed and guarded by the sentries posted by Chechensky.

I ordered that the Greek Orthodox Russian church be reopened and all services resumed. On the 12th – the Emperor's birthday – I required that all town officials turn out to greet me, that the city be illuminated and all church bells be rung the whole day long. Finally, I demanded from the new town elder a list of all officials and citizens who had volunteered to serve the Grand Duchy of Poland.

Having dealt with the town affairs, I sent out a courier to general headquarters with a dispatch outlining the success of my mission. An hour or so later a crowd came calling on me. My 'Swiss Guard' from the Don, standing with a lance at my door, shooed them away quickly; but I did agree to see a few of them, mostly city elders. They seemed mainly intent on safeguarding their personal property and I reassured them that even though I wore a beard and commanded a troop of cossacks we were not pillagers. After a while they came to realise that indeed this was the case.

I was peppered with invitations from people who had met me before, when I had travelled back from Tilsit and had stopped in Grodno for a few days. Some invited me for tea, others for dinner, but my comrades and I turned these down, dividing our time between our own pleasures and our official duties.

All the instructions given to the inhabitants and city officials were carried out to the letter. The Poles were seething with resentment at being forced to transform themselves from the status of armed knights to that of obedient servants of the Russian empire, and, worst of all, having to obey the leader of the Jewish community.

On the evening of the 13th, I received orders to march to Ganiondz. My group immediately proceeded to that place but because I had fallen ill, I was obliged to stay behind for five more days. I then got into my sledge and arrived at Tikochin where my men were waiting for me.

Having crossed the borders of Russia, and seeing that all the partisans under my command were sporting three decorations, while I myself had been completely forgotten because no one had interceded on my behalf, I did not feel it unseemly to put in a word for myself to the commander-in-chief:

> Your Serene Highness! While our national war was in progress, I felt it would be shameful to think of anything except how to destroy the enemy. Now that I am beyond our country's borders, I must obediently beseech Your Serene Highness to grant me the order of Vladimir 3rd Class and St George 4th Class.

In reply, I received in the village of Sokola on the 22nd a packet with both decorations and the following letter from General Konovnitsyn:

> Having received your letter addressed to His Serene Highness, I had the good fortune to report to the Emperor about your feats of valour and efforts during the present campaign. His Imperial Majesty has consented to give orders to have you decorated with the orders of St George 4th Class and St Vladimir 3rd Class. I inform you accordingly with great pleasure, etc., Vilna, 20 December 1812.

Some claimed later that if I had applied for St George 3rd Class, it would have been granted me as well. I probably did make a mistake, but the reason was the high opinion I held of this decoration. I felt I was still unworthy of it. How could I insist on the same order that was worn by the likes of Osterman-Tolstoy, Ermolov, Rayevsky, Konovnitsyn and Pahlen?

I had to stop in Sokola as a result of receiving orders from General Vassilchikov. Immediately afterwards I received new instructions from General Konovnitsyn to proceed to Ganiondz to join up with the corps of Infantry General Dokhturov and to come under the command of Eugene of Württemberg, and also instructions from Prince Volkonsky to the same effect.

My detachment, made up of the two cossack regiments (Popov's 13th and Bug's 1st), together with a mixed command of hussars and cossacks, was now at the head of the regular army's vanguard and my partisan activities came to an end.

CHAPTER 7

The Year 1812

'This partisan warfare, so difficult, so perilous, so energetic, for which one has to be constantly on horseback and alert all the time, and which requires both action and thought in the same person to the highest degree . . .'

From an obituary notice on General Hugo

Instead of an Introduction[12]

I recently had the opportunity to read Napoleon's notebooks. The owner of this fascinating volume lent it to me for a short time because he was about to set off on a long trip from which, in fact, he never returned. Despite the hurried reading, I enjoyed thoroughly the daring sketches and the surprising thoughts and imagination of this amazing man. In these pages Napoleon appeared exactly as he had on the battlefield: a truly original personality of giant intellect.

Alas, however, perhaps relying too much on the credulity of his readers, he tends to describe both circumstances and events in a particular light, not wishing to see things as they really were. It may be that he felt that this was the surest way – at least in the beginning – to capture people's minds and harness them to the victor's chariot. But, being a poet at heart, he fell victim to his own flights of fancy and gradually convinced himself of the truth of these false assertions which he had made in order to mislead others. He would have done this in much the same way as Rousseau fell in love with an idealised 'Julie' as a real person who adored him, or as Tasso became passionately convinced that the battle fought for Jerusalem unfolded exactly as he imagined it in his immortal work.

I may be wrong, but truth and credibility seem to be more on my side. Here are incontrovertible facts that are known to the whole world; yet look at the determination and impatience, almost annoyance, with which Napoleon contradicts in his notes the incontrovertible proofs and facts that are known to the whole world! A candid account does not warrant getting into such fits. Whatever the motive may be for littering this treasure trove

---

[12] This essay was intended as an introductory chapter to Davidov's *Diary of Partisan Warfare, 1812*. Davidov was putting the finishing touches to this piece in the 1830s.

of military and political observations with unfounded descriptions, it cannot justify the results. We are bound to witness, with some surprise, how this new historian goes about disputing and demolishing the accounts of the feats of arms performed by the armies and commanders who opposed him, and finally comes around to the accomplishments of Russian partisans.

He says, for example: 'Not one sick man, not one laggard, not one messenger, not one transport was seized during the course of this campaign, from Mainz to Moscow. Not a day went by that we did not receive news from France, and not a day went by that Paris did not receive letters from our army.'

Fourteen pages further on he adds: 'During our march on Moscow I never had enemy forces in our rear. All the time during my 20-day stay in this capital, not one messenger, not one munitions transport, was intercepted; not one fortified relay station was attacked; artillery and military transports reached their destination unhindered.'

Finally seven pages later, he addresses the same subject and repeats: 'During the campaigns of Austerlitz, Jena, Friedland and Moscow not one messenger was intercepted, not one transport with sick soldiers was seized; not a day went by that general headquarters was left without news from Paris.'

Words dropped from such Olympian heights no longer represent the irritable hissing of mediocrities who have been criticising our partisans for quite some time. These are thunderbolts tossed by Jupiter, and their rumbling sounds may have a lasting effect on public opinion, just as so many erroneous traditions have taken root in the minds of those too indifferent and lazy to investigate the facts, preferring to repeat carelessly the opinions uttered by others.

Because I am one of the accused, a sense of honour prompts me to refute the injustice of such terrible, crushing pronouncements. Like a new Leonidas, I must face the masses led by Xerxes. My opinion of service as a partisan may not be as glowing as that of some of my compatriots, but it has never descended to the level of scorn. I feel, in a sense, that I was born solely to play a role in the fateful year of 1812; but much in the same manner as a rank and file soldier firing blindly amid the smoke and confusion of the battle of Borodino, I have killed a dozen Frenchmen. No matter how much knowledge and talent were at my disposal, it was fate, just the same, which decided to diminish the enemy army by a dozen men and thereby to contribute to its eventual destruction by my comrades.

That is how I visualise my own contribution to the weakening of the enemy forces, according to the means offered to me by my superiors and the gifts bestowed on me by nature. Napoleon and his countrymen may be permitted to curse me for the blood of his soldiers that I have spilled, but he should not deny me my feats of arms nor presume to wipe away the blood splattered on my sword – those honourable stains for which I paid with my exertions and the constant risk of losing my life. This belongs to me; this is my plot in my country's field of glory. It is all the more dear to me because it alone stands out in my life, which was barren during my youth and devoid of distinction in my declining years.

How, though, am I to defend what is mine? Am I to publicise the ephemeral lines of my own notebooks in the hope that they will outweigh the impressions made in the minds of the public by this extraordinary man? That would be the height of impertinence, laughable and futile. And who will bother to read an account which may be deemed to be pure invention when the brand of refutation blazes on every page of his writings? Who will undertake to disprove the accusations that have been made about the activities of our partisans by presenting arguments that are more convincing than those levelled against them?

There are five main sources for these various statements. First, the official bulletins of the French army which, as we know, were composed by Napoleon himself; second, the *Moniteur*, which was the only official gazette of the French government; third, the letters of Marshal Berthier to the various corps commanders; fourth, the captured enemy documents which are preserved in the archives of the imperial headquarters; and fifth, the descriptions of the Russian campaign by certain writers whose sympathies are in no sense with the Russian cause. Once we have located these documents, we can publicise our own notes.

The campaign of 1807

Let us deal first with the above-mentioned statement by Napoleon to the effect that during the campaigns of Austerlitz, Jena and Friedland, not one messenger was intercepted, not one transport with sick soldiers seized, and not a day passed without news being received from Paris.

It is true that in the course of the Austerlitz and Jena campaigns, there was no report of a single partisan attack. I assume that the reason for this inactivity was that the Austrian and Prussian commanders were stunned by the decisive defeats inflicted upon them at the outset of both campaigns. This moral paralysis affected even the bravest of soldiers, to the point that Blücher himself, together with other Prussian generals, unabashedly laid down their arms at Ratkau. With more than 33 battalions and 54 squadrons under their command, in the event of imminent peril they could have headed for Hamburg or Lauenburg, crossed the Elbe, and continued to wage partisan warfare and inflict considerable damage on the enemy forces. I am convinced that if the battle of Jena had been postponed for sufficiently long to allow the Prussian army an opportunity to consider other military options, not only

Blücher, but even other rather less resolute and resourceful generals would have adopted such desperate tactics and reaped an unexpected advantage for their country. Be that as it may, however, Napoleon's comments regarding partisan warfare in relation to the campaigns of Austerlitz and Jena are justified and do not raise the least objection.

Nevertheless, the same does not hold true in respect of the campaign of Friedland (which I refer to as the campaign of 1807 in East Prussia).

Here, from the very beginning, the Russian army confronted the enemy with fierce determination. At Pultusk it repulsed part of Napoleon's army and fell back only because the battle was not fought at a location that suited us. At that moment the main forces of the French army were not directed at Pultusk but were aimed at Plotsk and Thorn. Facing this threat, the right flank of our army was deployed at Golomin and Makov. So whether we succeeded or failed, we could not remain at Pultusk, let alone think of pursuing towards Warsaw the French troops we had just repulsed.

Moreover, the least delay or slightest movement along the border of Eastern Galicia, which was then under Austrian rule, would entail losing communications with Russia or the need to violate the border of a neutral power. This consideration prompted Bennigsen to fall back immediately and transfer the theatre of operations to the confines of ancient Prussia. This turned out to be the wrong choice, although somewhat remedied when we intercepted Napoleon's courier sent to Bernadotte whom our army pursued towards Thorn. This led to the concentration of forces at Yankovo and the battle at Eylau – a hard-fought but indecisive engagement after which both sides claimed victory: we, because we had retained possession of the battlefield, the French because the Russian army subsequently fell back on Königsberg.

In fact, the French victory at Friedland was the enemy's only success during this campaign. But before this unfortunate event, a number of particular engagements gave a chance for our light troops to become accustomed to the ups and downs of military life and provided a form of active training that continued for almost half a year. Unexpected local successes encouraged us to undertake daring operations that were based on careful thought and observation, experience and habit, and which truly came into the category of partisan warfare. They were not the result of high command planning, but of individual inspiration and impulse. The trouble was that they tended to be isolated and unrelated, rather than part and parcel of a unified policy that demanded a joint effort in a perceived common cause. At this stage the ultimate objective was concealed from commanders and troops alike.

It was only after the passage of time, following disastrous setbacks in the Russian heartland itself, that the imminent peril to our country was fully recognised, and all our efforts were concentrated upon national salvation. Only then did we discern the advantages to be gained by the organisation of light troops into small parties in order to attack the enemy communications and supply lines which had become over-extended and highly vulnerable.

To sum up, I quite accept that partisan raids carried out during 1807 were not influenced or inspired by our high command; but I cannot agree with the assertion that such raids never took place. The *Moniteur* and the official bulletins – archives of truth when it comes to admitting setbacks suffered by the French army – will doubtless protest at my lack of fairness. And, of course, Napoleon's own notes, taking full account of the importance of official dispatches intercepted during this campaign, will report in his own words the distress that the army would have suffered in the event of these dispatches failing to reach their destination. They will also serve as a valuable tool, for they will contradict the very assertions made in the book that I myself am challenging.

Let us begin with Napoleon's notes and then call as witnesses the official *Moniteur* and the army bulletins. He writes:

> After the battle near Pultusk in December 1806, the commander of the Russian army, General Bennigsen, marched towards the lower Vistula to attack the Marshal Prince of Pontecorvo (Bernadotte) who had occupied Elbing. Napoleon left Warsaw on 27 January 1807, concentrating the army forces at Villenberg and moved against the left flank of the Russians, intending to throw them back on Frisches Haff. Snow and ice covered the ground. Bennigsen's army was in grave danger; the French army had reached the rear of the Russians when suddenly cossack troops seized an officer from the main headquarters of the Prince of Neuchâtel (Berthier). The dispatches which were found on him informed Bennigsen of this troop movement. Bennigsen, thoroughly alarmed, quickly moved towards Allenstein . . .

The *Moniteur* version of these events is as follows:

> The French army had not yet begun to move. All the other corps remained in their winter quarters in complete safety. It postponed action until the enemy's movements became more clearly defined, fearing that the least action might draw attention to the dangers to which the enemy could become exposed at any moment.
>
> With each passing day the intentions of the Russians became increasingly clear. They bypassed Osterode and entered Lobau. Then, at a signal from the French main headquarters, the troops were mobilised and advanced on the enemy's left flank, intending to threaten their rear. But in wartime unforseen circumstances may arise. An officer detached from the main headquarters had been dispatched to the Prince of Pontecorvo with a detailed account of the movements of the French army, informing him of the Emperor's intentions and instructing him to fall back as far as Thorn to lure the enemy even further. This officer was seized by cossacks and did not have time to tear up his dispatches. Thus the Russian general learned

in time of the danger that was looming and gained an eight-hour start. . . This enabled Bennigsen to arrive at Allenstein on 3 February with his entire army, fully prepared to encounter the French army which was headed in that direction. This turn of events was at first inexplicable, but the reason was discovered the following day when it was learned that the officer in question had been taken prisoner and had no time to burn the dispatches.

The *Moniteur* concludes its article by repeating:

> The enemy would have been destroyed if the officer sent to the Prince of Pontecorvo had burned the dispatches he was carrying. Everything had been calculated for the enemy to remain in the dark for another eight hours concerning the moves revealed by these dispatches.

The Russian army escaped destruction through circumstances entirely dependent on luck. This is a reminder that luck may intervene in all plans and events, and that whereas decisive actions that destroy an army and change the course of a campaign may be the fruits of experience and genius, they have to be accompanied by such whims of chance. A courier carrying such information is worth a hundred bearers of news comprising Parisian gossip or empty chatter from the Palais-Royal.

During the course of this campaign other couriers were seized, among them Montesquiou, the famous orderly of the French emperor: but since they are not mentioned in the official records, I will not dwell on them.

As for the sick soldiers, it is known that during the attack on the corps of Marshal Ney on 5 June near Gutstadt, and on the 6th near Ankendorf, not only the sick men, but the carts, the park, the chancellery and the marshal's own carriages were seized as a prize by Platov's cossacks who had swum across the Alle and the Passarge rivers. The proof that they actually penetrated the enemy rear is contained in *Bulletin No. 78* of the French army, dated 12 June 1807, Heilsberg, which describes the action near Ankendorf:

> Our losses were 160 men killed, 200 wounded and 250 taken prisoner. Most of these were seized by the cossacks who, in the morning before the attack, had penetrated the rear of the army.

From this we see that Platov's detachment, consisting of 10 cossack regiments, the Pavlograd hussar regiment and the First Jäger Regiment, together with 12 horse-drawn artillery pieces, prior to the main assault, had overrun the rear of the 14,000-strong corps that was eventually attacked from three different directions by an army of 80,000 men. I challenge any soldier: 'Would Platov refrain from capturing all that was so conveniently there for the taking?'

Furthermore, given that Platov's detachment seized all the important documents (now in Bennigsen's archives) from the corps and, according to the bulletin's own admission, took 250 able-bodied prisoners, is it likely that the sick men would have escaped the same fate? The suddenness of the raid by the hetman's flying corps would no more have given the French the chance to find a safe haven for these men than to relocate the artillery parks and supply wagons that were also captured.

But why play with words? Napoleon's intention is clear. When he talks about the unimpeded progress of his messengers and the absolute safety of the sick men, it is not so much their welfare that concerns him, but the need to prove that during the course of this campaign all his rear dispositions remained inviolate, and that our troops were unable to seize anything in those areas.

The following is also relevant. *Bulletin No. 53*, 22 January 1807, Warsaw, reports that General Victor (in charge of the army's Second Corps), while travelling to Stettin, was seized with his adjutant by a party of 25 hussars who were conducting searches in this area. And *Bulletin No. 60*, 17 February 1807, Eylau, states:

> In the region of Willenberg 3,000 Russian prisoners were freed by a party consisting of a thousand cossacks.

This is incorrect. The prisoners were set free not by cossacks, but by the Kiev dragoon regiment commanded by Major General Lvov, who was sent for that express purpose from the Sedmoratsky detachment which had occupied Johanesburg. He arrived in the enemy's rear when their army moved towards Eylau; and he managed to free not 3,000 but 5,000 Russian and Prussian prisoners who were being taken to Warsaw, bringing them back safely to Johanesburg.

Here is another instance to support my case. On 25 January, Bernadotte had beaten our vanguard at Morungen and pursued it late into the night towards Liebstadt, giving no thought to Looken, the first village which remained in the rear of the victorious corps to be secured by their advance. Unfortunately for the French marshal, on that same evening, the Sum hussar and Courland dragoon regiments reached Looken. The former was under the command of Count Pahlen, the latter under Prince Michael Dolgoruki, adjutant to the Tsar. Noticing that the sound of artillery fire was moving ever closer to Liebstadt, Pahlen felt it would be shameful to remain inactive while others were engaged in fighting. He decided to move on his own against the rear formations of the French corps. But not wishing, meanwhile, to leave undefended the village he had just occupied, which might enter later into the plans of the commander-in-chief, he sensibly and daringly took only three squadrons of dragoons and two squadrons of hussars and headed at full speed toward Ekersdorf and Himmelfort. He arrived at Morungen late at night. It was empty of troops, but filled with heavy equipment belonging to the French corps.

Pahlen's and Dolgoruki's men burst into the streets and awoke the sleeping guards, still basking in their earlier victory, with cold steel and musket shots. Our squadrons ransacked the town (even taking Bernadotte's underwear), so that when the marshal returned with his corps to Morungen on 27 January (when our army's offensive was already under way), he found nothing but dead bodies, carriages that had been hacked to pieces and papers from his chancellery scattered about by the wind.

Before concluding my remarks concerning the campaign of 1807, fairness requires that I do not ignore our own inability to extract full advantage from what was on offer, with the arrival of new masses of troops who had joined the army from the regions of the Don, Kuban and Urals. In truth, with the exception of the above-mentioned raids, only two of which can be attributed to cossacks, their service was largely restricted to guard duty and concerted action with troops of the line. This was completely at variance with their natural inclination, preventing them from displaying the qualities of mobility, enterprise and ingenuity that characterise a martial nation not yet crippled by the uniformity of methods and regulations typical of European states.

Platov's detachment, as mentioned, consisted of ten regiments of cossacks, one hussar regiment, one Jäger regiment and 12 horse-drawn artillery pieces. Their assignment, until March, was to form part of the vanguard of the main body of the army. From 13 March to 5 June they were stationed at Passenheim to secure communications between the main forces and the corps engaged in action at Narev. Then, up to the time of Tilsit, they remained in the ranks of the army proper. What advantage was derived from this? None, or very little. They attacked, were beaten back, advanced, retreated and finally fell back on Tilsit along with the rest of the troops. But my God! What a fantastic opportunity they had to display and give free rein to their natural abilities!

The following alternatives might have been considered. First, the majority of these regiments could have been retained on the right bank of the Alle between Zeburg and Heilsberg for action as independent groups against the enemy's rear, exactly as General Lvov had done with one regiment of dragoons while the French army was busy moving from Villenberg through Allenstein and Landsberg towards Eylau.

Second, at a later stage, rather than wasting three months in empty exchange of fire with newly drafted Polish troops in the area of Passenheim (troops which had taken up parallel positions facing them near Indenburg) our cossacks instead could have divided themselves into groups. They could then have carried out raids, on the one hand, between Hohenstein and Hillenburg on the communications of the main French army with Tornau, and on the other, through Horzelen and Prinsnitz on the communications of Masséna with Warsaw.

Third, during the offensive drive of the French army towards Heilsberg, the cossack regiments could have been launched from Heilsberg through Gutstadt along the left bank of the River Passarge towards Morungen and Muhlhausen. And finally, while our army was falling back from Friedland towards Tilsit, these regiments (after first retreating to Herdauen) could have made a sudden dash from there through Friedland towards Königsberg.

Such operations would truly have benefited our cause. Acting in the true spirit of partisan warfare in a country that was allied to us, and taking the field against a tired, inexperienced cavalry unprepared to fight off partisan raids based upon total surprise and invulnerability, our men would inevitably have sown destruction and panic in the rear echelons of the French army. Obviously they could not have held back the victorious progress of the great commander; but by diverting the greater portion of his cavalry they would have denied him the resource that enabled him to obtain quick and decisive results on the battlefield and to continue the relentless pursuit of his opponents.

Until now my objections have focused on a campaign that Napoleon only discusses fleetingly; but I come here to another war during which raids and probes became an integral part of military planning by the high command. The damaging effects of such on the enemy attracted Napoleon's special scrutiny.

The Russian campaign of 1812

The controversial statements relating to the year 1812 deserve to be considered individually. The first is Napoleon's own afore-mentioned boast that during his march on Moscow he never had to deal with enemy forces in his rear.

Here we face an immediate problem. How exactly are we to understand the words, 'During our march on Moscow'? Are they to be interpreted as 'during the actual march towards our capital' or as 'in the course of the Moscow campaign'?

In the former more restricted sense, Napoleon is right. Before he entered the city, our light cavalry carried out only guard duties and partisan warfare as such had not yet begun. The first raid took place near Tsarevo on 14 September on the very day when Moscow was occupied and the second raid on 21 September near the village of Perhushkov. I would be inclined to accept that wider interpretation and would not raise any objections had not the historian destroyed that perception when he continued to elaborate on the subject, stating that during the Moscow campaign, not one supply wagon was captured, not one messenger was intercepted, and so forth. This proves that he was referring to the entire campaign from the Niemen to Moscow, including the stay in Moscow and the retreat back to the Niemen.

As for the assertion that Napoleon never had to endure an enemy presence among his rear dispositions, we have to decide whether the words are to be understood in the tactical or strategic sense. In strict terms of tactics, Napoleon is again correct, because his army stationed in the Moscow neighbourhood was facing the countryside and had its back to the capital, its headquarters in the occupied Kremlin where they were fully in control.

Yet this fails to ring true. Napoleon was no mere commander of a fortified town or police chief whose field of action extended no further than the city gates. In command of immense military forces, with an extraordinary feel for inter-relationships, and familiar with all the intricacies of the art of war, his vision obviously extended far beyond city walls. Therefore he cannot possibly be trying to convince us that the rear dispositions of an army encompass only medical transports, food wagons and their escorts.

From these considerations it becomes abundantly clear that he is not talking in the tactical but in the strategic sense; not just with reference to Moscow and the Kremlin, but to the whole vast territory through which his army had travelled and continued to receive food and military supplies – an area of countryside where communication was maintained with other corps stationed on its flanks, with allied powers and with the French homeland, and to which the army would need to retreat in the event of failure.

Considered in this light, Napoleon's account is incorrect. Barely five days had elapsed since Moscow was occupied by the French army when its communications were already placed in jeopardy by Kutuzov's astute decision to move away from the road leading to Riazan to the road to Kaluga. This was a switch of positions which excited and amazed everyone in our army; yet this bold new strategy is never referred to by foreign writers, motivated either by envy or by ignorance. The new position at Tarutino, aggressive in a strategic sense and defensive because of its location and fortifications, serves to contradict Napoleon's views.

In addition to this, Dorokhov's detachment and Seslavin's party were conducting sweeps between the Smolensk and Borovsk roads toward Viazma; separate detachments under the command of Prince Vadbolsky were operating between Vereya and Mozhaisk, and another under Benkendorf between Mozhaisk and Volokolamsk; Chernozubov's group was active between Mozhaisk and Sychevka, Figner's in the region of Zvenigorod, and my own between Gzhatsk and Dorogobuzh. It is surely safe to conclude that, for a writer whose ambition was to be considered an historian by posterity, Napoleon's comments were far from being accurate.

'During my 20-day stay in Moscow . . .'

Napoleon's stay in Moscow lasted not 20 but 34 days. He entered the capital on 14 September and left it on 19 October. This remark is quite important because these additional 14 days were crucial in allowing us to consolidate the Tarutino position which had such a decisive influence on the fate of the enemy army. For in truth, if our army had set off 14 days earlier, not one of Kutuzov's plans would have come to fruition! There would not have been enough time to reinforce our army with the additional troops formed by Prince Lobanov and the recruits being trained in Tarutino to complement the troops of the line, and for the 24 regiments to arrive from the Don. These cossacks, together with the troops on hand, added up to over 20,000 light cavalry – the force that inflicted so much harm on the enemy during his retreat. The morale of the army would not have risen to the pitch necessary for the victory gained over the enemy vanguard on 18 October; and there would not have been sufficient time to open the supply lines that enabled us to pursue the enemy convoys and to maintain the steady flow of essential supplies from the rich southern provinces. All this took place between 5–19 October.

At the same time, these additional 14 days had an opposite effect on the enemy and completed their army's disarray. Shortage of food had already made itself felt after 20 days in Moscow. All available provisions were pretty much exhausted, increasing the number of marauders and adversely affecting discipline in all branches of service. Had this army marched out two weeks earlier it would not only have been spared famine, but would have also have covered the whole distance between Moscow and Smolensk on dry ground and in fair weather. The autumn weather was exceptionally warm; cold and storms materialised only on 7 November around Dorogobuzh, and by then the enemy would have already been beyond Smolensk. I do not offer reproach or criticism, but merely list here the sequence of events to permit readers to draw their own conclusion from those 14 days about which Napoleon keeps silent.

'Not one fortified relay post was attacked . . .'

Partisans were not expected to undertake attacks on these positions because this was not in the spirit of partisan activities. There were only two considerations that might prompt them to storm such a place: either to gain possession of a mail carriage, courier or official who had halted at a fortified post for a brief rest, or to cut enemy communications. To accomplish the former, however, a partisan does not need to expend energy on an assault; all he has to do is to hide himself close to the highway between two such posts and his victim will soon appear out in the open. As for the latter possibility, this is a non-starter; confronted by even the smallest detachment of infantry, the cossacks would be forced to relinquish occupation of a station taken at such a high cost, or die in defence of it – a total contradiction of the purpose for which they were sent into the field.

Even supposing the partisans were able to hold on to such a post, the group's success would result in more harm than benefit, because the men would be shackled to one spot and convoys could simply avoid the station by using détours; whereas, by keeping constantly on the move, turning up in several places during the course of one day, they would allow little to slip through.

The storming of such a fortified place, only to abandon it shortly afterwards, would be the height of folly and not a display of valour. A partisan group, no matter how many men at its disposal, could never accomplish its purpose. It is fair to point out, however, that when necessity dictated it, General Dorokhov never gave a thought to the number of troops defending a position. The small town of Vereya, for example, surrounded by a ditch and palisades, was powerless to resist his partisan detachment, which captured 377 soldiers, 15 staff officers and an enemy banner.

'Not one sick soldier, not one straggler was captured . . .'

It would have been more truthful to claim that not one hospital was taken while the army was marching to Moscow and while it remained there. As already stated, the French had no partisans to contend with at that time, and the sick were conveyed to towns and monasteries surrounded by walls and palisades. Convoys were left behind for their defence and for the protection of wagon trains containing foodstuffs and military supplies.

When the French army quit Moscow, the sick and wounded were not taken along, but were left in the capital. It is hardly likely that our partisans would have engaged in invading the city streets and scaling monastery walls to strike what might have been a useful blow for the motherland, but essentially repugnant to the heart of any true soldier!

Such operations, moreover, would have been full-scale assaults, devoid of any appeal to courage or nobility of motive – incentives without which our brutal profession would sink to the level of privileged butchery.

The reckoning, nevertheless, was not postponed for long. Perhaps it is not generally known that during the retreat of the enemy army there was not enough time to dismantle even one hospital, all of which fell unopposed into the hands of the victors.

As for the safe transfer of sick soldiers from one hospital to another and the safety of those in the rear who had become detached from their units and wandered about as stragglers, this is contradicted by the very presence of our parties in the same area. Is it believable that our many flying detachments on the prowl along the Moscow–Smolensk highway would idly watch these bands of marauders pillaging at will, without interfering with them? Even if our partisans elected not to get involved, is it likely that the local villagers would allow these bands to continue their raiding unopposed and not seek justifiable vengeance by attacking and destroying them and their belongings?

An indication that it was unsafe for retreating troops and supply wagons to travel along enemy lines of communication comes from the official proposal by Count Lauriston on 5 October calling for an end to the people's war, fomented and fostered by partisans, which was causing such harm to the French.

Field Marshal Kutuzov replied: 'The people consider this war as an invasion of Tartars and therefore feel that any means of deliverance from it cannot be criticised, but is praiseworthy and sacred.'

Matters did not end here. Alarmed by the increase of attacks in the rear of his army, Napoleon overcame his pride and reiterated Lauriston's proposal on 20 October from the village of Troitsky.

Marshal Berthier, in his letter to Prince Kutuzov, mentions among other things:

> General Lauriston was entrusted to put forth certain measures before your Serene Highness to bring in line military actions with those rules which have been observed in all wars so that countries would not suffer any more harm than that which is inherent to the nature of warfare.

To this the field marshal responded from Tarutino, on 21 October, as follows:

> It is very difficult to hold in check a population that has been outraged by everything that is going on, a people that has not experienced a war deep within its country for over 200 years and is now ready to die for it, unable to distinguish between what has become the norm and those measures rejected in ordinary wars.

Be that as it may, it was not marauders alone but foragers, too, who were victims in this struggle between armies and an entire nation. Larrey, Chief Surgeon General of the French army, comments:

The commanders of the enemy army encouraged our commanders in their hope for peace, assuring them that preliminary conditions would be agreed upon in the next few days. In the meantime, hordes of cossacks were surrounding the areas where our armies were deployed and captured every day great numbers of foragers.

M. Chambray, author of the *History of the Invasion of Russia*, notes:

To the exhaustion of the foragers was added the setbacks they suffered from cossacks who rode up as close as the city barriers of Moscow.

And on 3 September 1812, Napoleon himself sends the following order to Berthier from Gzhatsk:

Write to the generals in command or various corps to remind them that we are losing daily numbers of people due to the prevailing disorder in the method the troops are adopting to obtain food; that they must without delay agree among themselves on measures that should be adhered to and pursued in order to put a stop to incidents that threaten the army with destruction. The number of soldiers captured by the enemy daily reaches several hundreds; therefore, under the threat of severest punishment, soldiers must be forbidden to wander off alone in search of food. We must instead send bodies of troops for that purpose (following the guide-lines established for foragers), with commands detached from each corps, if the army is stationed together, or from each division if the army is divided into sections. Let a general or a staff officer be in charge of these joint commands and a sufficient body of troops always follow them to provide protection against partisans and villagers while foraging.

In the event of their coming across local inhabitants, they should obtain from them food and fodder by peaceful means, not causing them any harm and violence by confiscating their possessions. It is important that generals and corps commanders should immediately do everything possible to find the necessary means to put a stop to these disorders and ensure the successful carrying out of these instructions.

Do not neglect to write to the King of Naples (Murat) in charge of the cavalry that it is absolutely essential for the foragers to be provided with protection against cossacks and enemy cavalry sent abroad for this purpose. You will also suggest to the Prince of Eckmuhl (Davout) that he should not approach any closer than two leagues from the outposts of the vanguard. Impress on him the necessity of this measure so that the foragers, in their quest for fodder and provisions, always remain at a safe distance from the enemy.

Finally, you will remind the Duke of Elchingen (Ney) that he loses more men daily through foraging operations than in battles and that it is essential for these operations to be conducted with greater caution and not so far afield.

Despite Napoleon's reproaches and instructions, the foragers on the rampage were little better than marauders. Wandering about aimlessly and unsupervised in a foreign land, often without ammunition, they risked either capture or death. How could they subsist unscathed amidst an armed and angry populace bent on vengeance?

If, for argument's sake, the partisans and peasants were merely sitting tight, watching the excesses perpetrated freely by this rabble, why did Berthier and Lauriston need to propose measures to Kutuzov to ensure that military actions be carried out in accordance with all the established rules of war? Why did Napoleon have to concern himself personally with the organisation of foraging expeditions? Was he not apparently acknowledging that his marauding soldiers had got out of hand? Surely, the gist of the argument is:

> First of all we are losing many people every day because of disorders encountered in attempting to find food; second, we must agree on immediate measures that are to be adopted to put a stop to occurrences that threaten to destroy the army; third, the number of men seized daily by the enemy runs into the hundreds; and fourth, Ney is losing more men on foraging expeditions than in battles.

To sum up, the marauders in question are more likely to have been exterminated by local people than by organised groups of partisans, whose raids on enemy communications had a more serious aim than that of defending property against the dregs of the French army.

Not one messenger was intercepted . . .

Without mentioning the messengers who fell into my hands, I will only refer to those captured by other partisan units. Perhaps some will say that reports to superiors do not constitute documentary evidence that is true and unassailable; but that holds true only in the context of the number of men killed. In every nation and in every army that number has always been distorted to exaggerate enemy losses and minimise one's own. But when it comes to tallies of prisoners or intercepted messengers, and the dispatches in their possession, there can be no room for doubt because a captive or courier is personally conveyed to headquarters, interrogated there and added to the list of prisoners already being held. The dispatches seized are kept and itemised so they can be studied further at the main imperial headquarters. Here, then, is my supporting evidence:

Field Marshal Kutuzov's report to the Emperor dated 4 October states:

> On 23 September Major General Dorokhov, pursuing the activities of his detachment, brought the mail which he intercepted from the enemy in two sealed cases

and a third containing pillaged church belongings. On 24 September his detachment captured on the Mozhaisk highway two couriers with dispatches . . .

General Winzingerode's report to the Emperor from the town of Klin, dated 15 October, says:

During the course of the last few days Lieutenant Colonel Chernozubov captured two French couriers who were riding from Moscow carrying dispatches.

The field marshal informs the Emperor on 13 October that on the 6th a courier was captured near Vereya by Lieutenant Colonel Prince Vadbolsky; and General Winzingerode passes on to the Emperor on 20 October the following report from the village of Tchashnikov by Lieutenant Colonel Chernozubov, whose regiment was operating on the Mozhaisk highway between Gzhatsk and Viazma, relating the capture of a courier:

Having reached the village of Tepluha on the main Moscow highway with the regiment entrusted to me, where a relay of the French mail had been established, I managed to intercept the French dispatch carrier who had just ridden out of the village before I arrived. All the papers that we found on him I am conveying to your Excellency together with a French officer seized on the road. Thereafter I proceeded to Tsarevo along the same highway and on my way captured an officer and 37 rank-and-file men whom I handed over to the Sychev district police captain for delivery to the authorities at Tver. I was not able to reach Tsarevo because I ran into a large number of infantry who were accompanying a wagon train. Having wrested part of this train from the enemy, I turned back and on this day have settled for the night in the village of Holm, ten miles from the main road. I have the honour to report to your Excellency that in these undertakings I was seconded by the following Sychev officials: the leader of the nobility, Nakhimov, and the police captain, Boguslavsky.

M. Chambray, in his *History of the Invasion of Russia*, convincingly refutes those of Napoleon's assertions that I challenge here, stating:

Napoleon contradicts himself in this case in his letters of 2, 23, 24, 26 and 27 September, as well as in those of 6, 10, 23 and 24 October, 9 November, 2 December, and in many other letters which I do not mention because I found nothing worthy of note in them. Over and above these letters, the reports of General Baraguey d'Hilliers, which are annexed to this second edition, amply testify, not to Napoleon's error, but to his deliberate intention to mislead others in order to safeguard his glory and self-esteem from attack by others. He would undoubtedly have refrained from offering his version of the events that I dispute here had he known that parts of his letters, those of Berthier and other generals, accounts of troop movements and other precious documents indispensable for describing the invasion of Russia would one day be made public. In this fashion, events that would normally have been played down or overlooked have instead emerged as some of the best-known episodes of our time.

Here are some quotations from these letters:

We have not received any couriers since the last to arrive on 19 October. We are missing those who were supposed to come on 20 August, 21 September and 22 October.

Please bring to the attention of Marshal Victor the fact that we have not received any couriers and I am in the dark as to what is happening in his sector.

The Emperor has not received two couriers; perhaps this is due to our retreat to Senno which has opened a huge area of land to the enemy's control.

And M. Chambray concludes:

During Napoleon's retreat from Smolensk to Molodechno he received only two dispatches from France, and those only from Maret (the Duke of Bassano). To ensure the safe delivery of the first one of these, a Polish nobleman performed this daring trip and I will be silent as to his name so as not to place him in jeopardy. The second was delivered to him for a monetary reward. He met Napoleon at Kamen after the Beresina crossing.

We come now to the main object of partisan activity, namely the capture and destruction of enemy convoys with military supplies and foodstuffs, as well as detachments, commands and troops travelling to or from the enemy army. Whether or not the partisans achieved this purpose, we shall learn from creditable documents in my possession. But before proceeding, let us briefly consider the condition of French army communications at that time. Again the description is that of M. Chambray:

Napoleon's ignorance of Kutuzov's movements, which were boosted by the number of Russian partisans circulating around Moscow, placed him in a quandary as to the enemy's intentions. These groups, who disrupted the foragers with their relentless activity, had severed all direct communications between Murat, Bessières and Poniatowsky. Their raids were assisted by those local people who still remained in their homes and provided the Russian partisans with information about the movements of the French troops. By seizing several artillery trains and detached units between Moscow and Mozhaisk, Dorokhov and his men barred the way to further transports and road traffic. In order to restore communications, Napoleon dispatched, on 23 September, a body of dragoons of the guard, two squads of mounted artillery of the guard and one regiment of the line. This detachment was ordered to stop at the village of Viazem on the main highway about seven leagues from Moscow.

After a few days, on 26 September, he sent further troops to a point half-way between Viazem and Moscow. This group included the Broussier Division (part of Eugène's corps), light cavalry from the same corps, mounted Jägers of the guard and a squad of mounted artillery. Because the road from Mozhaisk to Smolensk was constantly patrolled by armed parties, Napoleon gave orders to send troops from the latter city in concerted units numbering no less than 1,500 men.

Now let us move on to documentary evidence. First, a report to Berthier by General Baraguey d'Hilliers, the military governor of Smolensk province stationed in Viazma, dated 20 September:

The numbers and the daring of inhabitants in the heartland of the province are apparently multiplying. On 15 September the peasants from the village of Klyushino, not far from Gzhatsk, intercepted a pontoon transport that was proceeding under the command of Captain Michel. The villagers were able to fend off our troops everywhere and cut to pieces the detachments that are sent out of necessity to look for food. These frenzied actions, which occur most frequently between Dorogobuzh and Mozhaisk, deserve, in my opinion, close scrutiny by your grace. Measures must be taken without delay either to put a stop to further unrest caused by the peasants or curb their insolence by punishing them for previous transgressions.

According to *Bulletin No. 23*, 22 October, Moscow:

Cossacks continue to prowl along our flanks. A detachment of 150 dragoons of the guard under Major Martaud fell into a cossack ambush between the Moscow and Kaluga roads. Hacking away at 300 men, the dragoons broke through but left 20 men on the battlefield. They were captured, together with the major who was seriously wounded.

A letter from Berthier to Bessières dated 22 September, Moscow, reads:

You have, of course, already been informed as to what took place on the Mozhaisk highway; but actually it was only a sudden attack by about 40 cossacks who came upon 15 artillery carriages at a village and blew them up. The Emperor dispatched Major Letord with 50 dragoons along the Mozhaisk highway precisely to the spot where we were stationed for the night. Major Letord had been instructed to stop all cavalry detachments that were on their way to join the army. As a result, his detachment will soon number 1,500 or 2,000 men. With this force he will safeguard the highway.

Next day Berthier writes again to Bessières:

> Five or six hundred cossacks who have cut off the Mozhaisk highway have caused
> us considerable harm. They have blown up 15 artillery carriages and captured two
> squadrons of reserve troops who were on their way to join the army. This amounted
> to nearly 200 mounted soldiers. These squadrons were part of the reserve under
> the command of General Lanusse who, due to his lack of circumspection, had
> placed them farther to his right. Afterwards, the cossacks tried to attack a large
> convoy of artillery shells, but were chased away by strong musket fire. As I have
> already informed you, Major Letord, with 200 riders, last night reached the man-
> sion of Prince Golitzyn situated on the Mozhaisk highway. According to the news
> which we received from you, and also information reaching us from the King of
> Naples (Murat), His Majesty has ordered Saint-Sulpice to march out with all his
> dragoons to reinforce Major Letord if the need arises. I assume that this need will
> not materialise because of the movement of troops dispatched by you to Podolsk
> and the Desna River. That action should remove the presence of cossacks from
> the Mozhaisk highway.

On 23 September Napoleon writes to Berthier:

> Please inform General Baraguey d'Hilliers and the Duke of Abrantes (Junot) that
> the cavalry and artillery, which are to protect transports, must follow them in step,
> pass the night forming a square near the transport, and must not disband under
> any circumstances. The head of the transport must spend the night in their midst.
> Any transport leader who does not adhere to these orders will be punished for gross
> negligence and will be held responsible in the event the transport is seized. Please
> confirm these orders to Smolensk so that each transport will be dispatched under
> the command of a staff officer and under the protection of 1,500 infantry soldiers
> and cavalry, excluding artillerymen, engineers and drivers. Let it be known that I
> am upset to see transports sent out with a weak military convoy. As a result of
> these instructions, have an order issued concerning the convoy arrangements and
> send it to the heads of the Fifth and Sixth transports. Independently of this order,
> I want you to present to me a full report outlining the dispositions taken regard-
> ing the transports and their convoys. I seem to recall that directives were issued
> detailing the methods by which such transports ought to be protected. If that is
> the case, these dispositions should be copied and sent urgently to all the com-
> mandants in charge of fortified positions extending from here all the way to Kovno.

Another letter was sent by Napoleon to Berthier from Moscow on 24
September:

> Please inform General Saint-Sulpice that I have received his letter. Tell him that
> I consider safe passage from Mozhaisk to Moscow as a very important matter and

that I am relying on him to safeguard this communication and to keep it open; that he must dispose his troops at the point where he is presently stationed, which is a central point; that he must open communications with the Duke of Abrantes (Junot) now in Mozhaisk; that I recommend he offer convoys to messengers who may ride by his detachment; and that Colonel Letord will come under his command. I leave it to him to position Letord at whatever point he deems best. Give him instructions and insist that he organise patrols to protect couriers. We must find out whether cossack detachments have been recalled from their mission to intercept them. I assume that he already dispatched two or three hundred men to the spot where the outfit of General Lanusse was seized several days ago. General Letord is marching out today or tomorrow, which will add one more patrol to the surveillance of the road.

Here is an excerpt from a letter from Berthier to Bessières dated 26 September:

The cannon fire which you heard yesterday morning to your right was directed at the observation detachment composed of dragoons of the guard who were sent into action in a faulty manner by Major Martaudome, who was captured or killed. We lost, in this senseless engagement, several dragoons of the guard, a major, a captain, a senior adjutant and up to 20 dragoons wounded. We also lost several infantrymen. A detachment commanded in haphazard fashion was attacked unexpectedly by 3,000 men with artillery pieces.

Napoleon writes to Berthier from Moscow, 27 September:

I have given permission to General Baraguey d'Hilliers to use the Polish regiment as he sees fit. So many detachments are proceeding back towards us that he should easily teach a lesson to the villagers.

Baraguey d'Hilliers to Berthier, Viazma, 30 September:

I have received Your Excellency's letter. I was saddened by its contents and to learn that the Emperor accuses me, not quite openly, of dereliction of my duty in organising the area assigned to me. In his opinion this has given rise to the disorders plaguing the area between Smolensk and Mozhaisk. That is why I hasten to answer as frankly and succinctly as possible.

First of all let me state this: I organised the military and the civilian government of Smolensk province, which is confirmed by the enclosed statute. But in order to achieve maximum success in an enemy region whose inhabitants are armed against us, two things are required: first, a sufficient number of troops to occupy the most important points and thereby compel the people to obey our authorities and forcibly evict their own representatives; and second, when there is no similarity between the language of the occupying army and that of the conquered people, we must have men who have command of both languages so that our orders and our needs can be understood by everyone. Up to now, with the exception of Smolensk which Your Excellency has provided with a strong garrison and where several co-operative landowners can be found, I have not been able to satisfy either one of the above requirements.

If we exclude fortified stations set up along the highway, then this will leave the following troops in the field: in Dorogobuzh about 200 infantry men and 15 hussars; in Viazma 210 infantry men and 40 hussars; in Gzhatsk 170 men. Your Excellency can verify these figures from daily reports. The day after my arrival here, in keeping with your orders, I sent three columns, each composed of 50 men, to inspect the region and to gather food provisions. Two of these columns were seized and did not return, as I already had the honour to report to Your Excellency. Several similar episodes have taken place since then.

Napoleon writes to Berthier from Moscow on 6 October:

Write to the Duke of Belluno (Victor) that the newly formed regiments in Königsberg and Vitebsk, from men left from other units, should not be used to provide cover for artillery transports. Such transports should be under the protection of full-strength battalions or units that are completely battle-tested.

And, in a separate letter to Berthier, on the same day, Napoleon writes:

Inform General Baraguey d'Hilliers about all the measures taken to form the 9th Corps and its location. Let him know that I fully agree with his demand that Viazma, Gzhatsk and Dorogobuzh be occupied by strong detachments. As a result I order you to direct the commandant of Gzhatsk and the Duke of Abrantes (Junot) in Mozhaisk not to allow troops to proceed any further on their way here, provided, of course, that they have not yet passed beyond these points.

Bulletin No. 25, 20 October, reports:

The enemy is sending many cossacks in the field who are proving to be troublesome for our cavalry.

Berthier to Davout, Viazma, 2 November:

It is absolutely necessary, Prince, to alter the troop dispositions while on the march to keep the enemy in check because they have so many cossacks at their disposal. We must organise daily marches as we once did in Egypt: the train of carts in the middle in as many ranks as the road will allow, with half a battalion at the head and several battalions in one rank on both sides of the convoy. In this manner, when they effect a turn, a full line of fire can be set up at once. You can arrange for intervals between the battalions to be occupied by several artillery pieces. Great care must be taken to see that no one is permitted to wander off unarmed under any circumstance.

On the same day Berthier writes from Viazma to Ney:

We must crack down on the activities of the cossack rabble and deal with them as we did with the Arabs in Egypt.

Bulletin No. 28, 11 November:

Since the engagement at Maloyaroslavets our vanguard has not run into the enemy, except for a few cossacks, who, like Arabs, are roaming around our flanks and showing off their riding skills to keep us on the alert. All this time we have not seen any Russian infantry, only cossacks.

Bulletin No. 29, 3 December:

The enemy, observing on the roads the evidence of the terrible tragedy which has overwhelmed the French army, is attempting to take advantage of it. Their cossacks, like Arabs in the desert, have surrounded the columns and are picking off any wagons and carriages that have fallen behind.

And, from the same bulletin:

Officers and soldiers have endured much from weariness and hunger. Many have lost all their belongings due to the loss of draught horses and some from cossack ambushes. The cossacks have captured a great number of stragglers, pillagers, engineers, staff officers out on patrol, and wounded officers travelling without protection.

General Baraguey d'Hilliers was in command of a division being formed in Smolensk. He disposed his troops along the road leading from Smolensk to Yelnya. The approach of the Russian army in that direction should have prompted him to keep his division together. He did not do so. On 9 November three Russian partisan detachments attacked one of his brigades which, notwithstanding its considerable strength of 1,100 infantrymen and 500 cavalry, decided to lay down their arms. The remaining portion of the division barely managed to find refuge in Smolensk. The partisans captured many French depots, the largest of these in Klementievo. The majority of the horses used to draw supply wagons and stabled in the Smolensk region, but relatively far from town, also fell into the hands of the cossacks.

The Emperor made his displeasure known to General Baraguey d'Hilliers for the fact that, while he had known about the enemy's movements, he did not gather together his troops. The Emperor removed him from command and exiled him to Berlin. There he was supposed to go on trial.

Apart from the irretrievable loss of men and horses caused by the lack of foresight of General Baraguey d'Hilliers, the Emperor was greatly saddened that a French corps composed of 1,100 men and 500 cavalrymen could lay down their arms when confronted by partisan detachments.

In *A Critical Analysis of the History of 1812*, by P. de Segur, Gourgaud writes:

> General Augereau, with his brigade, was captured by the Russian partisans; Denis Davidov and Seslavin joined forces for this enterprise . . .

I can assure the reader that this is not the last of the documents in my possession, but I hesitate to expand this introduction unduly, and I am under the obligation to use only those documents that were made public by the enemy. To my regret I am unable to refer to those partisan strikes which, while known to both opposing sides, were only mentioned in the reports sent to Prince Kutuzov. That is why I shall not expand on the raid of 20 October near Kamennoy and Pleskov in the rear of the French vanguard, in which Figner captured five officers and 360 men and seized an enormous transport of food supplies that the French had gathered in different villages.

Other operations which I am bound to pass over in silence include the raid near Bykosov, 22 October, when Seslavin uncovered the movements of the French army, potentially very dangerous for us, which I mention in my memoirs as one of the turning points of the whole campaign. There were also raids near the village of Shalimov, 24 October, in which the partisan Kudashev took two commissioners and 400 men prisoners; next day, another near Medyn, in which Colonel Ilovaysky defeated the vanguard of Prince Poniatowki, capturing General Tyshkevich, one colonel, many officers and men, and five field pieces; and on 26 October an attack near the Borovsk road in which the partisan Prince Kudashev captured 400 wagons with provisions and munitions and seized about 400 men. On 2 November there was an action near Molodechno, when Colonel Tchernishev captured three messengers and freed Generals Winzingerode and Svechin, as well as Major Narishkin and supply officer Polotov. And finally, on 28 November, there was a raid near Borisov, in which the partisan Seslavin opened communications with Chichagov and captured 3,000 men and many officers.

All these raids and reconnoitres, variously successful, carried out while the French army remained in Moscow, managed to intercept supply trains with food and munitions as well as foraging expeditions. They made it almost impossible for messengers to get through and reach other army corps, to relay dispatches to central Europe and France, or to receive news from there. They barred the way to adjutants and officials carrying orders and prevented them from reaching different army posts. This prevented systematic co-operation between various army units and disrupted daily troop movements, the success of which depended on maintaining the element of surprise. Such movements were discovered by the partisans and met with unexpected resistance. We see examples of this at Maloyaroslavets, Slavkovo and Smolensk, as mentioned in my notes.

These partisan operations inevitably created even more damage to the enemy when the army left their warm quarters in the city and retreated back along the road which had been devastated earlier and now offered no refuge, but only the prospect of cold and hunger. The tireless audacity of the partisan bands kept them in a constant state of alert, both by night and day, depriving them of rest and leaving them exhausted. How could they tell if a night attack were imminent, whether there was artillery lurking behind the masses of cossacks and whether an exchange of fire might suddenly expand into a full-scale battle?

Moreover, the incessant forays and raids against those units which had wandered away from the marching columns instilled a general fear among the enemy of becoming separated from the main body of troops while seeking food and shelter. Based upon official records kept at Russian army staff headquarters, we see that as many as 15,000 men and officers were taken prisoner by raiding parties.. To this figure we must add an immense number of carts with provisions, uniforms, munitions and artillery carriages, thousands of horses, draught oxen and so forth.

Given this evidence, my question to any unprejudiced person is this: 'How much confidence can be derived from those parts of Napoleon's notes in which – apparently angered by the recollection of painful past memories and a no less painful present – he decides to make several assertions: that during the Moscow campaign the enemy did not appear in the rear of the French army even once; that the army never lost one supply train or artillery transport, not one unit, not a single messenger or courier or even (and this strains all credibility) a single straggler?' And, who is telling us all this? Napoleon himself, who twice barely avoided capture by our cossacks and whose place, as commander-in-chief should always be, as everyone knows, behind the front lines.

The first of these incidents is recounted not by me, but by the honest and forthright General Rapp, who was by Napoleon's side. His account is as follows:

Napoleon spent the night within half a mile of this location (Maloyaroslavets). The next day we mounted our horses at 7.30 to inspect the place where we had fought the day before. The Emperor was riding between the Duke of Vicenza (Caulaincourt), the Prince of Neuchâtel (Berthier) and me.

We had hardly left the huts where we had spent the night when suddenly a crowd of cossacks appeared. They rode out of the woods ahead of us and to the right. As they were arranged in pretty good order we mistook them at first for French cavalry. The Duke of Vicenza was the first to guess correctly.

'Sire, these are cossacks!'

'It cannot be,' answered Napoleon.

They were already galloping towards us with terrifying yells. I grabbed his horse by the bridle and turned it around myself.

'But they are ours!'

'No, they are cossacks, hurry up!'

'It is really them,' said Berthier. 'Without a shadow of a doubt,' added General Mouton.

Napoleon gave several orders and rode away. I moved forward with the convoy squadron. We were overpowered; my horse received a lance blow six fingers [four inches] deep and stumbled over me. We were crushed by these barbarians. Fortunately they spotted the artillery park some distance away and dashed off in that direction. In the meantime, Marshal Bessières had sufficient time enough to arrive with mounted grenadiers of the guard.

The same affair is mentioned in *Bulletin No. 27*, 27 October:

The Emperor moved his main headquarters to the village of Gorodnya. At seven in the morning 6,000 cossacks, sneaking through the woods, rushed out with a general 'hurrah' to the rear of our position and seized six cannon in the nearby artillery park. The Duke of Istria (Bessières) galloped over with the entire guard cavalry who slashed at this horde with their sabres, sent them tumbling into the river, recaptured the artillery pieces and seized several wagons belonging to the enemy; 600 cossacks were killed, wounded or taken prisoner; 30 guardsmen were wounded and three were killed. The horse that General Rapp rode was killed. The fearlessness of this general, displayed so many times, is always in evidence. Major Letord of the dragoons distinguished himself. At eight o'clock order was restored.

This affair, known to the French army as 'The Emperor's Hurrah', took place the day after the battle of Maloyaroslavets. Before daybreak Platov detached a portion of his forces with General Ilovaysky on a raid across the River Luzha, several leagues above Maloyaroslavets, to engage the rear dispositions of the enemy troops who had taken part in the earlier battle and still occupied the field. Ilovaysky attacked the artillery park composed of 40 guns that had been moving along the Borovsk road while Napoleon was on his way from Gorodnya to Maloyaroslavets to join up with the troops of the Viceroy of Italy (Eugène Beauharnais).

The cossacks split their forces, one group overrunning the artillery park and the other attacking Napoleon and his convoy. Had they been aware of his identity, they would obviously not have exchanged this prey for the eleven field pieces wrested from the park which were never recaptured by the French cavalry despite the assertions of Rapp and *Bulletin No. 27.*

It is true that this cavalry repulsed the cossacks at a time when the latter felt the need to return to their main force. They were pursued as far as the river, which they forded with the captured guns. But the fire of the horse-drawn artillery of the Don cossacks under Platov from the right bank of the River Luzha halted the enemy cavalry in their tracks. They fell back and gave up the pursuit.

No less false are the assertions of the *Bulletin* concerning the number of killed, wounded and prisoners, as well as the alleged capture of the wagons seized from the cossacks. Partisans and cossacks do not possess wagons except the ones taken from the enemy; and even these are used only on long trips, not on raids lasting just a few hours. Partisan trains usually consist of draught horses carrying packs on their backs.

Here is another episode. The partisan Seslavin, after a fight, occupied the village of Zabrezh where he captured General Dorgeance and 11 other officers. Chambray, in his *History of the Invasion of Russia,* relates as follows:

> On 4 November Napoleon left Molodechno at nine o'clock in the morning and moved his headquarters to Monitsa; Loison was supposed to arrive in Oshmiany the following day. Since Smorgony and Molodechno were occupied by his armed forces, Napoleon, taking advantage of safe passage on the road, decided to leave the army and make his move secretly. On 5 November, at eight o'clock in the morning, he left Byenitsa and arrived in Smorgony at one in the afternoon. Having decided to depart, he gathered his generals: Murat, Eugène, Berthier, Ney, Davout, Lefèvre, Mortier and Bessières. He told them he was leaving the army and heading for Paris where his presence was now required. He turned over the command of the army to Murat and at seven in the evening departed in his usual carriage which was followed by a sleigh. He took only three generals with him: Caulaincourt, Duroc and Mouton. The first sat with him in the carriage, the other two in the sleigh. A mameluke and a squadron leader from the Polish Uhlans, who was to serve as a translator, were in the driver's seat. Napoleon travelled incognito under the name of the Duke of Vicenza and, assuming that the road was not under any threat, took along only a small escort of Neapolitan cavalry.
>
> Loison only reached Oshmiany in the afternoon and, because of the intense cold, quartered his men indoors. The Russian colonel, Seslavin, who was also headed for Oshmiany but followed side roads to the left of the main highway, arrived there in the evening with a regiment of hussars, a contingent of cossacks and

artillery pieces. Unaware that the village was occupied by an infantry division, he broke in with his cavalry but was immediately forced to retreat. After firing several cannon shots, he set up bivouacs at a short distance from the road. Napoleon arrived safely in Oshmiany, but could easily have fallen into Seslavin's hands, and this undoubtedly would have occurred had the partisan leader been aware of his passage.

This is how it happened. One hour before Napoleon's departure for Oshmiany, Seslavin, unaware of his plans, was simply seeking out the enemy and spoiling for a fight. He broke into Oshmiany with the Akhtyrka hussars and cossacks just as his cannon opened fire on the warehouse located in the village. The main guard standing outside the house prepared for Napoleon was cut down and the warehouse set on fire. The French troops, scattered among the houses where they had taken refuge from the cold, began to run out in the street without any order, confused and disoriented in the darkness. Some, seized by panic, ran down the road towards Tabaryshki. Others who were quartered outside the village ran back into it and started to fire on Seslavin from every side. Not having any infantry with him, he countered them with swords and lances but found that the fight was too unequal and fell back. At that very moment Napoleon rode into Oshmiany and after changing horses, continued his trip through Medniki and Vilna and from there to France.

If Seslavin's attack had taken place an hour later, Napoleon could not have avoided capture. Of course, such a conclusion would have been contrary to all rules of dramatic art, the interests of Parisian restaurateurs, the pretty ladies of the Palais-Royal and the general's small armed escort who completed such an unexpected trip at other people's expense. On the other hand, what glory could have been gained by the Russians. We could have brought everything to an end right here at home and without any help from foreigners!

Seslavin is not to blame because success in such cases depends on fate and not on calculations of mere men!

I cannot be accused of yielding to anyone in my hatred of those who would attack the independence and honour of my country – not the kind of hate which festers under the surface but which comes out into the open. My comrades in arms recall, if not my successes, at least my efforts to inflict as much harm as possible on the enemy during both the patriotic and foreign wars. They also remember my astonishment and admiration at Napoleon's feats, my heartfelt feelings of respect for his troops even in the midst of battle. As a military man myself, I gave him his due as the foremost soldier of all time, anywhere in the world. I was thrilled by bravery no matter what uniform it wore, or in what ranks it appeared. Bagration's 'bravo!' shouted to the French grenadiers at Borodino in the heat of battle echoed in my soul.[13]

That is what I felt when my heart was beating under the hussar uniform. And I feel the same now whether driving a plough or in the quiet of my study. No, it was not hatred, but love of truth that guided my pen. I have not invented anything, but merely gathered together arguments designed to contradict assertions appearing in Napoleon's notebooks, obviously written haphazardly, hurriedly and without documentation.

The reader must decide where the truth lies. But, in any event, he must in all fairness concede that as a Russian I never abandoned decency and politeness in my expressions while refuting pronouncements of a man whose memory has been shamelessly assailed by some of his own countrymen who served under him, and even by people who profited from his generosity.

---

[13] This amazing episode took place during the struggle for the Bagration Flèches shortly prior to 10 a.m., just before Bagration was mortally wounded, when the 57th Grenadier Regiment pressed forward its courageous attacks under the murderous cannon fire of the Russian artillery.

CHAPTER 8

Occupation of Dresden, March 1813

At the end of the patriotic war of 1812, and as our army entered enemy territory, certain elements of our military forces received new assignments and dispositions. My partisan detachment, as mentioned, was part of the vanguard of the foremost corps of the regular army.

At first it appeared that this assignment was not much different from the one we had been given previously and that it still offered sufficient ways and means for me to satisfy my restless yearning for brave exploits – but things turned out very differently. There were to be no more independent, intuitive, daring raids: instead, there were calculated marches according to mapped-out guidelines, delivered to us by duty officers from corps headquarters. We were now strictly forbidden to engage the enemy without special permission. The last raid I had conducted, prompted by youthful ardour and reckless courage, proved unhelpful to my foreign service record, and – let's be frank about it – dimmed my future prospects, which suddenly became a source of fear and concern.

The vanguard corps into which my partisan detachment was now incorporated consisted of 8,460 infantrymen, 3,109 regular cavalrymen, 3,535 cossacks and 69 battery pieces, plus some light and horse-drawn artillery with their attendants, and totalled altogether about 16,000 men. The corps was under the command of Lieutenant General and Adjutant Baron Winzingerode.[14]

The individual commanders were General Adjutant Prince Troubetzkoy, Major Generals Nikitin and Bakhmetiev, Count Witt, Talyzin and Knorring, and the handsome and brilliant Lanskoy.

Everyone knows in what pitiful state the remnants of that enormous Grand Army, which had once overrun Russia, were now fleeing homewards. It is easy to imagine the insignificant resistance which the enemy put up against

---

[14] Baron F. T. Winzingerode (1770-1818) was an Austrian officer who went from Austrian to Russian service and back several times. Alexander used him to protect the road to St Petersburg during the 1812 invasion of Russia. Subsequently, he was captured by the French, then rescued again by the Russians. At the battle of Leipzig, he commanded the cavalry of the Allies and later participated in the 1814 campaign in France.

our main forces as they marched from the Niemen to the Elbe. The opposition we encountered was only from a few units.

Our forces were divided into two streams: the first, under the direction of Count Wittgenstein, was marching through northern Prussia towards Berlin, preceded by three light detachments under Major Generals Tchernishev and Benkendorf and Colonel Tettenborn, with full authority to act according to circumstances. The second, which comprised the main body of the principal army, and to which was attached the imperial headquarters, was marching through the Grand Duchy of Warsaw and Silesia towards Dresden.

Ahead of it was the corps under Winzingerode and two detachments – that of Lieutenant Colonel Prendel and mine – assigned to him. Both of these detachments were under the overall control of Winzingerode, who had forbidden them (or at least me) either to engage the enemy or to move from place to place without his knowledge or that of the general who had jurisdiction over me.

Around the middle of February, Russia concluded peace with Prussia, and the Prussian forces were moving to join us.

The army under the command of Count Wittgenstein was reinforced by the corps commanded by General York and General Bülow; the corps under Marshal Blücher marched out of Breslau and now constituted the vanguard of the main army. Winzingerode's corps went to serve under his command and kept its place in the front line.

On 20 February, Tchernishev seized Berlin. The enemy, after evacuating that city, moved in two columns towards the River Elbe, one towards Magdeburg, the other towards Wittenberg. The former was followed by Tchernishev, the latter by Benkendorf.

At the end of February, Tettenborn was dispatched towards Hamburg while Benkendorf and Tchernishev remained on the Elbe to keep Wittenberg and Magdeburg under observation.

A special and independent detachment under the Tsar's adjutant, Guard Officer Orlov, was on its way to Grossenheim.

The main headquarters of Count Wittgenstein was in Berlin; the imperial headquarters and the main headquarters of Prince Kutuzov, who was in command of the combined allied forces, was in Kalish.

The Viceroy Eugène was at the head of a French army 60,000 strong, made up of remains of the Grand Army and of various garrisons and reserves that had arrived from behind the Rhine. It was disposed as follows:

Marshal Davout, with 17,000 men, was to defend the Elbe from Dresden to Torgau. Under this command was Reynier's 7th Corps, Gerard's 31st Division, the Bavarian Corps under Rechberg and the Saxon troops of Lecoq and Libenau. Wittenberg, Magdeburg and the whole distance between them was defended by Grenier and Lauriston. There were 34,000 troops in their command, under the personal authority of the Viceroy Eugène.

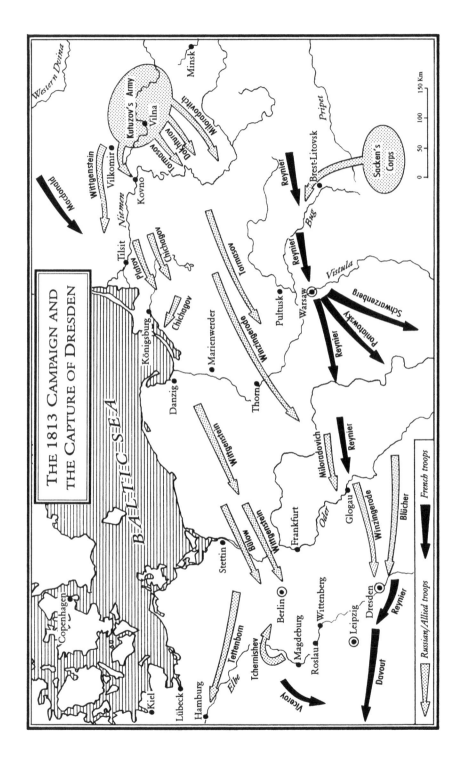

THE 1813 CAMPAIGN AND
THE CAPTURE OF DRESDEN

Marshal Victor commanded troops on the lower Elbe. His corps comprised no more than 6,000 men.

The rest of the troops were stationed in Leipzig with the main headquarters of the Viceroy and the corps headquarters of Marshal Davout.

Here I must recount two circumstances that had a direct influence on my adventures.

This period, when we were on the march from the Vistula to the Elbe, represented a brief spell of tinsel glory for our armed forces, although necessary in order to attract Germany to the common cause and gain the support of those who were still wavering. The French continued to flee; the myth of their invincibility was slowly dissipating. Some of their former allies were joining the victors, but others, shaken by the unexpected turn of events and still swayed by the genius and unbelievable resourcefulness of Napoleon, continued to hold back. We had to take advantage of our present successes before the arrival of new forces from France and, with our combined strengths, capture as much weakly defended territory as possible. This promised two important advantages: to extend the area available for future military operations in the event of Napoleon suddenly appearing from behind the Rhine, and to grip the imagination of those still unconvinced by the frequent, pompous announcements of new provinces, cities and capitals falling into our hands.

What a rich harvest for those who basked in easily acquired fame! The leaders of the allied armies took new heart and dreamed of triumphal entries into the capitals of Europe, with the city keys being cast at the feet of the Emperor, ranging from Blücher – not yet destined to bask in the glow of Katzbach, Brienne and Waterloo, and who was thirsting for glory of any kind and at any price – down to each and every corps commander eager to feed his vanity with yet another captured city.

Small towns, of course, were freely accessible, and these were left to feed the ambitions of small fry like us, the lower ranks of hungry would-be heroes. To my misfortune, there were only two decent-sized capitals available at that time. One of them had already been seized by Tchernishev; the other was Dresden, and in fact Blücher and Winzingerode were both heading already for this fair city. They did not comprehend that the measure of any famous exploit is the amount of effort needed to accomplish it. The taking of Berlin by an entire army or a large corps would not have attracted general attention, whereas its capture by a light detachment justly brought fame to Tchernishev.

I must add that after the crushing defeat of Napoleon's immense armies in Russia, no one expected the war to resume, and certainly not on the same scale as before. In any event, prevailing predictions tended towards peace, taking into account that hundreds of thousands of troops were converging on the Rhine, and that preparations to meet this onslaught were at that moment still largely on paper.

Given the prospect of early peace, the commanders of the many armies that were already assembled seemed anxious for their names to be linked forever with the memory of the last shot that was fired and inscribed on the final page of this historic sequence of events. It was a noble aspiration, and my superiors were quite single-minded in this regard. That is why Blücher was seized with the desire to capture Dresden personally and elbowed aside Winzingerode towards Goerswerde; Winzingerode, in turn, and for the same motive, pointed both Lanskoy and me in the direction of Meissen. Yet for some reason, Winzingerode was finding various pretexts to delay carrying out his orders, and kept creeping slowly towards his goal. I could never understand this kind of behaviour and could not foresee that my superiors had been scheming in vain, nor that fate had singled me out to trick them and smash my own head in the process.

Another circumstance concerns an army decree that had apparently been proclaimed within the borders of Russia, which forbade any kind of dealings with the enemy, and more particularly, any form of conditional agreement. It is possible that such a decree existed, but no such orders or directives ever reached our groups during the whole Russian campaign. Similarly, I was not informed for two months that I had been promoted to the rank of colonel, or about my occupation of Grodno. As a result of my negotiations and the truce I concluded with the Austrian General Freilich, I received a warm commendation from Field Marshal Prince Kutuzov and was awarded the order of St Vladimir 3rd Class by Emperor Alexander, who had then arrived in Vilna.

These two circumstances, namely the desire of my superiors to capture Dresden themselves and the existence of an order forbidding negotiations with the enemy, turned out to be the hidden underwater rocks on which my corsair vessel, sailing ahead so bravely and carefree, was to founder.

In the meantime, our troops were moving ahead. My party, as I mentioned before, was under the orders of Lanskoy, who commanded Winzingerode's vanguard and remained to his right, heading for Muskau, Shpremberg and Hoerswerde. At the village of Bernsdorf we caught up with the Tsar's adjutant Orlov, already set to march on Grossenhein. Orlov told me that he planned to cross the Elbe so as to threaten Dresden from the left bank.

It must be noted that on that same day, 7 March, Blücher's corps was still located in Silesia, and more than three days' march from Buntzlau. Winzingerode's corps was on the way to Goerlitz, and Lanskoy was entering Bautzen.

In Bernsdorf, according to Lanskoy's orders, I detached Squadron Leader Chechensky with the 1st Bug Cossack Regiment under his command to inspect the roads and neighbouring area of Dresden, as well as to gather information on the city itself.

Now let us have a look at what was going on in Dresden prior to my arrival in Bernsdorf and my junction with Chechensky. For this purpose, I refer to the description of the Saxon General Odeleben, who wrote an eye-witness account:

On 12 February I left the capital for Plauen, which is in Westland, after turning over the government of the kingdom of Saxony to a committee of government officials called the Immediate Commission. Half of the Royal Guard Regiment followed the King, the other crossed over to Königstein where the government treasury and the famous paintings of the Dresden gallery had been transported for safekeeping. The hussars, part of the cuirassiers of the guard and the Zastrow Regiment under General Libenau were quartered in both the Old and the New City.

On 23 February, General Reynier, who had stopped briefly in Bautzen, entered Dresden with VII Corps and quartered some of the men in the settlements on the left bank of the Elbe, with the others in the New City, in lieu of a vanguard. This corps did not number more than 5,000 men, taking into account the 1,400 Bavarian troops under General Rechberg dispatched to Meissen, who had left the moment Reynier arrived in Dresden. The Saxon cavalry joined forces with him and he was under strict orders to defend the Elbe crossings at Dresden and Meissen. For this reason, he transferred to the left bank all the boats that could be used by our troops to effect a crossing. He also set up mines around two of the supports of the magnificent bridge linking both halves of Dresden, moved hospitals and military supplies from the New to the Old City, and erected several bastions and palisades around the New City.

A commotion arose in the city; the people prevented the troops from mining the bridge for a while, but Reynier finally prevailed and two bridge supports were ready to be detonated.

In the meantime, on 28 February, Davout entered Meissen with his corps 20,000 strong, set fire to a beautiful wooden bridge adjoining the city and arrived in Dresden on 1 March. With his arrival, the preparations for the defence of the crossing went into high gear, but severity and oppression of all strata of the population increased to an incredible level. Reynier turned over the command of VII Corps to General Durutte and left the city.

The 7th and the following night was spent removing the artillery from the newly erected fortifications in the New City and the transports and all sorts of heavy equipment were moved to the Old City.

On 8 March at 9 o'clock in the morning, paying no attention to the written requests of the King and the entreaties of the inhabitants, Davout ordered the mines set off on the bridge and two spans blew up into the air with a dreadful noise. That was the signal for him to march out to Meissen, leaving Durutte with VII Corps and about 3,000 French soldiers reinforced by several battalions and squadrons of Saxons under General Lecoq.

Durutte began to carry out his instructions. He set up one battery on the bridge at the break caused by the explosion to keep the length of the whole bridge under artillery fire, as well as the main street leading into the New City. Another battery was set up near the castle on the Wallergarten and a third one at Friedrichstadt where he considered the most likely attempt on the left bank would be made, due to a bend in the river that made a crossing easier.

The defence of the New City fortification was entrusted to two companies of infantry and ahead of them the palisades were manned by Saxon sharpshooters. Major Eshky, commanding Saxon troops, was left in charge of that part of the city.

This was the situation in Dresden when Chechensky and the 1st Bug Regiment appeared with no more than 150 cossacks.

On the morning of the 8th, while on the march from Bernsdorf to Königsbruck, I heard a heavy roar coming from the direction of Dresden, and learned from the inhabitants of the neighbouring villages which lay in my path that this noise must have come from the explosion of the Dresden bridge where French pioneers had been digging for some time and were only waiting for orders from Davout to blow it up.

This accursed sound was to blame for all the unpleasant things that I had to endure later. It awoke my quest for honour, which had been stifled by the punctiliousness of Winzingerode.

I quickly deduced that part of the city situated on the right bank of the Elbe had either been totally abandoned or merely contained a garrison which my party could cope with, and therefore we could batter at the gates with a definite hope of success.

I thought, 'If I can only gain entrance into the New City, everything will be accomplished: this will be the thin end of the wedge, and the glory of taking possession of the entire town will belong to me alone and nobody else. The only other people could turn out to be Orlov, Prendel or some Prussian company commander.' It never entered my head that it might be Blücher or Winzingerode, because they were so far from Dresden. My young blood was on the boil, but obedience to superior rank gripped me by the collar. Being under the direct command of Lanskoy, with whom I was actually on friendly terms, I did not dare embark on this undertaking without his knowledge. A courier galloped over to him at Bautzen with this note which I wrote word-for-word as follows:

I am not so far from Dresden. Please let me have a try at it. Maybe success will crown my attempt. I am under your command; my glory is your glory.

Because of the slow riding pace of Saxon postmen, I did not hear from Lanskoy for a good seven hours. He wrote to me:

> I have long been seeking permission to send you on a partisan expedition, but met with refusal on the grounds that you might be needed here within 24 hours. I feel that these measures are too timid, so authorise you to make an attempt on Dresden. Go with God.
>
> Lanskoy

Having received authorisation, I immediately sent an invitation to Orlov to join the feast which I was planning, and in the event he was unable to come, I asked him for reinforcements, observing the French saying: 'God is on the side of the big battalions'. After sending this message to Orlov, I marched out of Königsbruck at four in the afternoon. My party had hardly got under way when a cossack brought me the following report from Chechensky:

> Right up to the walls of the city, I couldn't find out anything from the inhabitants, except that there's no one in town, and that's why I galloped with 50 cossacks to get a closer look; but as soon as I got to the gates, I was met by a violent cross-fire from behind the palisades. Thank God, except for three horses, all went well. I have set up pickets and await your further orders.
>
> Squadron Leader Chechensky, 8 March

I replied:

> Hold tight, I am hurrying to join you with my group.
>
> Denis Davidov, 8 March, 5 o'clock in the afternoon

Chechensky now sent a second report:

> All day long, the enemy kept knocking down the pickets that I had set up around town. Fulfilling Your Excellency's orders. I did not pull back one step, although I clearly saw that my persistence would not do any good. Suddenly the mayor rode out with an appeal that the city be spared. I didn't show any sign of surprise, but couldn't begin to guess what this could mean. However, I told him that if during the night the residents would chase away the French troops occupying the New City to the other bank, the town would not suffer; failing this, there would be no quarter given to anyone. The mayor asked for a two-hour delay and went back to town. I shall remain with the regiment until his return to our day-station, and as soon as a reply is received, I will report to you in full. On this day, during the exchange of fire, Ensign Romodanov was mortally wounded; four cossacks of the line were wounded and nine horses killed.
>
> Squadron Leader Chechensky, 8 March

In reply, I quickened my pace.

My party was already about three miles away from Chechensky, on the hills covered by a pine forest from which the road descends to Dresden, when a new envoy, sent by him, arrived with this note:

> Our Dear Denis Vasilyievich! The town's mayor appeared and said that the commandant of the city wishes to speak with our officer. That's why Loewenstern went into town. The commandant told him that if we had the least bit of infantry, he would immediately evacuate the city; but he could not surrender it to cossacks alone.
>
> Alexander Chechensky

What could we do? Circumstances no longer appeared in the same light. We had to resort to cunning, which in such instances tends to be successful. I left 100 cossacks at the place where I had received this last note from Chechensky, with orders to set out bivouac fires along the hills in four places and to light no fewer than twenty fires at each spot; indeed, the more the better, to make sure that they would not go out, but burn as brightly as possible and remain clearly visible from town. In charge of this affair I put the smartest of the cossack officers, leaving him responsible for carrying out my instructions and allowing him to gather several local people from the nearest settlements to give him a hand. I hurried with my other 400 cossacks and 50 Akhtyrka Hussars towards Chechensky and we joined forces immediately.

My first concern was to make good use of the surrounding area and deploy my forces to make the enemy believe that there were more of us than actually was the case. I set up bivouacs all along the outskirts of the city, facing the New Town, posting the front ranks of my units in the open and concealing the rest behind the buildings. In that situation, I awaited full daylight, admiring the bivouac fires that my cossacks had set up on the heights and burning as if they belonged to a detachment of 3,000 men.

At that moment, I received a letter from Lanskoy, which hit me like a deadly bombshell! He wrote:

> My dear Colonel!
> Notwithstanding the permission I gave you, I find myself forced to change your direction as a result of orders which I have received from the corps commander. And so, my dear friend, instead of Dresden, I now ask you to leave Köningsbruck and make for Radeburg, but do send horse patrols along all the roads leading to Dresden and clear all the neighbouring areas. Deploy your troops to the right of Radeburg in the direction of Meissen and clear these nearby areas as thoroughly as possible. Give orders to requisition all the boats that are on this side of the Elbe and send patrols towards Torgau for this purpose. Arrange to erect a bridge

at Pilsnitz, which you should hold until Madatov gets there. Madatov will station himself between you and the postal track which runs from Bischofswerde to Dresden so as to cover the movement of our corps which is definitely moving away from the Kalisch road. Its headquarters are being moved to Goerswerde to clear the area for the Prussians. Benkendorf's cossacks are in Torgau; instruct your patrols to make contact with them. Independently of this, please issue orders to the local authorities to prepare as many food supplies and as much forage as possible for the corps which undoubtedly will remain for some time on this side of the Elbe because of difficulties in crossing it.

(Signed) Lanskoy
I am riding to Kamentz

I must confess that reading these lines came as a cruel blow, but I soon recovered my wits and decided nonetheless to continue my activities.

My reasoning was as follows. What, I asked myself, does Lanskoy want to accomplish by sending me to Radeburg and Meissen? First, to collect boats and provisions for the supply of the corps. Second, to ensure that my party and Madatov's detachment protect and cover the movement of our corps from the Kalisch road to Goerswerde. But the preparation of food supplies is much more easily achieved through the city authorities who have control over the local police of the area; and I would certainly be carrying out Lanskoy's directives more effectively by seizing the city, rather than by turning off to Radeburg or Meissen. As for assembling boats, there are none to be had, since no enemy commander would leave them for the benefit of his opponents on the opposite shore. So it is pointless for me to worry about obtaining things that are unavailable to us and securely in the hands of the enemy.

Then there is the question of cover for the movements of Winzingerode's corps. Wouldn't it make more sense, in order to carry out Lanskoy's wishes and those of the corps commander, for me to station my group at the point from which all enemy patrols spread out to track our troop movements, instead of scattering my party along the several main routes and risk neglecting the side-roads and paths that the enemy scouts might take? Furthermore, is it not obvious from Lanskoy's expressed intentions that his new orders were written on the assumption I was still in Königsbruck and not, in fact, already near Dresden? In any event, my lot has already been cast: I am standing beneath the palisades of Dresden. My first attempt was unsuccessful because the negotiations were conducted with Chechensky, who was commanding only 150 cossacks; but here I am with a party of 500, of which the enemy either knows already or will soon discover. Moreover, there are the fires which would even have fooled me had I not known who lit them and kept them going. During the course of the day, Orlov may come to join me, or at least send me help. Prendl is also near by. All this may brighten the prospects, and God willing, everything will turn out all right. Besides, only the most obedient sergeant major would, in my place, decide to carry out Lanskoy's orders quite literally and sanction a retreat, under enemy fire, at the cost of his honour.

If these orders had arrived before the beginning of the negotiations, it would have been an entirely different matter. Chechensky's foray could have been regarded as a typical cossack reconnaissance and nothing more. But a demand for the city's surrender has already been made. Threats in the event of a delayed response have been expressed, and the enemy has clearly observed the bivouac fires before the city gates, dispersed over the hills to prove to them that they are not just dealing with a couple of hundred cossacks.

That's how I reasoned with myself. Incontrovertible arguments, but alas, short-sighted and lacking in depth. How is it that I couldn't get it through my head that it was not just a matter of collecting boats and gathering food supplies for the troops; not just about giving protective cover to the corps while it was moving to Goeswerde, but actually a decision to remove both me and Lanskoy from the area along which Winzingerode was planning to march on Dresden? That is what this man was demanding of me through the good offices of Lanskoy, who like me, did not comprehend the implications of the order, and innocently transmitted it, counting upon my sweet disposition, and proceeded from Bautzen to Kamentz, while I remained where I was, convinced that I was being useful and still unable to see how dangerous the consequences would be for me.

As soon as it was daylight, I again sent Loewenstern as a messenger under a flag of truce to demand the surrender of the city and announced that I had arrived with cavalry and infantry (whose fires could be seen on the hills) which signalled the impending start of an assault in case of their refusal. The reply came that General Durutte wanted to talk to a staff officer empowered by me. I sent him Lieutenant Colonel Khrapovitsky of the Volynia Uhlan Regiment, and to make him look more important, I added to his many medals some of my own decorations! Durutte was stationed in the Old City. During the crossing of the Elbe by boat, Khrapovitsky had his eyes blindfolded with a handkerchief, as is customary. (A print depicting this trip by Khrapovitsky was offered for sale in Dresden by some local speculator.) He was led by the arm to the quarters of the French general and the negotiations began. The Saxon General Lecoq and the members of the Immediate Commission were allowed to attend. By Durutte's side was his first adjutant, Captain Frank.

In the meantime, what I was expecting did actually take place. Orlov, occupied by preparations for the crossing of the Elbe, could not spare his whole detachment, but sent me instead 100 cossacks from Melentiev's regiment; and Prendl's detachment appeared on the Bautzen road.

Despite the arrival of these troops, however, the negotiations, with their inevitable discussions, and sometimes becoming quite aggressive and vindictive on both sides, lasted the whole day. It was only at 9 o'clock at night that the delegates ratified the conditions in the names of Durutte and myself.

One of the difficulties arose from my intention to strike out certain paragraphs which I considered totally unnecessary, namely:

1. The paragraph dealing with the provisioning and quartering of my troops, which called on me, through my representative, to arrange to have civil servants designated by the town authorities.

2. The paragraph stipulating that the inhabitants should not be harmed.

3. The paragraph mentioning the protection and preservation of the King's property as well as his private domains, and setting up guards to protect the Cadet Corps building, the royal library and the Japanese palace – all routine duties which could be carried out automatically by any commander with the least sense who might come to occupy a city!

For his part, Durutte, while agreeing to the surrender of the New City, did not accede to my demand that before leaving it to move to the Old City, the troops defending the fortifications should give a salute to the Russians, standing at attention in parade fashion, with a guard of honour beating the drums. These difficulties occasioned a tussle and evaporated only by evening.

I let the requested paragraphs stand in the articles of capitulation, but wrote under them 'Unnecessary Articles'; and Durutte agreed to order his troops to salute my men, as long as this was not mentioned in the articles being signed. I was satisfied because I wanted the people of Dresden to see for themselves (and not through the newspapers) that the French had been humbled before the Russians.

There remained one article, however, that brought down on my head all the vultures and scavengers who haunt the resting-place of past events. They reproached me for agreeing to the article which called for the cessation of hostilities in the New City itself to a distance of a one-mile radius.

In truth, this agreement on my part would have been objectionable, even unforgivable, had it not been spelled out that *each one of the parties to this agreement was obliged to notify his opponent of the likely resumption of hostilities in this area 48 hours beforehand.* And here was my thinking as to our position in relation to this clause: without boat transport, which was concentrated on the enemy side of the river and in their hands, and taking into account the weakness of my party's composition, I could not undertake any action against Durutte, who was occupying the Old City of Dresden with infantry and artillery. He, on the contrary, with the troops and boats at his disposal, could always launch an attack on me in the New City and make me regret having dared to come out and challenge him with my cossack command alone. Therefore, as far as my party and myself were concerned, this article protecting us from an attack by Durutte was not only valuable, but vital; and to this day I cannot understand his madness in believing that the same article safeguarded him from the crossing of the Elbe by our troops – as if we necessarily had to cross the river at Dresden and couldn't do the same eight, fifteen or twenty miles farther up- or downstream!

Well and good. But did I have the right to conclude this agreement only because it was beneficial to ourselves? Was I conducting this war alone against Napoleon? I was a minuscule part of the enormous combined forces; how could I presume to oblige this giant army to observe an agreement advantageous to me, but possibly harmful to the designs of the high command and the common good?

The army corps of Blücher and Winzingerode were those nearest to Dresden. But officially I knew for certain that the first was in Buntzlau, on the border of Silesia and Saxony, beyond the range of the present military events, and the other in Goerlitz. If Winzingerode had been anywhere near my detachment, I would never have dared do what I did. I would never have approved of such an article, or else, instead of the 48-hour delay, I would have designated another deadline more in keeping with the time that he would need to move from the place he currently occupied to the city of Dresden.

On the one hand, however, I saw Winzingerode in Goerlitz, about 70 miles away (that is three days' march or, put another way, at a 72-hour distance from Dresden). On the other, this one article seemed to leap out at me as being preponderant over all the other articles and by the fact that its importance was almost concealed among the various conditions. I realised that if it was not agreed upon, I would not be able to complete what I had started and that Durutte would not surrender the city to me. What could I do? I had to agree to this article, but I had to ensure also that Winzingerode would not be hindered by the shackles that I had accepted. Moreover, this freedom of action for him had to be arranged in such a way that the hour of his arrival in Dresden would exactly coincide with the hour when the armistice would expire, because the least delay in this junction with me would bring about my inevitable defeat. Taking into account that Winzingerode's march would take three days from Goerlitz to Dresden, he should definitely get there on the 13th towards evening. Guided by this supposition, as soon as I had taken possession of the New City, I reported to General Lanskoy that the cease-fire agreement would end on the evening of the 13th and asked him to inform Winzingerode accordingly.

On the evening of the 11th, I sent a written notification to General Durutte that I would resume military operations in town and in the surrounding areas in 48 hours' time, as had been agreed in the surrender document. In this fashion, I completely untied the hands of General Winzingerode as to where and when he should take action and fended myself off from attack by Durutte until our general's arrival.

To my surprise, his forward infantry elements reached Dresden on the evening of the 14th, which placed me and my party on the edge of the abyss for an entire day: scheming behaviour on his part that was understandable but equally based on faulty reasoning! As I shall explain, by the 14th I was no longer in the New City, but my party's shameful exodus could not be attributed to me. In what way could I be accused of being rash and inconsiderate by agreeing to the article later singled out for criticism? How did it hinder Winzingerode's operations in the town and the surrounding areas, which, by and large, was the reason for my being reproached? And what harm was done to the movements of the army, considering that I had secured Dresden and kept my own group out of harm's way?

When the conditions had been ratified, I immediately sent a copy with the following report to General Lanskoy:

> Yesterday, I carried out a strong reconnaissance towards Dresden. Squadron Leader Chechensky, in command of the 1st Bug Regiment of cossacks, distinguished himself as usual. One junior officer was killed, four cossacks wounded and nine horses killed or wounded. A frightened enemy entered into negotiations, as a result of which I shall occupy half of Dresden tomorrow, and I have the honour of enclosing a copy of the conditions which were ratified by me for Your Excellency's perusal.
>
> Colonel Davidov, 9 March 1813, under the palisades of Dresden

But when we finished shifting about from one town to the other, and the debates, demands, refusals, agreements and alterations in the articles ended with the conditions finally being ratified, and when everything became calm and eventually settled down, then came time for further reflections on the subject. Dark thoughts swirled in my head, and as I considered matters from several points of view, my armed exploits appeared in a somewhat different light. At best, I saw the honour of Russian arms splendidly upheld as a result of a weak detachment of cossacks storming a capital defended by forces ten times more numerous in infantry and artillery. I envisaged my name mentioned in the accounts of military actions, and eagerly devoured by readers all over Europe. At worst, I saw Winzingerode making haste to occupy the capital of Saxony in person and alone, not thanks to a small detachment from his corps. I could imagine him concocting an elaborate account of how he defeated the enemy and made a triumphal entrance into the city, entertaining hopes of great and rich rewards from our monarch, and suddenly seeing his hopes dashed by my stunning and surprising success!

If I was right, if he really intended to get to Dresden, how furious he must be at my interference, and what sort of intermediary would there now be between me, a speck of dust, and our Emperor! Anyway, as Hetman Khmelnitsky used to say, 'What will be, will be, and what will be is what the good Lord will give us.' I repeated these words to myself in a sober voice, sank down on the straw spread before my campfire and fell innocently asleep.

Before daybreak, I gave orders to my party to prepare for a parade entrance into the city – to clean themselves up and groom their appearance as far as possible. We put on new clothes. I was sporting my curly beard, black as a raven, and a dark overcoat, red trousers and a red hat with a black border. I carried my Circassian sword at my side, around my neck hung the orders of St Vladimir and Ann studded with diamonds, and the Prussian Order of Merit and that of St George were pinned to my lapel. Khrapovitsky and Chechensky boasted similar outfits, but Loewenstern wore an infantry uniform, as did Beketov and Makarov with their regimental uniforms, and Alabiev in the cossack dress of Count Mamonov's regiment.

At 10 o'clock in the morning, the civil servants, deputised by the city, made their appearance. They rode out to meet this rough, uncivilised-looking cossack leader, and stared with amazement when they heard this bearded fellow replying to their greetings with thanks in halting (and somewhat coarse) French.

Afterwards, I spoke to them at length about the high destiny that awaited Germany if it lived up to the call of honour and dignity worthy of its name; of the debt of gratitude they owed Emperor Alexander, and about the means that they had at hand to express this best. I told them that I, a mere cossack horseman and soldier, did not understand a thing about politics, but that, to my way of thinking, I felt confident that if only Saxons would give the example and rise up for so just and sacred a cause, they would gain the good graces of the magnanimous Russian monarch, who had entered the country for Germany's sake and not for himself, since his task had already been fulfilled at home. In a word, I reeled off God knows what nonsense, without the slightest effort. Everything I said had been spontaneously borrowed from the proclamations that had been broadcast throughout Germany. Reading these daily provided me with a quantity of silly, ready-made phrases, and I was much indebted to them. I had piles of them stacked in my memory, like a supply of sausages to feed to the Germans. I trotted them out here, but became so dazzled with them that afterwards I almost found myself addressing my cossacks in the same lofty, empty terms.

On that day, from early morning on, Durutte instructed the inhabitants of the Old City to make their way to the New City and remain there until midday, when the garrison would march out. So there was a great gathering of people in this part of Dresden. Many of them, foreseeing the imminent liberation of the Old City from the French, did not bother to return and stayed in the New City until Durutte left for Leipzig.

At noon, my whole party got on their horses, and observing the order I had outlined, entered the gates of the fortifications. Here the garrison was lined up. They gave us a salute and stood to attention while the drums rolled. Commanding the honour guard was the same captain Frank, the first adjutant of General Durutte, who had been his emissary at the talks. I thanked the garrison by gently doffing my hat, called Captain Frank over and invited him for lunch. Then we set off, and the lead singers of the Bug Regiment broke into a song, 'Pine for me, my darling!'

The weather was lovely. The number of curiosity seekers was unbelievable. There wasn't an empty spot anywhere along the main street. Heads were poking out from every window of the two- and three-storey houses, and the roofs were covered with people. Some waved handkerchiefs, some threw their hats up in the air, and everybody screamed and shouted: 'Hurrah for Alexander! Hurrah for Russia!' And in this vast chorus celebrating these great names, I also heard mine here and there, like a small flute among the noisy trumpets and kettledrums.

They set aside a flat for me at the house of a banker by the name of Preiling, right on the main street. All the notable officials of the city awaited me there, but I rode past them to the river bank to organise lookout posts along the Elbe. In the meantime, my group was setting up bivouacs along the main street, so that they would remain handy and prepared.

After attending to these duties, I dismounted and went back to my flat where I greeted the city officials. Among those I remember were the director of the Cadet Corps, a portly red-haired general in a red military uniform with yellow lapels, the head of the Japanese palace, and a Mr Lipius, an elderly powdered gentleman. As for the others, I have forgotten what they looked like, let alone their names. In chatting to them I made use of other people's wisdom, just as I had with the deputies, but with certain changes. They all seemed happy and I was no less pleased than they were. We exchanged bows and parted.

I immediately dispatched a courier to Lanskoy with my report:

At noon, I entered New Dresden with my troops. Tomorrow, 11 March in the evening, I am calling off the truce that I had concluded with Durutte; herefore on the 13th, in the evening, we should be free to act inside the city, as well as on its outskirts. I respectfully beg Your Excellency to bring this circumstance to the knowledge of the corps commander. Any delay in the arrival of the infantry and the artillery into the New City could easily deprive us of what we have acquired.

Colonel Davidov, 10 March 1813, the New City of Dresden

On that very same day, the Saxon General Lecoq marched out of the Old City of Dresden with the Saxon infantry and Libenau with the cavalry. The former headed for Torgau, and the latter went to join the King in Plauen in Westland. They were replaced by Bavarian troops under Rechberg, coming from Meissen.

The next day, after inspecting the picket outposts, I went to visit the Cadet Corps and the Japanese palace under escort of Akhtyrka Hussars. I remember that while looking over the sketches drawn by the cadets, I, in my role of cossack, much surprised the director with my memory, when I pointed out to him on the map of the Plauen plain and its surrounding area, all the details of Daun's position during the Seven Years' War in 1758. I reminded him that the Austrian cavalry had been placed in the plain between Dresden and Plauen, and that Daun himself, at the head of the infantry, had occupied the heights from Plauen to Windberg. St Cyr had stood on the heights of Genshen to defend the rear of the army, and the Posendorf gap. I also reminded him that Brentano – first in Strelen and then in Niker – had the idea of measuring with a compass the plain between Plauen and Podshapel, and begged permission to draw the general's attention to the fact that this plain appeared wider on the map than it actually was, as it did not extend for more than 400 paces. My red-haired general stared at me with wide-eyed surprise, just as the deputies had done the day before when I addressed them in French, and instead of discussing with me Daun's position during the Seven Years' War, threw up his arms and loudly exclaimed: 'Are you really from the Cossack nation?' I assured him very seriously that I was, and we parted.

Things turned out differently when I paid a visit to the Japanese palace. Alas, in this treasury of art works, I ran up against the impregnable Plauen position! There were no memories here of the Seven Years' War, no battles or raids. There were only statues, easels and other antiquities completely foreign to my ignorant modern sensibility. I strolled through the halls admiring everything and offered no opinions or judgements as I had to the Cadet Corps. Here I was a true native Bashkir horseman.

On that day, Prince Madatov and the Tsar's adjutant, Orlov, also came to visit me, just for an hour. Like true friends, they congratulated me on my success, little suspecting, any more than I did, the surprise that awaited me when I read Lanskoy's letter which reached me as soon as they left. This is what Lanksoy wrote:

Many congratulations, dear Colonel, upon the capture of the New City of Dresden. I forwarded to General Winzingerode your report together with a copy of the capitulation agreement that you concluded with the French General Durutte and sent to me. This truce, however, was wrongfully concluded without permission of your superiors, especially since neither I nor even General Winzingerode had the right to authorise it.

I believe that the occupation of Dresden will give great pleasure to the highest authorities and in their expression of joy, they may overlook the article concerning the truce. But you have forgotten something no less important: it is the boats, rafts and ferries that I asked you about. They have not been assembled but if they were, I haven't heard about it. It should not be asking too much to get hold of the boats on which the enemy got across the Elbe, otherwise this may cause all the advantages of the truce to be on their side and not on ours.

Lanskoy

P.S. I have just received the report concerning your entrance into the city and which I am forwarding as well to the corps commander.

I answered him as follows:

My dear Serge Nicolaievich!
Please allow me to ask you where and when it was forbidden to conclude a conditional truce with the enemy when this goes beyond the range of general orders, does not cause the least harm, and is not only of advantage, but also necessary and life-saving for the one who concludes this truce? However, if this sort of prohibition actually exists I was completely unaware of it, because we partisans, during the whole course of the war of 1812, did not receive any kind of orders, decisions and other commands from army headquarters. As far as I am concerned, only one official document ever reached me – the one which contained Prince Kutuzov's praise and the decision of the Emperor to bestow on me the order of St Vladimir 3rd Class, upon my capture of Grodno as a result of conditions of truce.

The agreement and conditions entered into with Durutte were valuable, because thanks to them, I captured Dresden. The truce was, and continues to be, life-saving because, as a result, I can safely face Durutte's infantry and artillery with only cossacks at my disposal. Without this truce, he could strike me on the back of the neck and chase me out of the New City any time he felt like it. Maybe they'll say that my truce has tied the hands of our corps commander. But where is His Excellency? Three days' march from here. Therefore, assuming he is marching out of Goerlitz this morning, he cannot get here until the day after tomorrow. By then the truce will have ended, because as I already informed you, in accordance with the agreement I am sending a written notification to Durutte that military action will resume on my side in 48 hours, to coincide precisely with the arrival of our corps.

In this manner, I am simultaneously leaving freedom of action to General Winzingerode and making sure that my own party is safe and protected from imminent danger until he arrives. As far as cavalry is concerned, it will not be of any benefit here. If you were to arrive with your whole detachment, even if the cavalry of our entire corps were to materialise, without infantry and artillery we would be powerless to achieve anything in operations from the New City against the Old City.

Now a word about your order concerning the gathering of shipping transport for the river crossing. The enemy made their crossing of the Elbe not by means of boats – they got across on dry land over bridges that existed at the time in Dresden and Meissen. But now the first has been blown up and the other destroyed by fire. When they crossed over to the left bank, the enemy troops took with them every available vessel between the frontier of Bohemia and Torgau. We had to expect this. No one in his right mind, protected by the river and the destroyed bridges, would fail to complete his defence by transferring to his side all boats capable of being used by the enemy to effect a crossing. Orlov did not find any boats on the Elbe; he made use of some he located on the Elsterwerde canal, which is God knows how far from me and was never mentioned in my orders.

Your Excellency's most obedient servant,

Denis Davidov

11 March 1813, New City of Dresden

Already from early that morning, I had instructed the city officials to take measures for the gathering of food supplies and forage in town and nearby settlements to meet the needs of a 40,000-man army for at least a whole month. At the same time I ordered them to bring down to the banks of the Elbe all materials necessary for the construction of rafts and ferries, with the intention of frightening Durutte into believing that a crossing was imminent. I felt that this ruse was justified in the event that Orlov did actually manage to cross the Elbe, especially since he had promised me to launch an assault to the rear of the Old City of Dresden at the first opportunity.

On the 12th, most of the heavy equipment and a fairly large number of French troops started to march out of Dresden towards Leipzig,[15] and the Bavarian troops under Rechberg headed for Meissen. During that day Lieutenant Colonel Prendl and his unit arrived in the New City. In the evening, my picket lookout alerted me to the rumble of artillery wheels and the sound of marching troops on the opposite side of the Elbe. I assumed that this was caused by the enemy pulling out of the Old City and galloped towards the remains of the bridge spans that had been blown up. I got quite close to the enemy battery stationed at the other end of the spans, but although I listened in to their conversations in French, I was unable to make out anything clearly. I learned later that the noise was in fact caused by some of Durutte's retreating troops, alarmed by the crossing over to the left bank

---

[15] Leipzig was to be the scene of the famous Battle of Nations seven months later. The battle lasted for several days and remained inconclusive for a while. But eventually, Napoleon, outgunned and outnumbered, had to fall back, sustaining heavy losses. It dealt a heavy blow to his reputation and marked the renewed ascendancy of Prussia. A new Europe was soon to emerge, and France had to prepare to fight for survival. The battle of Leipzig was second only to Borodino in terms of losses and casualties.

by Orlov's advance troops, and not caring to be attacked by him and me simultaneously. Durutte had already been aware of Orlov's plans, and had indeed mistaken my preparations to build rafts and ferries for a genuine intention on my part to cross over to the Old City at the first sign of Orlov's successful crossing.

It seemed that fate was smiling on me and inviting me to take possession of the remaining half of the Saxon capital, when suddenly at dawn on the 3th, Winzingerode fell on me out of the blue. He had not gone to Goerswerde, but had galloped post-haste from Bautzen to Dresden. I will spare the reader the details of our interview, since it mostly consisted of a monologue, as is often the case between a superior and a subordinate. The accusation was contained in three points, which he belaboured at length:

1. How had I dared to march on Dresden without permission and despite the fact that I had received a different direction and assignment?
2. How did I dare to enter into negotiations with the enemy, which had been strictly forbidden while we were still within the confines of Russia?
3. How could I presume to enter into an armistice with the enemy, which, he emphasised, neither he nor Blücher had been authorised to do?

This last step he called a crime of state, worthy of exemplary punishment.

In answer to the first question, I told him that I had approached Dresden not on my own but at the order of General Lanskoy; but fearing that my accuser might insist that I produce the relative paper in which the permission to march on Dresden was contained, and recalling that there was also a disparaging comment about Winzingerode himself, I hastened to add: 'General Lanskoy has arrived – I saw him. Your Excellency can ascertain this from his lips.' As for the prohibition to hold any negotiations with the enemy, I showed him the disclaimer contained in my letter to Lanskoy.

None of this, however, did me any good. 'No matter what the circumstances,' he argued, 'your fault lies in that you were acting in disregard of the prohibition to enter into negotiations and conclude truces with the enemy. It is no excuse to plead ignorance of orders issued to the whole army, and therefore I cannot save you from facing a court martial. Turn over your command to Lieutenant Colonel Prendl, and be good enough to proceed to the imperial and main headquarters. It is possible that they will be more indulgent there. I myself do not condone and never employ indulgence in the military service. Goodbye.'

That is how my feat of arms was rewarded, which I dare say was bravely and rather cleverly done.

I turned over my command to Prendl.

Anyone who has been torn away from men under his care and command, with whom he has shared for such a long time hunger, cold, joy, sorrow, hardships and dangers, will understand the agitation that gripped my soul when I turned over my party to the authority of another person. From the Borodino battle to the entry into Dresden, I felt my fate, my life, was linked to theirs. I did not simply take leave of subordinates – in each hussar and cossack I was leaving a son, in each officer a friend. Among the latter were men like Khrapovitsky and Beketov, with whom I had forged an alliance that made us blood brothers. This stemmed from a constant camaraderie, instinctive empathy and continual readiness to risk our lives for each other – not to mention the memories of wonderful, hallowed events that we had shared together. Oh, how a stale piece of bread at a bivouac, the smell of gunpowder and the shedding of blood bring people together! Five hundred men were sobbing when they saw me off. Alabiev rode with me. He had no command of his own and was free to go; but whereas service in the group had given him the chance to distinguish himself and to be promoted, riding with me would only earn him heartfelt gratitude – and he chose the latter.

I had not yet left my quarters when they came to see me – a deputation from various social ranks of the Meissen region with representatives from the city council. Having learned of my misfortunes, they hastened to offer me their expressions of gratitude for having kept the men under my command in such admirable order, as a result of which, according to them, the town had enjoyed tranquillity and safety, as in the past. With this, they presented me with the following document, which I still possess:

> When, on the 20th of this month the Russian Imperial Armies closed in on the city of Dresden, the undersigned deputies of the Meissen region, together with deputies of the city council, went to meet Lieutenant Colonel Davidov at the commander's headquarters of the Russian Imperial Army, at the gates of the New City of Dresden, to entrust to the care of His Excellency the town, the inhabitants, the King's property and the effects held for the public in stores and warehouses, and to beg him to preserve them from the consequences of war activities, in keeping with the concluded agreement now in force.
>
> Afterwards, this much-desired agreement was confirmed: the royal buildings and warehouses were placed under guard and the occupying forces were quartered in good order and assured of sufficient forage needed for a numerous cavalry. Strict discipline was observed everywhere, and quiet and safety were ensured throughout. The undersigned did not want to overlook this opportunity to attest to the true facts of the matter and reiterate the expression of their sincere gratitude.
>
> Their signatures followed. New City of Dresden, 24 March 1813

I was boarding the post carriage when I received the news of Orlov's successful crossing. A few more hours and the Old City of Dresden would have been in my hands. Fate turned over my prize to another person. I rode out to be held to account through the same gates of the New City which, two days previously, I had entered with my group, full of joy and enchantment!

In Kalisch, I went to the chief of the main headquarters of both allied armies, Prince Peter Mikhailovich Volkonsky. The prince immediately took the papers from Winzingerode to the Most Serene Prince Kutuzov. Without a moment's delay, the prince in turn went to seek audience with the late Emperor. He reminded him of my past service in difficult times, and of Grodno. The Emperor said, 'No matter how things stand, victors are not to be judged.' Those were his words.

Winzingerode was right in his prediction about indulgence: the hearts in which a Russian chord is to be heard, a chord of our fatherland – those hearts I do not fear.

Within a few days, Te Deums and artillery salutes celebrated the capture of Dresden. I listened to them while wandering through the streets of Kalisch. However, the next day, Kutuzov sent for me, offered a profusion of apologies, showered me with compliments and sent me back to Winzingerode with instructions that he return to me the same group which had been under my command. I was grateful to him. He couldn't have done more; his authority had its limits.

I found our corps in Leipzig. Winzingerode did not return my group to me, under the pretext that it was now scattered over a vast distance, but his promises to form a new unit did not cease until I finally asked for permission to be returned to the Akhtyrka Hussar Regiment to which I belonged.[16]

Napoleon was approaching; the allied armies were marching to meet him, and we had to expect a major conflagration. I wanted to play a part in it with sword in hand, and not in the retinue of anyone else. Meanwhile the official news of my capture of Dresden was published as follows:

> General Winzingerode reports from Bautzen that Neustadt, or the part of Dresden which lies on the right bank of the Elbe, has been occupied by his troops.

Nothing more.

Later on, I served in line regiments or commanded detachments, but only temporarily and not with aims of my own, merely at the guidance of others. The largest command I received (two regiments of Don cossacks) was entrusted to me that autumn, after the armistice; yet even this was not detached but under the command of Colonel Count Mensdorf in the Austrian service, from whom I gained a great deal. He showed respect for me. I felt

---

[16] His regiment, later attached to Blücher's army in 1814, was to see action in France during the battles at Craon and Brienne, after which he was promoted to the rank of major general.

unlimited loyalty towards him, and greatly admired his noble manner, his culture, his heroic spirit, his military gifts and his high moral standards. He is now, as I hear, lieutenant general field marshal and military governor of Bohemia.

Epilogue

Here end the military writings of Denis Davidov, which span a period of 30 years. From a story contained in his *Diary of Partisan Warfare*, we know that he did eventually get to Paris, and in 1814, returned a little drummer boy, Vincent Bode (whom he had probably saved from a dire fate) to his ageing father. That same year, he returned to Moscow, where he was writing various poems and elegies. After peace was concluded, he was appointed to lead the headquarters staff of two different infantry corps (the 7th and then the 3rd). In 1819, he married. In 1821, he had his name struck off the list of front-line cavalry generals. Finally, he got bored with peacetime service and tendered his resignation in 1823.

Upon the accession to the throne of Nicholas I in 1825, he again resumed active service and carried a sword at his side, as in the olden days. The Persians had invaded Georgia, and Davidov hurried there. In ten days he covered the distance from Moscow to beyond the Caucasus and eventually, after a lively pursuit of enemy forces, sighted Mount Ararat. He occupied himself by building a fort, and when winter brought a lull in military operations, he went on leave to Moscow for six weeks with General Ermolov's blessing. Back in the Caucasus, the change of climate apparently had an adverse effect on him and he was forced to return to Russia for treatment and recuperation. Until 1831, he busied himself running an estate, enjoying a quiet, peaceful family life, and continuing to write poetry.

In 1831, there was an insurrection in Poland, and he was back to the military life. Galloping to join the main army headquarters, he was entrusted with several regiments of cossacks and dragoons (four in all) and engaged in a series of fierce engagements with the rebel forces. On 7 June 1831, at the head of the vanguard of General Ridiger's corps, he sustained a three-hour assault by the main enemy forces and stood fast, while the remaining Russian forces bypassed them and achieved victory. For his part in the battle, Davidov was promoted to the rank of lieutenant general. After other various engagements, the uprising was finally put down and Davidov returned home to Moscow and his family.

This marked the end of his military career, and literary matters continued to occupy him until his death at the age of 54 in 1839. Although this is not a very long lifespan, considering that he had joined the army at the tender age of 17 and remained in the service on and off for 30 years, it does appear to have been a very full life!

To this day, Davidov remains a much-beloved and heroic national figure in Russia. An impressive monument to his memory stands in the cemetery of the Novo-Devichey Monastery near Moscow, where all great and famous Russians are buried. Underneath his bust is an inscription which spells out: 'Denis Davidov, Hero, Created Partisan Detachments During the Patriotic War of 1812'. There are fresh flowers on his grave every day.

The Bennigsens and Winzingerodes of that era are largely forgotten. They are not really considered heroes or, for that matter, true Russians, but merely foreign generals from Hanover and Austria in the service of the Russian army. The memory of Suvorov, Kutuzov, Davidov and Bagration, on the other hand, continues to burn brightly, and remains a source of inspiration and pride for those who keep the Russian heritage and past glories alive.

Brief Biographical Sketches

Bagration, P. I. (1765–1812). Georgian prince who participated in all major campaigns during the wars on the Continent, commencing in 1805. Commanded the Russian Second Army in 1812 and managed to evade encirclement during the early months of the war and to join up with the main Russian forces at Smolensk. Mortally wounded at the battle of Borodino, where he displayed exceptional bravery.

Bennigsen, L. L. (1745–1826). Count of Hanoverian origin. Served in the Russian army with distinction; active participant in the plot against Emperor Paul. Commander-in-Chief of the Russian army in 1807, and temporary head of the general staff in 1812 until recalled at the insistence of Marshal Kutuzov.

Chechensky, A. N. Russian officer and partisan leader during the war of 1812. Apart from the facts related by Denis Davidov, not much else is known about him or his career.

Chichagov, P. V. (1767–1849). Admiral and naval minister. Commanded the Army of the Danube in the war of 1812 and then the Third Western Army; he was accused of not having done his utmost to prevent the French army from crossing the River Beresina. In 1814 he left Russia, never to return home.

Ermolov, A. P. (1777–1861). General who participated in all the Russian military campaigns from 1805 to 1815. In 1812 he was chief-of-staff of the First Army. He was later suspected of sympathising with the activists of the unsuccessful plot of 1825 (Decembrist Movement) and was forced to retire from the army in 1827.

Figner, A. S. (1787–1813). Russian officer and famous partisan leader. He had a grim record of executing all French prisoners he captured during the war of 1812 and earned a bloodthirsty reputation even among the Russian military.

Khrapovitsky, S. S. Russian officer and partisan leader during the war of 1812. Apart from the deeds ascribed to him by Davidov, little is known of his career or eventual fate.

Kulnev, J. P. (1763–1812). General famous for his personal courage and original character, who met a hero's death at the battle near Kliastitz. He participated in the Russian campaign in Finland of 1818 which Davidov describes in great detail.

Lanskoy, S. N. (1774–1814). Russian general, of whose career little is known except what is related in Denis Davidov's memoirs.

Orlov. Russian officer, aide-de-camp to the Russian Emperor, who served with distinction during the 1813 campaign. No other details of his career are known.

Orlov-Denisov, V. V. (1775–1843). Count, cossack general during the 1812 war, in which he commanded a partisan detachment. Head of Emperor Alexander's personal escort, he was later promoted to the rank of lieutenant-general for distinguished conduct at the battle of Leipzig in 1813.

Rayevsky, N. N. (1771–1829). General who distinguished himself in the campaigns of 1812 and 1815. Commanded the Seventh Infantry Corps at Borodino where he put up a stubborn defence of the central redoubt, later referred to in history books as the 'Rayevsky Battery'.

Seslavin, A. N. (1780–1858). Russian officer and famous partisan leader during the war of 1812, known especially for his daring and enterprise. He served as colonel and commander of the Sum Hussar Regiment, then as head of a partisan detachment, and was eventually promoted to the rank of major-general in 1813.

Suvorov, A. V. (1730–1800). Count of Rymnik, Prince of Italy. The most venerated general in Russian history, who held every rank from corporal to generalissimo. He took part in six major foreign wars, defeating the Prussians, Turks, Poles and French. Under his command, his troops were never defeated and his military record remains unblemished to this day. In his final campaign in 1799, facing an enemy force four times larger than his own, he led his army over the Alps to safety in a spectacular march. He led Austro-Russian forces against French armies, but unfortunately never met Napoleon in battle.

Short Bibliography

Anonymous. *Napoleon's Critical Situation During the Crossing of the Beresina by the French Army*. St Petersburg, 1833 (in Russian).

Beskrovny, L. *The Patriotic War of 1812*. Social Economic Literature, Moscow, 1962 (in Russian).

Bogdanovich, M. *History of the Patriotic War of 1812*, vol. III. S. Stugovitski, St Petersburg, 1860 (in Russian).

Bourgogne, Sergeant. *The Memoirs of Sergeant Bourgogne, 1812–1813*. Heinemann, London, 1899; Arms and Armour Press, London, 1979.

Chandler, D. *The Campaigns of Napoleon*. Macmillan, New York, 1966.

Clausewitz, C. von. *The Campaign of 1812 in Russia*. Greenhill Books, London, 1991.

Davidov, D. *Collected Works*. Government Publisher of Artistic Literature, Moscow, 1962 (in Russian).

Duffy, C. *Borodino and the War of 1812*. Scribners, New York, 1973.

Durdent, R. *Campagne de Moscow en 1812*. Eymery Paris, 1814.

Elting, J. *Swords Around a Throne – Napoleon's Grande Armée*. Free Press, New York, 1988.

Haythornthwaite, P. The Russian Campaign: A Reputation Damaged in *Napoleon, The Final Verdict*. Arms and Armour Press, London, 1996.

Manfred, A. *Napoleon Bonaparte*. MYSL Publishing House, Moscow, 1986 (in Russian).

Nicolson, N. *Napoleon 1812*. Harper & Row, New York, 1985.

Popov, A. *185 Year Anniversary of the Patriotic War of 1812 – A Compilation of Articles*. Samara, Russia, 1997 (in Russian).

Tarle, E., *Collected Works of Eugene Tarle,* vol. III. Academy of Sciences Publishing House, Moscow, 1959 (in Russian).

Weider, Ben. *La Sagesse de Napoléon*. Ed. Lemeac, Ottawa, 1983.

Wilson, General Sir Robert. *Journal 1812–1814* (ed. A, Brett-James). Kimber, London, 1964.

Zhilin, P.A. *Destruction of Napoleon's Army in Russia*. Science Publishing House, Moscow, 1968 (in Russian).

Index